DATE DUE

NOV 0 8 '87		
NOV 7 '87		
MAR 1 4 '95		
FEB 1 4 1995		

Peace in the Western World

Also by Matthew Melko (and Richard D. Weigel)
Peace in the Ancient World (McFarland, 1981)

PEACE IN THE WESTERN WORLD

by
Matthew Melko
and
John Hord

STANLEY A. MARCUM, CARTOGRAPHER

McFarland & Company, Inc., Publishers
Jefferson, North Carolina, and London

Library of Congress Cataloging-in-Publication Data

Melko, Matthew.
  Peace in the Western world.

  Bibliography: p.
  Includes index.
  1. Europe—History. 2. America—History. 3. Peace.
I. Hord, John K. II. Title.
D104.M45 1984   940   84-42606

ISBN 0-89950-120-6

Printed in the United States of America.

McFarland Box 611 Jefferson NC 28640

Acknowledgments

This book was greatly improved because a number of scholars were willing to take time to read the various cases and to help us avoid some errors of fact and interpretation. We would like to express special thanks to:

Charles Berry, Wright State University (Spanish Imperial and Costa Rican)
Alice Vines, University of Dayton (British)
Joseph Held, Rutgers University (Hungarian)
Erving Beauregard, University of Dayton (Brandenburger and Swiss)
Martin Arbagi, Wright State University (Venetian)
Michael McKenny, Canadian Civil Service (Canadian)
Denis Sinor, Indiana University (Hungarian)
Richard F. Swann, Wright State University (Canadian and Pacific)
James B. Nelson, Union Theological Seminary (Polish)
Bela Bognar, Wright State University (Hungarian)
Carl Mollins, Canadian Press (Canadian)
David C. Gordon, Wright State University (Scandinavian)
Geoffrey Blainey, University of Melbourne (Pacific)
Mark Fabryci, Wright State University (Polish)
Joseph E. O'Connor, Wittenberg University (Polish)
Victor Sutch, Wright State University (British)
Keith D. Suter, U.N. Association of Australia (Pacific)

We are also indebted to John Ray of Wright State, who encouraged Stan Marcum to draw our maps; and to Leroy Eid of the University of Dayton and Reed Smith of Wright State who helped us find readers. Jeffrey A. Garrett redrafted the Pacific Peace map.

Then we would like a fanfare for Betty Snow, who typed the manuscript, made the corrections, put back today what we took out yesterday and worried more than we did about Making the Deadline. She was helped by Shirley Vanover, who supervised our work-study students: Amanda Romero, Nancy Long and Marietta Kelly. Glena Buchholz, Lisa Paxton and Diana Bertke helped with proofs and index.

As always, the Wright State reference librarians came to our aid in many ways. Inevitably the greatest burden fell on Diane Marketti, the social science specialist, but we were helped by Emily Lehrman, Karen Kimber, Howard Jarrell, Laura Sandmann, Margaret Roach, Kathy Chilson, Barbara Ford-Foster and Marlene Johnson. Joy Iddings was a great help in getting us books from Interlibrary loan. At the Florida end of our operation, we are indebted to the staff of the John C. Pace Library of the University of West Florida and Betty Powell, who handled interlibrary loans in Fort Walton Beach.

Finally, one author wants to let Nelle Melko know he appreciates her sympathy and patience during the evenings of the last six weeks of working on the manuscript when he appeared to be in the living room, but was really exploring the Rialto or the Outback.

Table of Contents

List of Maps and Tables

It is remarkable that in most languages the word peace has no plural. We speak of war and wars—but not of peace and peaces. This linguistic anomaly has profound causes. Peace is regarded as the background, or prevailing melody, of history, interrupted by countless wars, as the heavens are dotted with stars. But in truth, war and peace are the heads and tails of the coinage of history. They are the two faces of Janus. We can regard peace as the front and war as the back, or vice versa, just as we choose. — Richard Coudenhove-Kalergi.

1

Peace in the Western World?

Peace? In the Western world? The expression sounds incongruous at best. In all Western history since the extinction of the Pax Romana, only the nineteenth century, the celebrated Pax Britannica, has achieved any such reputation. But during this supposed peace one finds the Spanish Carlist wars, the Swiss Sonderbund war, two [Franco-Sardinian]-Austrian wars, the Crimean War, two or three wars between Prussia and Denmark, one between Prussia and Austria, one between Prussia and France—and then of course there is the famous Balkan situation, not to mention assorted rebellions, revolutions, liberations, occupations and military interventions. Like Mark Twain's death, the death of war in nineteenth-century Europe seems to have been greatly exaggerated. And this is the best case available?

Certainly war provides the heroics of history. A bit of research in any local library in the card entries under "war" can yield a stack sufficient to prop up a sofa. Under "peace" the yield is thin. Worse, the war studies will be about the reality of war, the peace studies, usually only about the hope of peace—peace movements, peace treaties, proposals for peace in some indistinct future.

The Congress of Vienna ended a second Hundred Years' War between Britain and France. For over 150 years since, the two have been at peace, but what does history call this peace? It has no label; yet peace between Britain and France since 1815 is, nevertheless, a fact.

When we talk of peace, we often think of everlasting world peace, an ideal that seems unlikely to be achieved. During wartime, however, when we talk of peace we mean something more specific and obtainable. We mean peace for our country, peace for ourselves. We are thinking of peace for somebody in some place.

That finite peace, limited in time and place, can be studied by case history is an insight of Richard Coudenhove-Kalergi (1959). He observed that while peace does serve as a background, a firmament for the more brightly conspicuous stars called wars, peace also, like war, is made. Even the critics of specific examples see this quality: "They rob and kill and call it empire! They make a desert and call it peace!" to note one acid assessment of that other famous Pax (which, incidentally, does qualify as a Peace). Excluding such paleolithic survivals as the Tasaday, peace is an artifact, and by definition an artifact has inherent qualities that are subject to identification and study. Moreover both peace and war have the special quality of being artifacts over time: Unlike a painting or sculpture, more like a piece of music existing through a developing range of instruments and interpreters, peace is an artifact continually rebuilt and adapted as it goes along. Thus as with war, perseverance is a necessity; unlike war, continuation rather than termination is (usually, and at least officially) the objective.

Again like war, peace can be studied on a number of different levels and approaches. One may study the internal mechanics of an internal peace like Switzerland's. One may study so specific an international peace as that between France and Britain. One may study the general mechanisms of such a supposed general peace as nineteenth-century Europe's. This study arbitrarily defines units of peace temporally and geographically, simply because the available data make that the easiest course. Since this is the second volume of a series (though it may be read by itself), the criteria follow closely those used in the first, **Peace in the Ancient World** (Melko and Weigel, 1981).

1. Peace is defined as an absence of physical conflict.

2. The area in which peace occurs may be any definable region, whether it is a political unit, a group of such units, or a clearly discernible region within a larger political entity.

3. The period in which peace occurs must last a century or more.

4. If after a century of peace conflict brings that peace to an end, but then peace resumes for another century in the same area, these shall be considered as two phases of the same peace period.

5. If two contiguous areas have peace in the same period, this shall be considered a single peace period.

6. If peace begins in one area and later expands to a contiguous area, the whole shall be considered as a single peace, providing that the contiguous area also has at least one full century of peace.

7. Minor interruptions to peace are discounted.

8. If a government(s) of the area of peace is fighting somewhere else, that does not negate peace within the peace area.

To elaborate and explain:

1. Absence of physical conflict. This definition has been criticized as purely negative, as being something other than "real" peace. Quite possibly so; nevertheless one must begin somewhere, and this quality has the great merit of being the only ingredient which always forms some part of all the more angelic models. As of this early state of the study, to specify more alluring qualities would seem somewhat more akin to philosophy than to social science, a following of one's own preferences rather than an open search for an applicable synthetic model. Of course this is hardly to say that no further genuine qualifications exist, and one aim of this study is to find them.

2. Geographic size. There is no obvious intrinsic reason to say that a geographically small peace is somehow less of a peace than a geographically large one. If Venice or Costa Rica can maintain peace for a century, that is just as important to the peoples involved as was the peace of the vast Spanish Empire to its peoples. Therefore the only geographic constraint on selection of peace areas is that enforced by the data base. Liechtenstein, Monaco, Andorra would presumably all be peace areas if only there were decent availability of material, meaning secondary and tertiary studies, from which their models could be built. And since modern scholarship is besotted with national development, this bias in the data also heavily influences choices. Even well-known interior regions (e.g. Ruthenia, the Rhine Valley, the Massif Central, the Spanish Meseta) which might conceivably include some very enlightening peace areas simply cannot be addressed. Likewise for all the modern period the effective unit of study is the nation-state, even if at the time included in a larger polity, as Scotland was within Great Britain or Iceland and Norway within Denmark.

3. Duration. The choice of one century is essentially arbitrary, a subjective judgment based partly on the consideration that when a significantly smaller span of years is used the number of cases begins to rise almost exponentially, partly that a hundred years is long enough a time that necessarily all the initiators of the Peace will be long dead by the end of it. Indeed they should be long enough dead that only rarely will the rulers of the peace area at termination have any personal knowledge of or acquaintance with the initiators and their methods. Duration for a full century implies some degree of successful institu-

tionalization, and the increasing lack of such necessity as peace periods grow shorter may be the reason for the much greater number of short cases.

4. Interrupted Peace. There are only four examples of this in the West: the interruption of the long British Peace by the English Civil War, the interruption of the Norwegian regional division (nation-states again!) of the Scandinavian Peace by assorted incursions from Sweden, the interruption of the Spanish home division of the Spanish Imperial Peace by the War of the Spanish Succession and the anarchy of 1831-1850 in Brazil.

5 and 6. Contiguous Peace; Expanding Peace. These two categories have merged considerably as the analysis proceeded. The English Peace for example expanded to include Ireland and Scotland through conquest and dynastic succession, and Scotland, at first contiguous, became integral to the British Peace at large. The Spanish Peace expanded to include a host of more or less contiguous areas with slightly different peace periods. In the Pacific Peace Australia and Hawaii are hardly contiguous, but the oceanic colonial environment and the in-pressing outside world combined to make them similar enough for joint discussion and contrast. The Scandinavian Peace never included all Scandinavia at once, but the factors of contiguity and expansion both influenced its existence at one or another time. The exact degree to which contiguity makes for singularity must be left to a more developed state of the study, but as of now contiguity and expansion do seem relevant inputs to the equation.

7. Outbursts of Violence. It has proven very difficult to arrive at any objectively acceptable formula for the labelling of "unacceptable" violence. Such simple proportions as one death in ten thousand per year from formal violence have not proven satisfactory, if for no other reason than, in most cases, lack of data. The authors have argued, for example, whether the some four thousand apparently sociopolitical (racial) lynchings in the United States between 1890 and 1930 constitute a significant interruption to the peace of that period, and if so, whether the old Union states would still constitute a separate regional peace area. Or again, a Peace may be interrupted by highly localized but very intense short-term violence: the revolts of the ex-Muslims in Spain, the Comunero revolt in Paraguay, the Canudos campaign in Brazil. So long as these are localized and short-term, the subjective judgment is made that they do not constitute significant breaks in the Peace. It is again to be hoped that a later stage of the study will resolve this.

8. External Warfare. The government of a Peace may be fighting elsewhere. This has certainly been the most controversial qualification, and critics who accept the validities of the enterprise and the first seven criteria will nonetheless balk strongly at this one. Nevertheless it seems to be an important possibility. Only two of the twelve case studies herein were at peace outside their peace areas throughout their peace periods. Indeed it seems rather often the case that the opportunity for advancement through external war was a major contributor to the diversion of disaffected spirits from internal dissension, and one of the most hackneyed cliches of tactical diplomacy is that when in trouble at home, a government should stir up trouble abroad. This is again hardly the most angelic criterion possible, but then this world is not usually considered the principal abode of the angels in any case.

These criteria are applied to Western history, which is the history of Europe from the dawn of the middle ages to the present, and includes the periods of exploration and settlement in which Europeans inhabited many areas of the globe.

The criteria having been presented, Table 1 lists the cases that have been selected.

Five cases were not included because they were unsatisfactory in one way or another. These were the following, with tentative dates: the Bohemian, 1197-1394; the Italian, 1538-1701; the Dutch, 1794-1940; the West Indian,

TABLE 1

THE PEACE PERIODS

Peace or Sub-Peace	Dates
Venetian	1033–1310
Hungarian	1312–1428
Polish	1410–1606
Brandenburger	1486–1627
Spanish Imperial	
Spain	1492–1808*
America	1535–1780
British	
English	1485–1940*
Irish	1690–1919
Scottish	1746–1940
Scandinavian	
Icelandic	1262–
Norwegian	1371–1940*
Danish	1660–1801
Swedish	1721–
Finnish	1809–1918
Swiss	1856–
Brazilian	1654– *
Costa Rican	1842–1948
Canadian	1885–
Pacific	
Australian	1788–
New Zealander	1872–
Hawaiian	1824–
Polynesian	c.1880–

*Interrupted

1818– ; the American (United States), 1890– , which would have been combined with the Canadian as the North American Peace. Any of these cases may be valid under the criteria, but we did not explore them thoroughly. The Bohemian was ruled out because of possible interruptions, though these may have been no more severe than those that occurred in contemporary Hungary; the Italian and West Indian because of territorial interruptions; the Dutch because of aesthetic and definitional ambiguities; the American because of debatable interruptions and because the total length would have been almost a decade short of the required minimum length.

    Each of these individual case studies is divided into origins, characterization, termination (where applicable) and reflections. Characterization analyzes both the nature and the development of the Peace: setting within the larger world, kind or leadership involved, kind of polity involved, economy, society, culture, foreign policy. The individual case studies are followed by syntheses of each point of analysis, a general comparison of peace in the Western world with the findings on cases in the Ancient world set forth in the previous volume of this series, and recapitulation of findings.

    This study can hardly be called exhaustive. In so small a compass as a single volume provides, exhaustiveness is hardly possible; it must therefore be left to the future. Some boldness has been used to suggest and fill lacunae which appear only in the light of peace study, but if in this troubled twentieth century any enterprise calls for boldness, the study of the successful achievement of peace should be it. Presumably some of these findings will be challenged, but if such controversies as this book arouses include some systematic further address of the nature of peace as it has actually been experienced, then this series will not have been undertaken in vain.

2

The Venetian Peace
(1033–1310)

In the millennium after the fall of the Roman Empire, the Italian Penin-sula was a particularly troubled area. It was subject to invasions by Goths, Lombards, Franks, Normans, Germans and Magyars from the north and by Byzantines and Saracens from the sea. In the frequent periods when central control was wanting, it was subject to succession wars, usurpations, wars among small states, along with conflict between the Western Christian church and the German Empire, political, social and religious revolutions and commercial wars among sea powers.

The city of Venice, however, seems to have been an exception to this pattern. Situated on the Rialto, a group of islands in an Adriatic lagoon off the east coast of Italy, Venice was partially divorced from the Italian political pattern, and generally involved in Mediterranean commerce which in this period centered around the Byzantine Empire.

The peace of Venice, which lasted from the eleventh to the fourteenth centuries, included only a group of Islands bounded by mainland territories, extending some 30 miles from Chioggia on the mainland to the west to Jesolo on the mainland to the east. While the total area was probably under 100 square miles, and the Rialto under two square miles, the population was considerable. With 80,000 people in 1200 increasing to 120,000 in 1300 (perhaps 160,000 for the Lagoon area), Venice was one of the largest cities in Europe. It is true that Venice also controlled some mainland territories, but the citizens of these territories were not considered Venetians and their circumstances were different. They did not enjoy the long period of domestic peace, though they may have shared the peace of the first century.

Effectively protected by its navy, Venice was more in danger of internal disturbances, although it is true that these disturbances were sometimes precipi-tated by currents from abroad. So it was that an uprising in 1033 brought Domen-ico Flabanico (1033–42) to power as doge (roughly, duke). Then, despite multiple conflicts on the mainland, despite vigorous Venetian participation in interna-tional affairs, despite the growth of rival naval powers, and despite several natural disasters, the city of Venice remained at peace until a well-organized aristocratic rebellion was suppressed with great difficulty by Doge Pietro Gradenigo (1289–1311) in 1310.

The doge was first elected in the ninth century at a public meeting of the city's entire male population. He was, of course, a man known personally by the citizens who elected him. His position was one of great power, since he acted as chief judge as well as chief administrator. But the citizens had a voice in major laws he proposed, in taxation, and in declarations of war and peace.

The Orseolo family, in power at the beginning of the eleventh century, showed a marked tendency to try to make the doge's position hereditary. After several years of conflict, the efforts of Domenico Orseolo to seize the throne were defeated, and it was awarded instead to Domenico Flabanico, who was known for his anti-dynastic views. After his time, there was never again a direct father to son succession. Flabanico was not remarkable in other respects. Laws against hereditary succession already existed, and he simply resumed the practice of following them.

Characterization

As time passed, and as men built fortunes in commercial enterprises, a patrician class arose that quietly and gradually acquired control of the city from both the doge and the public. The doge was restricted by the creation of an advisory council that gradually clipped his powers while investing him with honors, until by the fourteenth century he was simply one of a number of powerful patricians. At the same time common citizens lost their right to elect a doge, and finally even their right to acclaim the doge selected by the council.

The oligarchy that accumulated this power had first acquired wealth through commercial enterprises extended around Italy and throughout the eastern Mediterranean. The key to Venetian success was the creation of a large fleet of commercial vessels and the development of skilled sailors to operate them.

The commercial orientation of the Venetians was probably a factor in peace. They preferred acquiring wealth to fighting wars, and peace usually favored their enterprises. They also preferred acquiring wealth to defending their religious beliefs. The mainland controversies between the pro-German Empire Guelphs and the pro-papal Ghibellines did not touch Venice before the fourteenth century. Nor did the Venetians shrink from making trading agreements with the Moslem Arabs and Turks, the position of the Christian Church notwithstanding.

For Venice, the main source of power was a navy. Given limited population and resources, the Venetians developed their power in this area in an innovative way. Borrowing from what they had seen in the Byzantine Empire, they developed a huge shipyard, the Arsenal, a name that was to become the prototype for centers producing military power. As the Arsenal evolved, workmen became more skilled and specialized, learned to stockpile standardized, replaceable parts, and developed a skilled reserve force of workmen who could be mobilized when a new fleet was needed quickly. Rib and plank construction, much faster than the earlier layering technique, began at this time and may have evolved from the requirements of the new organizational situation. Though the Venetians built trade and war vessels of different construction, each could be used for the other purpose. Thus the Venetians were disproportionately strong in naval power and commercial vessels, compared to other nations and cities which used conventional craft methods and were distracted by the need to develop a system of agriculture, to sustain land militias, and to defend religious and political positions.

Not that the Venetians were uninvolved in other people's affairs. They carried on an active and aggressive foreign policy, expanding into Dalmatia across the Adriatic, participating (mostly for commercial reasons) in several crusades, tackling the Byzantine Empire when it interfered with their commerce, and on one occasion defeating a fleet put together by the German Emperor, Frederick Barbarossa. This, incidentally, was the only naval battle they fought near their home ground, and had they lost, they probably would have been

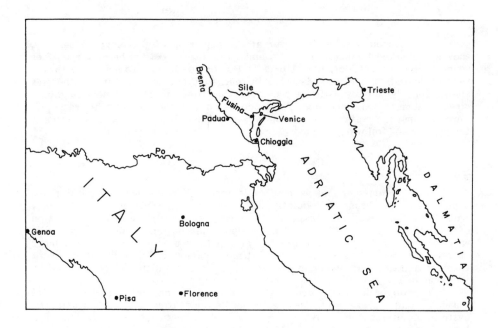

VENICE AND SURROUNDING AREAS

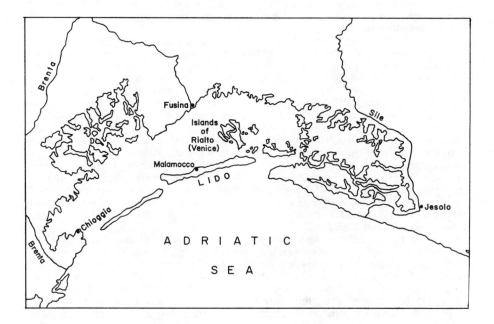

invaded. Generally they restricted their contacts with Italy to commercial exchanges, and they refrained from becoming involved in mainland politics. They did join a Lombard League against Barbarossa and supported a revived league in the thirteenth century against Frederick II. But their support consisted of naval operations, acting as League treasurer, providing podestas (hired city managers), and offering sanctuary to exiles of captured towns. Although Frederick at one point occupied Fusina, two miles across the Lagoon, he never threatened Venice, even verbally. It was a whale versus elephant situation.

When they did have to engage in land fighting, as in a minor war with Padua over the diverting of the course of the River Brenta (1143), the Venetians engaged mercenaries. Not only did they lack experience in land fighting, but they feared that a Venetian general might use his army to take over the city, something that did happen in other Italian cities with the emergence of the **condottieri.**

By the twelfth century, the Venetians found themselves in a situation that should have taxed their resources to the utmost, and can hardly have been conducive to peace. On the eastern shore of the Adriatic there had developed a powerful Hungarian Kingdom under the Arpad Dynasty. To the southwest lay a powerful Norman kingdom in Sicily and Italy. To the northwest was the Holy Roman Empire now entering a stage of expansion and power under Barbarossa (1152-1190). To the southeast was another Roman inheritor, the resurgent Byzantine Empire, reaching a peak under the Emperor Manuel I Comnenus (1143-1180).

How could a city carry on an aggressive foreign policy, maintain trade routes carrying as far as the Black Sea, and defend domestic peace under such conditions?

For one thing, the great powers had many other concerns, and were not as focused as the Venetians. The Hungarian land forces could drive the Venetians from the Croatian and Dalmatian coasts, but they were formed of feudal levies that had to return periodically to the farms. The Byzantine Empire could raise a powerful navy in times of crisis, but neglected it in favor of other ventures when the need for a fleet was not imperative.

Then there were several factors that added vitality to a number of Italian cities, including Genoa and Pisa as well as Venice, though the latter were too involved in mainland politics to achieve long periods of peace at home. For one thing, these cities were able to organize various undertakings with greater speed, skill and concentration of energy than the larger political entities. They were able to keep their profits and apply them to the next venture without having to worry about taxation or feudal obligations. The city administrators were themselves merchants, so there was a uniformity of outlook on policy, and little divergence of interest or perceptions. The prevailing merchants' viewpoint also meant very low taxes compared to mainland states. Another advantage they had was the ability to form a series of short-term corporate enterprises of various sizes for various purposes. While these enterprises were risky, their numbers provided a form of insurance, so that the fate of the Merchant of Venice would have been exceptional, as indeed Shakespeare indicates it was.

Finally, the Venetians were a menace if crossed, but also useful when accommodated. Trade, not conquest, was their end. They could participate in the sack of the city of Constantinople, as they did in 1204. But their usual role was to bring luxury goods or, if needed, grain from distant lands. In the eleventh century they had procured an enormous trade advantage when they were given tax exemption within the Byzantine Empire by Emperor Alexius Comnenus as a reward for naval help against an attack by the Norman leader, Robert Guiscard. This meant that for the next century they had the same privileges as the Byzantine merchants, who were at a tremendous tax disadvantage.

Not being a power primarily involved in the acquisition of territory, they could serve a broker's role, as they did in making their city the site of peace talks between Barbarossa and a league of Italian states headed by Pope Alexander III (1159-1181) in 1177. A contemporary German churchman commented that Venice had been chosen because it was a place in which "the courage and authority of the citizens could preserve peace between the partisans of each side. . . ."

On the whole, though, you could not say that the Venetians were a peace-loving people. They preferred trade to fighting, but were always prepared to fight, and were not unwilling even to engage in piracy if an opportunity presented itself. The Byzantines perceived them as arrogant and insufferable. But at home their system was based on trust. A man's reputation for reliability and fair dealing was everything if he were to make further corporate agreements. And on the ability to make such agreements, all his enterprises depended.

Clever and self-reliant though the Venetians were, this was not a period of great aesthetic creativity for them nor for the Latin world in general. When they sought to celebrate the rise of their city in the eleventh century, they looked to Byzantium for a model. The splendid Church of St. Mark, a chapel rebuilt for the doge in the eleventh century, was largely executed by Greek masterbuilders and artists. The style of the period is distinctly Byzantine. The Western style, which has come to be known as the Renaissance, did not come into its own until the fourteenth century, after the Venetian Peace had ended.

The rebuilding of St. Mark, by the way, provides the only miracle we have noted in the history of Western peace. The relics of St. Mark had been lost when the original basilica had burned more than a century earlier. When the new chapel was consecrated, prayers for the recovery of the relics were answered when a portion of masonry gave way, and an arm appeared through a hole in the wall.

If they produced no great art themselves, they did produce one famous piece of literature: **Desciption of the World** written in a Genoese prison in 1298-1299 by Marco Polo.

If Venice was undisturbed through this period by warfare, it was by no means always quiet and pleasant. In 1106 the city of Malamocco on the neighboring island of Lido was destroyed by a hurricane and flood that also brought severe damage to the Rialto, where 24 churches perished. In the same year the Rialto had two devastating fires, one of which leaped the Grand Canal. In 1172 the Doge Vitale Michiel brought a plague-decimated fleet back to the Rialto after a disastrous mission to Byzantium, thus bringing the plague to the city. He fled from an infuriated Assembly and was assassinated in the street. In 1268 the Venetians, though rich in spices from the east, were unable to purchase grain from Italy, and famine resulted. Although these disasters were extremely unpleasant, and although they might have been mitigated by better planning, nevertheless Venetians were permitted to drown, burn or starve without suffering the additional vexations of war.

Termination

It was quiet evolution of government rather than disaster or adventurous foreign policy that brought the peace to a close. The power of the patricians in the late thirteenth century became apparent when, in 1289, Pietro Gradenigo was elected against the protests of the citizens, and certainly in 1297 when the Great Council, in effect the registered aristocracy of the city, closed its membership to all whose parents or grandparents had not been Council members. This led to a rebellion against the Council in 1299, but this was quickly nipped.

Then, after being worsted by Genoa in a series of naval battles, Gradenigo discarded previous policy and became involved in a mainland political conflict in Ferrara. Unfortunately the Pope favored the other side, and put Venice under interdict, opening her possessions throughout the Mediterranean world to confiscation. The doge was accused of being a Ghibelline, and this added to his unpopularity. The result was a second revolution, this led by members of old aristocratic families, headed by Bajamonte Tiepolo. There was a great deal of street fighting and the peace was broken, though the fighting lasted at most a few hours and the casualties may not have been great.

A long period of tension and rule-by-terror followed the rebellion. The terror arose from a secret court, the Council of Ten, which was created to investigate the rebellion of 1310 and soon became more powerful than the doge, the Great Council that created it, or any of its members. This unhappy period culminated in a long war with the Republic of Genoa, also a naval power, which saw Venice besieged, her surrounding islands overrun, and her strength exhausted. The Rialto, however, was not invaded, and it could be argued that they have preserved their Peace to the present day.

Tiepolo's 1310 rebellion came about because a doge, already unpopular as a symbol of suppressed citizens' rights, allowed himself to become involved in the complex religious and political struggles of the mainland, struggles that had brought disaster to the cities involved and which his predecessors had taken every precaution to avoid.

The inner weakness of Venice in the period following may have been reflected in reduced efficiency at sea. At any rate Genoa was sufficiently successful in naval battles against Venice to entertain the hope of carrying a war successfully into the Adriatic. The resulting six-year war (1374-1380) was disastrous to both cities.

Reflections

Venice was an island power, protected by a navy. As such, she might engage in conflicts with the ships of other navies, such as those of Genoa or Pisa or the Saracens, but these did not venture to attack Venice in her home waters, which in any event were remote from the main lines of trade.

The lack of internal insurrections may be attributed to commercial prosperity and governmental stability. Even though the manner of election changed and power shifted, there always was procedure. There was never anything like a succession struggle. And had Gradenigo stayed out of continental involvements, it is unlikely that he would have been challenged for mere unpopularity, so long as prosperity was maintained.

Sismondi (1966:116-7) points out that the pattern of development within the Venetian nobility was quite different from that of other Italian cities. The nobles of other cities aroused resentment and excluded themselves from the government of the cities by their turbulence and flouting of the law. The Venetian nobles operated within the law, had no vassals to espouse their causes, no castles into which they could retreat when they wished to defy the government. So "they conducted themselves as citizens, and thus soon became masters of the state." Islands, being detached and defined entities, provide their inhabitants with an opportunity to form patterns that are at variance with those of the mainland with which they are associated.

Certainly the Venetian outlook contributed to peace. The Venetians preferred prosperity to the defense of honor or the triumph of righteousness. They fought naval engagements when they had to, to protect their islands or their trade, but they did not become involved in mainland conflicts. In this approach they repeated the patterns of their Ancient Mediterranean predecessors, the Phoenicians (Melko & Weigel 1981: 47-54), and provided a model for another long period of peace that was to follow.

In reading this chapter, Martin Arbagi wondered to what extent Venetian prosperity rested on the special privileges they extracted from Alexius Comnenus which in effect gave them extraterritoriality (diplomatic immunity) in his domains. Venetian merchants could trade tax-free. Venetian manufacturers operated without the fearsome government regulations which so hampered the native Byzantine artisans. Thus Venetians (and within a few decades, merchants from other Italian city-states such as Genoa and Pisa) could systematically bleed the Empire dry by depriving it of tax revenues, and also bring on economic recession and unemployment in the great cities of the Byzantine state because they could undercut the natives. When the hapless Byzantines tried to get out from under, as it were, the Venetians did not hesitate to use gunboat diplomacy to enforce their claims. . .   To what extent was the Venetian Peace a product of this imperialism?

The Venetian Peace was certainly not large, and the Venetians would hardly be described as peaceful. Yet for nearly three centuries, surrounded by great powers and a continually changing and treacherous political situation, they preserved domestic peace for their city. It was not a very large city, but it was a very large achievement.

3

The Hungarian Peace
(1312–1428)

By the thirteenth century, both the German and Byzantine Empires, which had played such a major role during the period of the Venetian Peace, were on the wane. The future great powers of Europe—Russia, the Ottomans, the Austrian Habsburgs, Spain and France—had not yet emerged. In this interim several major powers arose in the Balkans and eastern Europe, most of them experiencing what were to be remembered as "golden ages" in their respective histories. Two of these, Hungary and Poland, and perhaps a third, Bohemia, managed to achieve more than a century of internal peace.

The Bohemian Peace, if it were achieved, lasted through most of the thirteenth and fourteenth centuries. The doubt about the peace concerns two dynastic struggles that preceded and followed the reign of Wenceslas II (1283–1305). These may have been severe enough to have prevented any continuous century of peace for Bohemia, and for this reason the period is not considered at greater length here. But the fact that Bohemia was generally stable and peaceful during the fourteenth century was of great importance to the development of peace in Hungary. The Hungarian Peace, in turn, was to have important consequences for Poland. The Polish Peace, however, was of a different magnitude, and occurred, moreover, in what has come to be perceived as a different period of European history. It will be considered in the next chapter.

Origins

The Plain of Hungary is a bowl formed by the Carpathian Mountains and the Transylvanian Alps. Into this plain, between the seventh and tenth centuries, came the Finno-Ugrian Magyars to join, perhaps to rule, the Slavs who were already established there. A ruling dynasty was established from the Arpad family, which came from Bulgar stock. This rule was usually fairly stable, but never completely free of invasions, religious uprisings and succession struggles.

The last of the Arpads died at the beginning of the fourteenth century. This century was later to be characterized by some as the greatest century of the Middle Ages, the High Middle Ages. Others saw it as a period of waning, of change for the worse. In any event it was dynamic and hardly peaceful, a century of Jacqueries, rebellions, insurrections and plague. It was an age of feudalism and it has been argued that such ages are never peaceful, since the continual changes in vassal relationships normally involve a quantity of fighting and bloodshed that are taken for granted, like violent crime and automobile fatalities in the twentieth century.

13

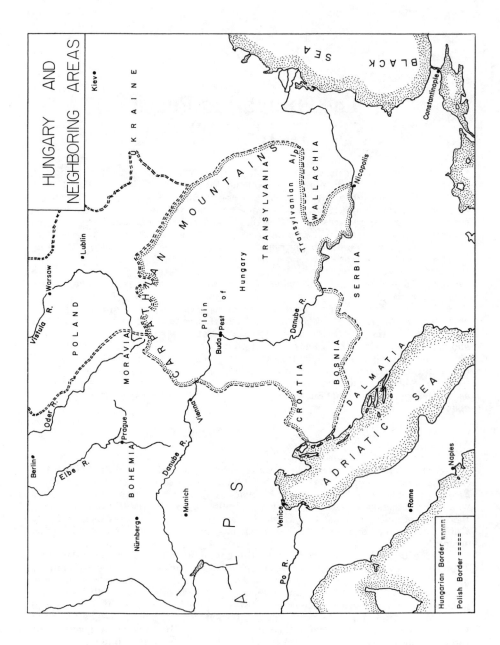

When the last Arpad king, Andrew III, died in 1301, a succession struggle followed among interested royal families of Europe. This was finally won by Charles Robert (1308-1342), who came from an Angevin family that had holdings in Italy. He subsequently engaged in a number of conflicts against dissenting Hungarian nobility before peace was established. His son and successor, Louis (1342-1382), rounded off his father's domestic policies and entered into complicated and widespread diplomatic and military activity which netted him a ring of client states and the throne of the great neighboring state of Poland. Louis was succeeded by his son-in-law Sigismund of Luxembourg (1387-1437), whose position at home was more precarious and whose interests abroad were even more extensive and complicated than those of Louis. In the last year of Sigismund's long reign, 1437, a major peasant revolution broke out in the southeastern region of Transylvania. This was followed by a succession struggle and frequent attacks by the Ottoman Turks. The kingdom recovered strongly under the leadership of Janos Hunyadi and his son Matthias (1458-1490), but after the death of Matthias, Hungary stumbled again into revolution and succession warfare, and finally conquest at the hands of the Turks.

The Hungarian Peace extended also to Croatia, the total territory involved exceeding 120,000 square miles. It can be tentatively dated from a decisive victory by Charles Robert over the powerful Amades and Csak Clans at Rozgony in 1312, though there were further conflicts that may have involved violence as late as 1317 or even 1323, and it lasted until the second of a series of Hussite invasions from Bohemia in 1428.

The peace was disturbed in 1403 when Ladislas of Anjou, a rival claimant to the throne, invaded Croatia to be defeated in a single battle. It may have been disturbed also as the result of a succession struggle that followed the death of Louis, and by some border incursions preceding the major invasion of 1428.

Characterization

The foreign relations of the Hungarian monarchs were unusually diversified. Many of their adventures were dynastic, bringing Hungary some glory perhaps, but little in terms of wealth and power. It was rather wealth and peace at home that enabled them to engage in such adventures. Louis, for instance, became king of Poland as the result of an arrangement with heirless King Casimir. But Poland was lost when Louis left no male heirs. Louis also engaged in a long, expensive and unsuccessful attempt to maintain his brother on the throne of Naples. Sigismund lost sole claim to Dalmatia, which had been decisively won by Louis, not because of external invasion but because his rival claimant, Ladislas of Anjou, sold his interests there to the Venetians after he had lost all hope of obtaining the throne of Hungary. Sigismund became German emperor in 1410 and king of Bohemia in 1420, but these acquisitions weakened his power in Hungary without strengthening Hungary itself.

The general milieu of Europe in the fourteenth century appears to have been a factor in the peace. French influence predominated. Bohemia, Hungary and Poland all were developing Western-style feudal monarchies, national institutions and consciousness of the idea of a national culture derived from a French model. Frequently these monarchies supported and trusted one another. When Bohemia did attack Poland in 1330, Charles Robert, who had been married to both a Bohemian and a Polish princess, intervened in behalf of Poland and finally arranged an armistice. The Polish and Bohemian kings, Casimir III and John of Luxembourg, were then guests at his palace in 1335. Out of this summit meeting came trade agreements and contingency plans for military defense from Balkan incursions. The Polish princess, Elizabeth, was the mother of

Louis, who ultimately succeeded to the Polish throne. He was only marginally interested and never learned Polish, but the union of his daughter with a Lithuanian prince was to lead to the Polish Peace.

This security to the northeast and northwest gave Hungarian monarchs a free hand in dealing with the tumultuous Balkans. These campaigns did not contribute much to peace in Hungary, but they did not do much harm either. The only possible threat was a gifted king of Serbia, Stephen Dushan, who made alliances with Venice and Croatian nobles during the time of Louis. The Hungarian monarch, in turn, had the support of Stephan, Ban of Bosnia, whose daughter he later married. But most of the campaigns of Charles Robert and Louis seemed designed to assert the authority of the king of Hungary, notably two campaigns that Louis carried to Naples in behalf of his brother. Sometimes such campaigns were moderately successful, sometimes they were checked. But the rulers never seemed to seek more than nominal suzerainty, and always seemed to consider withdrawal as an acceptable option.

Historians often see the Balkan policies of the Hungarian monarchs as having to do with preparing a buffer defense against the growing power of the Ottoman Turks. But is is very difficult to see that the monarchs before Sigismund perceived the Ottomans to be much of a threat. The Balkan states themselves appeared to have no hesitation in pledging loyalty to both the Hungarian and Ottoman monarchs at the same time, which indicates that they did not see themselves simply as a Hungarian defense line. Nor did the Hungarian monarchs seem to regard the Ottomans as very high on their list of problems. Hungarian forces defeated those of Murad I in 1377, but there was no follow-up campaign. Sigismund organized a complicated coalition against the Ottomans, but this ended in a decisive defeat at Nicopolis on the Danube in 1396. After that Sigismund fortified his southern frontier against possible future attacks, but had no time for further experiments in preventive warfare. What proved to be far more important for the defense of Hungary was the dramatic appearance of Tamerlane on the scene. His Mongols actually captured Sultan Bayazid II in a pitched battle outside of Ankara in 1402. This slowed down the Ottomans for a few decades so that Sigismund's fortifications were not tested during his lifetime.

The domestic peace of this period probably derives from the personal qualities of the monarchs and the willingness of the Angevin rulers to accept existing trends. They tried to appease the Hungarian nobility and Charles Robert did not attempt to introduce any major reforms or radical foreign ideas. Both monarchs genuinely sought to adapt themselves to the country.

The initial success of the Angevins may be partly attributable to the insignificance of their Italian holdings and their distance from Hungary. Any monarch coming from this region could not involve Hungary in problems of his homeland, and he would probably prefer to concentrate his efforts on the larger of his territories. This, in fact, is the way it worked out. Charles Robert was austere, sometimes brutal, capable, respected but not loved. His position was hard-won and he was determined to hang on to it, cautious about excessive risk. Louis "the Great," who was raised in Hungary, was noble, magnanimous, and straightforward according to an account of a Venetian envoy. He was also distinguished for physical courage in battle. Sigismund, though capable and hardworking, was for a long period resisted as a usurper. In 1401 he was actually imprisoned by his own nobility for several weeks, but released when it was found that there was even less agreement on a successor. Ultimately, he consolidated his position through his marriage to Barbara Cillei, a member of one of the leading noble families. But whereas the Angevins had regarded Hungary as the center of their power, Sigismund was dragged into the affairs of Germany and Bohemia when he became Emperor (1410) and then king of Bohemia (1420).

The government of the Angevins was more autocratic than that of their

Arpad predecessors. The diet of the nobility, created by the Arpads, met only on one occasion under the Angevins, and then only to hear reports from the monarch on decisions already taken. But the nobility was kept in line by the implementation of a series of policies which must have been favorably received. Charles Robert bestowed estates confiscated as a result of his own succession war on families of his supporters. Louis continued to favor these families so that by the end of his reign about one-third of the land was owned by about 50 or 60 great families. In 1351 Louis issued a series of laws that formalized developing codes of landholding. Under these codes, land could not be sold nor divided among successors. If no heirs could be found, the land reverted to the Crown. This pleased the nobility at the time, even though in later centuries it made Hungary a land of large estates and created problems of land reform, since it made mortgaging impossible.

Although the Laws of 1351 were promulgated under the principle of **una et eadem libertas,** which may be freely translated "the same freedom for all," and although clan names common under the Arpads lost their vogue under the Angevins, there was still a class distinction among different levels of the nobility: prelates, magnates and common nobility. But it does appear that the lesser nobility did have greater power with the formation of county assemblies, in which they debated, and a royal supreme court that did allow a lesser noble to challenge a greater. Further, Louis decreed a tax of one-ninth of all produce to be paid by peasants to landowners. This protected the smaller landlords since the larger ones could not win their peasants away by offering lower payments and obligations. It also protected the peasants from exploitation by the landlords.

Under the Angevins, the peasants themselves, whether they had been descendents of free men, freedmen or slaves, were also considered to be equal to one another, a free peasant class: the **jobbagy.**

From the burghers, the kings found little support. The burghers never had adequate resources, and many of them were German, that is, immigrant-dominated, and therefore little involved in political activities.

In short, the government and land policies of the Angevins insured their own popularity, but contained the seeds of future problems for their successors, since the landowners were likely to become very powerful in relation to the crown. Under Sigismund they began to express this power. The diet regained strength since it governed during his long absences. Many were new nobility who obtained their estates at the expense of barons who had sided against Sigismund.

The military structure which made Louis powerful was established under Charles Robert. It was based on the obligation of all great nobles to supply powerful contingents of heavy cavalry. Small nobles served under the great nobles. Sigismund added a second-line army of peasant soldiers. Under the Angevins this made a formidable, high-spirited army, which Louis in particular kept busy. But there was always a danger that such powerful nobles would unite to pursue their own interests, and in Sigismund's reign the threat that some might do so made his position precarious.

Having access to the Adriatic through Croatia, Louis even established an admiralty, and maintained some ships in the Adriatic to reduce Venetian influence in Dalmatia. This navy was retained through 1420.

The Angevins were able to maintain an elaborate court and carry on a complicated foreign policy on a relatively low house and property tax partly because the country was rich in gold and Charles Robert concentrated on the development of mines, encouraging prospectors to explore, but insuring that landowners and king were amply rewarded for their findings. By Louis's time the mines were producing 3,000 pounds of gold a year, five times as much as any other European state. After some experimentation, he also borrowed the Florentine idea of gold coinage of unchanging content, reducing 35 kinds of locally produced coins to a few gold coins produced by the state.

While the peasant had to pay taxes to government and landlord as well as a tithe to the Church, times were prosperous and there is little evidence of complaint. A 1380 census showed 50 boroughs, 500 market towns, and over 25,000 villages, the population totaling three million. This represented an increase of a million since the beginning of the thirteenth century. Craftsmen were organizing gilds and the monarchs were encouraging trade by standardizing frontier duties, granting franchises, concluding customs agreements with neighboring powers, abolishing internal duties and standardizing weights and measures. Hungary exported woven textiles and metal goods along with livestock products, receiving raw linen for further weaving along with luxury cloths and spices. Prosperity was both a consequence and a cause of peace. The Angevins created the conditions that made prosperity possible and prosperity helped to minimize factors that were dangerous to peace.

The Peace was further cemented by the religious unity of the period. Much of Europe was unified under the Western Christian Church. The Angevins, particularly Louis, were Christian gentlemen, and church, state and knights were in harmony. Sigismund continued the policies of Louis, but he was more a cosmopolitan man of the Renaissance world. Religious policies, for him, were decided in terms of political expediency.

This was also a period of culture in Hungary, although it was primarily a beneficiary of a cultural florescence that involved most of the subcontinent. Under Louis the court was more interested in science and national history. Sigismund's court was open to poets, most of them alien, but poetry and ballads began to be written in Hungary as well. Gothic churches abounding in French influence were raised under Charles and Louis and the Kolozsvari family, father and sons, produced some notable sculpture. The crafts of silversmithing flourished and universities were founded at Pecs (1367) and Buda (1389). The taste of the court itself was sometimes superficial and uncertain. By the time of Sigismund, Renaissance morality dominated the court. The king himself was a humanist with a streak of cruelty and neither he nor his wife, Barbara Cillei, was much given to marital fidelity.

Termination

There were several junctures at which the Hungarian Peace may have been interrupted. On the basis of sources available, it is difficult to say whether any of these were sufficient to interrupt the Peace and thus whether at some future date the Peace may have to be withdrawn. Bohemian "marauders" apparently entered Hungary during the period of Charles Robert's intervention between Bohemia and Poland (1330-1335). His armies drove them out. At the death of Louis there was a succession struggle involving his wife Elizabeth and daughter Maria. The Bosnian Prince Tvartko intervened, and ultimately the queen and her chief supporters were murdered. Then Sigismund, who was betrothed to Maria, in his turn, intervened and was crowned king. There was considerable political activity, certainly, and some harsh dynastic interaction. This could have been accompanied by open warfare among the nobility, but sources available do not indicate that it was. Again, in 1401, when Sigismund was imprisoned, there may have been some fighting. In 1403, when Sigismund tried to designate his own successor without consulting the nobility, some of them invited another Angevin, Ladislas, to intervene. He did enter Hungary, but was defeated by Sigismund's supporters in a single battle, and was forced to withdraw. Finally, Sigismund on several occasions ordered retaliatory mass executions, a style that was also to be adopted by the Hohenzollerns in Brandenburg. But we do not know how many times this occurred, how extensive the executions were, or whether they actually took place in Hungary. All of these possibilities, however, make the case for the Hungarian Peace rather fragile, perhaps no better than the case that could have been made for peace in thirteenth and fourteenth century Bohemia.

In any event, the Peace, if it were a Peace, apparently came to an end with invasions by the Turks in 1415, and by Hussites in 1423 and 1428 followed by an economically and religiously inspired peasant rebellion in 1437, the last year of Sigismund's reign. The invasion of 1428 spread far into Hungary, with much destruction, marking the end of the troubled Peace.

Peasant dissatisfaction stemmed from a gradual increase in obligations that accrued as Sigismund became more dependent on the newest class of prelates and magnates. The jobbagy were being taxed in cash above the ninth assigned by Louis. Their freedom of movement became increasingly restricted; their sons were drafted for military service, previously a privilege of the nobility; they were increasingly called upon to supply labor services; and as trade increased, they were compelled to pay in cash rather than in kind, which could mean making forced sales of seed or stock that were needed for capital expansion or maintenance. The rebellion, led by Anatol Nagy, involved both Hungarian and Romanian peasants. A number of battles were fought and the peasants were first victorious but ultimately defeated. Those who were not killed in battle were impaled.

Meanwhile, the Hussite controversy had arisen. In the fourteenth century a Moravian, Jan Milic, had challenged the Church for its wealth, its complacency, its separation from the people, and its loss of spiritual ardour. His cause was taken up by John Hus, a professor at the University of Prague. As an advocate of the simplification of church services and their presentation in national languages, Hus became leader of a movement that was anti-Roman and anti-German. His execution by the Council of Constance in 1415 led to a long series of political and military conflicts between Hussites themselves. This in turn ushered in a religious conflict that was to occupy Europe for more than two centuries. The Hussites twice invaded Hungary in the 1420's.

Since it was social as well as religious, the Hussite heresy further fanned the animosity of the jobbagy and some of the lesser nobles against the provincial, orthodox greater nobility. In 1437 they finally rebelled when the Bishop of Transylvania did not collect debased coinage for three years, then tried to collect back tithes when the currency had been improved. In a way the Hussite rebellion might be seen as a fortuitous outside factor, except that the execution of Hus, in violation of a guarantee of his safety, was ordered by a council presided over by the German Emperor. In 1415 that emperor was Sigismund.

The 1437 rebellion, with its many peasants uprising and official reprisals, definitively ended the Peace. In the same year Sigismund died and there was a prolonged succession struggle during which a Bohemian warlord occupied part of Hungary. In retrospect Sigismund's relatively peaceful settlement of a disputed succession was not a dependable precedent; any such dispute was an invitation to the nobles to divide among their own candidates. Later in the century the strong leadership of the Hunyadis controlled the nobility for some decades, but this too proved temporary. Moreover the Ottoman power was growing again, and if its attention was temporarily diverted from Hungary by Balkan problems, this too was just a respite. After the pause under the Hunyadis, peasant rebellion, succession struggles and external invasion again overwhelmed the Hungarians.

Reflections

The Hungarian Peace was, then, first of all a product of external factors, of the temporary absence of great powers in Eastern Europe. The many rising powers bordered on enough small competitors and were themselves unstable enough that war on each other was still difficult to prosecute seriously. Perhaps more remarkably, the reigning monarchs of the time understood this and avoided spectacular adventures. Expansion involved more the rules of dynastic succession than force of arms, and in Hungary Charles Robert and Louis did not neglect their position at home for the sake of these efforts abroad.

Internally, Hungary benefited from strong and competent leadership. The father and son, Charles Robert and Louis, each had the right temperament for his task. The less spectacular father was the model of a builder, undertaking the challenges necessary to build confidence in the dynasty. Louis used his father's accumulated capital, playing the role of a great monarch, a lover of justice, promoter of knowledge, patron of the arts, brave and chivalrous leader. Sigismund was overtaxed, less personally attractive, sometimes cruel and treacherous. But given his responsibilities, he was certainly competent. After the Peace, John Hunyadi had the capacities of a reformer, probably the competence of Charles Robert and greater support, but the external situation had changed enough that no one could save the Peace.

Long reigns also helped. Hungary seems to have been very unlucky in its royal successions. Charles Robert left a male heir but Louis and Sigismund did not, and quite possibly only the long reigns of the Peace prevented more disputed successions that would have meant war.

Necessarily the kings conciliated the nobles. Charles Robert and Louis were able to restrain them from political challenge by allowing them to better their economic positions, but Sigismund did not manage this and had to yield political power as well, realizing that any attempt at dictatorship would have meant running civil war.

The Peace was an age of religious unity and royal support of religion, whether from sincere devotion as in Louis' case or for political reasons as in Sigismund's. The economy was encouraged by low taxes and this kept prices stable regardless of major gold production. Government policy enabled the peasants and artisans to share in this prosperity. But under Sigismund both Crown and nobility began to increase their exactions and expenditures, giving cause to the lower orders for the later revolts.

The Hungarian Peace seems to be the center of a relatively calm period in the history of Eastern Europe, which contrasts with the widespread social disturbances, religious uprisings and civil wars extending elsewhere from Russia to England during the waning of the Middle Ages.

4

The Polish Peace
(1410–1606)

Origins

The Slavic kingdom of Poland appeared under the Piast Dynasty in the tenth century. It soon diminished its own success by a system of divided successions that were accompanied by internal wars and external attacks from Germany, Russia, and Baltic pagans. After a period of Bohemian dominance, however, the country was reunited under two strong fourteenth-century Piast monarchs and then expanded by the marriage of Jadwiga, daughter of the Polish king, Louis of Hungary, to Jagiello, Duke of Lithuania. The descendents of Jagiello presided over a period of physical expansion and cultural development that saw Poland rise to become one of the great powers of Europe.

Lithuania had been one of several Baltic states until the fourteenth century, expanding into Russia after that nation had been weakened by the Mongols. Otherwise the Baltic coast between Germany and Russia had been occupied by smaller states of Baltic, Slavic and Teutonic origin. They were perpetually subject to conflicts with one another and to invasions from Poland, Russia and Sweden. The Polish Peace began after the combined power of Poland and Lithuania ended the raids of the troublesome Teutonic Knights on their northern border with a decisive victory at Tannenburg in 1410. Except for a couple of Mongol incursions into Podolia, peace was maintained then for almost two centuries until a rebellion of nobles broke it in 1606.

In Europe, this was the time of the great intellectual movement that has come to be known as the Renaissance and of the great challenge to Christian unity and dogma that has come to be known as the Reformation. Both of these movements were to have important repercussions in Poland.

Though the combined territory of Poland and Lithuania was very large, the Peace was restricted mostly to Poland itself, which in this period included several territories bordering the Vistula: Great Poland, Little Poland, Galicia and the dependent Duchy of Mazovia, not officially incorporated into Poland until 1526. The total area was about 120,000 square miles. Lithuania, however, through much of this period was subject to raids and formidable invasions from Turks, Mongols and Russians as well as a serious feud among its own nobility.

Characterization

The problem of the last two Piast monarchs was to recreate the Polish state. Ladislas I (1306–1333) established himself as a fighting leader capable of defeating external enemies and commanding respect from his own nobility. His son, Casimir (1333–1370) consolidated his state by making peace, conceding

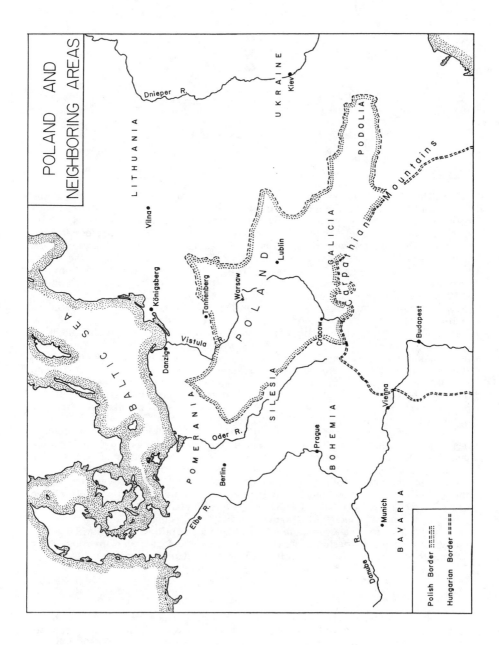

POLAND AND NEIGHBORING AREAS

Polish Border ::::::::
Hungarian Border =====

Silesia and Pomerania—two areas the Poles had been claiming—to neighboring powers, Bohemia and the Teutonic Order. Casimir then concentrated on domestic policy, creating an effective taxation system that included towns, clergy and gentry and working toward the codification of Polish law and using it to protect townsmen, peasants and Jews against the power of the great nobles.

In Casimir's time Poland was a medium-sized state surrounded by a medley of powers. On the northern border were the warlike Teutonic Knights, a German crusading order that had been invited by a Polish prince to combat heathen Prussians in the thirteenth century. They conquered the Prussians, but then invited settlers in from Germany and became a more dangerous threat to Poland than the Prussians had ever been. To the west there were the German states, weakly united under the Empire but including the powerful Bohemian state of the emperor Charles IV and the vigorous Habsburg state. To the south was the Hungary of Louis the Great. To the east was Lithuania, like Hungary, Poland and Bohemia, newly powerful in the fourteenth century. Beyond these states the great Mongol power was on the wane, but newer great powers were beginning their rise, the Ottoman Turks around Brusa and the Russians around Moscow.

Lithuania was converted from a rising menace to a protective bulwark by the marriage of Jadwiga and Jagiello. The combined power of Jagiello, King Ladislas II (1386-1434) of Poland and his cousin Vitold, grand duke of Lithuania, made it possible to subdue the troublesome Teutonic Knights. This done the cousins clarified their own relationship by establishing a formal union of Poland and Lithuania in 1413. In 1569, representatives of the Polish Diet (**Sejm**) at Cracow and the Lithuanian Diet at Vilna met at Lublin in Little Poland to negotiate a unified Sejm that was to meet in the Mazovian city of Warsaw on the Vistula, near the Lithuanian border. Separate councils were still maintained to consider local affairs, and there persisted a sense that territory was either Polish or Lithuanian. But there was to be only a single coronation ceremony and only the common diet was to advise on foreign affairs.

Through the fifteenth and sixteenth centuries there was much fighting in Lithuania, but the fighting never approached the Polish border. The Ottomans were either stopped or headed in other directions. Russia was weak in this period, and was more likely to be attacked than to attack Polish and Lithuanian forces. Similarly, the Hungarians served the Poles as a southern bastion against the Turks. And when, in the sixteenth century, the Hungarians did not appear strong enough, Sigismund I (1506-1548) steadily supported Habsburg claims to the Hungarian throne, refusing to take it himself and refusing to support the claims of his son-in-law, John Zapolya of Transylvania. Sigismund wanted Hungary, supported by the Habsburgs, as a bulwark against the power of the Turks and he appeared to recognize that his own claim might lead the Austrians to turn on him, instead of devoting their attention to the Turks.

The age of Polish Peace is the age of development of the first Western crowned republic, and the Peace lasted just so long as the republic held the confidence of its citizens. This citizenry was essentially the **szlachta,** a word sometimes translated nobility or gentry, but—since Poland had no system of hereditary ranks or titles—actually referring to the entire class of freeholders, from the very large to the very small. The other two traditional Estates, clergy and burghers, continued to exist, but in reduced roles.

This had begun just shortly before the Peace itself. In the 1300's Poland had been an almost standard Western polity: king, Council of State consisting of the high clergy and great landowners, towns populated by merchants and artisans from all over Europe, a gradual shading-down of cultivators through villeinage and serfdom. Then in 1374 Louis of Hungary, trying to buy the szlachta's support, freed them of all obligations to the Crown. Under Jagiello the freeholders of each province began open meetings in the form of a Sejmik, a little Diet, and these claimed the right of consultation on all matters affecting their provinces. Casimir IV (1447-1492) wanted the smaller freeholders' help against the great landowners and so in 1454 recognized this claim, and Poland became a federation of six provinces, each of which had to be consulted separately about everything. This proved too cumbersome, and sometime between 1468 and 1496 king and szlachta evolved the finished Polish bicameral parliamentary system. The great clerics and landowners, the former Council of State, became the Senate, which had the right to advise the king but not to decide. If they agreed against a royal proposal it failed; if they were in dispute the king had to remain at least officially in favor of the existing law. Such proposals as came out of this process were then forwarded to the Sejmiks, which debated them thoroughly and elected delegates to the general Sejm, giving them binding instructions on the province's wishes. These delegates sat as a Chamber of Deputies with the full powers of all the Sejmiks collectively. Each matter was decided by consensus, theoretically by unanimous agreement, but in practice by the passive acquiescence of any minority too small and disinterested to force concessions. In 1505 the Crown agreed in writing that no law would be promulgated without the consent of the Sejm; in 1572, with the extinction of the royal line and henceforth open election of kings, Poland became "a republic in fact as well as in name. . . . The **Szlachta** now anointed themselves with the majesty that once belonged to the Crown and looked upon their king as a chosen representative with strictly limited authority" (**Cambridge History of Poland,** vol. I, p. 369). Moreover the szlachta used this growing strength to reinforce their position: The burghers, largely foreign and disinterested anyway, were forbidden to buy land and thus to become members of the szlachta; the peasants were· gradually degraded until in 1496 they were formally bound to the land. During all this period, with the situation continuously evolving in their favor, the szlachta had no reason to upset the system and thus Poland remained internally at peace.

The nature and function of the Polish economy during this period is a matter of debate among historians of Poland. Certainly it was a period of great increase in grain production, but the style of production remained manorial. Certainly there was a great increase in trade with the west, Polish grain being exchanged for finished products and luxury goods. Some modern historians have perceived Poland to be an economic colony of the West. This trade relationship was profitable for the West and the Polish nobility, but not for the Polish burghers or peasants. It seems improbable, however, that anything like a colonial relationship was perceived at the time. Much more likely, both the Westerners and the Poles were engaging in a mutually beneficial exchange. The absence of the development of craftsmanship or cottage industry in Poland, however, when so much else was imported from the west, is not easy to explain. Mark Fabrycy suggests that it may have to do with the dominance of the szlachta, trained for military and farming activities, leaving few people who had resources and interest in commercial developments.

The increase in Western trade came about because the Ottomans closed off trade with the East by the conquest of Constantinople in 1453. A decade later the Poles had triumphed over the Teutonic Knights on their northwestern border, giving them control of the Vistula River and the port of Danzig on the Baltic Coast. By the end of the fifteenth century, more than 500 ships a year were arriving at Danzig, bringing in cloth, livestock, salt, iron, wines and beer, Mediterranean fruits and vegetables. It was not a trade in luxury goods. The Poles were exporting various grains and vegetables along with lumber and forest products. The trade was profitable for Poland, but it did lead to an intense development of agriculture and lumbering under the aegis of the nobility, while Western Europe was passing into a stage of early industrial development.

Poland enjoyed a period of considerable cultural development in the sixteenth century under Sigismund I and Sigismund II August. Sigismund I was a typical Renaissance prince, entertaining a brilliant court. He married an Italian princess, Bona Sforza, who brought many humanists in her entourage. The University of Cracow, reconstituted in 1400, became a center of literature and science. It was at Cracow in 1543 that a member of the faculty, Nicholas Copernicus, published **The Revolution of Heavenly Orbs**, a book that marked a turning point in European man's conception of the universe and his scientific thinking.

The sixteenth century was a golden age of literature and art for Poland as it was for many other European countries, though the artists are not well known in the West. After Western models had been introduced in the fifteenth century, the sixteenth century produced native-born and educated artists and poets. Two of the best-known were Nicholas Rey (1505-1569) and John Kochanowski (1530-1584). Rey wrote both satiric and religious poetry, drama, didactic poems, epigrams and prose. He was known for his portrayal of character and an earthy touch. Kochanowski created some literary masterpieces that are still read and admired by Poles, though little known outside the country. His range was also wide, though he preferred poetry, anecdotes and shorter pieces.

There were many other poets and writers, historians, composers, sculptors and architects. Their creations were very much in the spirit of the Renaissance but distinctly national as well, much more than imitative. This wave of creativity was generated by and for the nobility and clergy. The burghers played a small role as creators or consumers.

Poland was a very diverse empire. Its recognized law codes evolved as far apart as Europe and Russia, among other sources; there were six official languages including even Hebrew; Lithuania, half the kingdom, was largely Greek Orthodox instead of Roman Catholic, and Poland was the home of the Jewish Pale.

Poland also contrasted with much of Europe of the sixteenth century in its relative tolerance to ideas challenging dogmas of the Catholic Church. A pattern of tolerance established by Casimir Piast and continued by Jagiello—a lukewarm convert to Christianity anyway—had made Poland an oasis of religious freedom, a haven for the persecuted of other countries. The continuity of tolerance was assured in the sixteenth century when Sigismund August swore fealty to the Catholic Church in order to gain support for his marriage to the Calvinist daughter of Nicholas Radziwill. Thereafter, though he officially supported the Church, he was unwilling to take action against the spread of Reformation ideas. This would have been difficult to accomplish without violence, since the children of the gentry were often educated in Calvinist Switzerland, while Lutheranism spread among the burghers who, as in Hungary, often came from Germany. The nobility were particularly receptive to Calvinism, since, unlike Lutheranism, it did not advocate royal control of the Church. Hence it was supportive of aristocratic dominance. James Nelson points out that although this toleration had royal sanction, it was applied variously in different locales. A person who had mobility could move from areas of intolerance, but a bound serf could not.

Protestantism was eventually unsuccessful largely for three reasons. The szlachta were interested in it at least as much as a weapon against overpowerful prelates as otherwise; when the need for such a weapon subsided, so did their interest. Protestantism was thoroughly divided against itself and causing more and more trouble elsewhere in Europe, a divisiveness that had increasingly less appeal to a Poland that depended on consensus structures for its existence. And in the 1560's a most remarkable cleric, Stanislaw Cardinal Hosius, began a Catholic revival that eventually monopolized Polish intellectual life. In Poland Protestantism died not of persecution but of inanition, and of religious wars there continued to be none.

Termination

Peace ended as a result of what appeared to be another shrewd piece of Polish diplomacy. When the Jagiello line came to an end the Poles, led by the Chancellor John Zamoyski, elected the Swedish crown prince Sigismund Vasa king (1587-1632), making an ally of a potential enemy and forming an alliance against the rising danger of Russia.

But Sigismund had the great fault of not being Polish. He was not raised to the Polish consensus, he felt no loyalty to it, and when the Sejm's requirement for effective unanimity interfered with his wishes, he felt no compunctions against trying to change this, or against acting on his own without consulting it. Zamoyski fought this successfully during his lifetime but died in 1605. In 1606 Sigismund tried to establish a permanent standing army, a regular yearly subsidy of the Crown, and Sejm decisions by simple majority rather than near-unanimity. Nicholas Zebrzydowski, a relative and protege of Zamoyski, used the occasion to assume leadership of the opposition and invoked the old medieval right of rebellion against a contumacious king. A Sejm of 1609 ended the rebellion, declaring general amnesty and the inviolability of the standing constitution. The king was defeated, but royal absolutism came to be the permanent bogey of the szlachta. Their answer, formally beginning in 1652, was the **liberum veto,** whereby a minority even of one could dissent and thereby paralyze the Sejm. Then in 1655, with the szlachta demoralized and partly treasonous, Sweden invaded and occupied almost all of Poland; soon after this was settled there was another rebellion. The **liberum veto** came to be more and more frequently abused and the szlachta repeatedly declared insurrection, and the resulting civil wars could be bitter and prolonged.

Reflections

The Polish Peace was maintained at home by royal agreement with the szlachta for a sharing of authority, abroad by a diplomacy that sealed the country against attack. Domestically this meant an ever-growing influence for the Sejm, but so long as the Crown accepted this the system seems to have worked. Abroad it meant alliance, then unification, with Lithuania and presumably might have ended the same way with Sweden. Agreement with the Habsburgs fended off any threat from Germany, though also preventing expansion in that direction. It is a maxim of international relations that states tend to ally with their neighbors' neighbors, but in Poland's case alliance with the immediate neighbors is much more the pattern and seems to have worked.

Although Poland like Hungary was predominantly Catholic, the Peace was maintained by tolerance of minorities rather than by religious unity. This tolerance excluded the religious wars that broke the Hungarian Peace.

The Peace saw a great period of Polish culture; this declined afterwards. The szlachta became thoroughly conservative and humanist contacts became scarce as Poland was continually at war.

A study of leadership indicates that a century passed between the building of the medieval Polish state by Ladislas I and its consolidation by Jagiello. Sigismund II had the trappings of magnificence. There were no political reformers among the Jagiellos, arguably because none were needed. Sigismund Vasa's efforts at change failed disastrously, though in retrospect they were very probably needed.

Both the Hungarian and the Polish Peace came into existence during a period between the waning of the medieval empires and the rise of their modern successors. The governments of each derived their revenues from a peaceful subsistence economy that also permitted the development of crafts and trade. Each reached a high level of cultural development and then collapsed from failure to develop a cohesive and adaptable political system, though in Poland's case this failure came only after two centuries of success. Historians would look back on each of these periods as a golden age.

5

The Brandenburger Peace
(1488–1627)

<u>Origins</u>

  The history of the Germans is difficult to contend with because of the multitude of political entities existing through tumultuous times. For Germany as a whole there appear to be no centuries of peace. Rebellions or invasions can be found in every century. It seemed likely, however, that more than one of the individual margravates, duchies or bishoprics would have enjoyed a century of peace somewhere along the line. But how to find them? There were often more than 300 such entities in Germany at a given time, and over the past 1,000 years there must have been at least as many political units.

  A review of several representative individual histories—among them Bavaria, Wurttemberg, Pomerania and Saxony—indicated that regional waters were as troubled as the German sea in general. Often these provincial areas were subject to local rebellions when Germany as a whole was relatively undisturbed. And then a rather unhopeful sunset cast produced an unexpected strike in Brandenburg.

  Certainly Brandenburg seemed to be an unlikely area in which to look for peace since it was later to be linked with Prussia, traditionally viewed as the center of German militarism. The link with Prussia, however, was not forged until the seventeenth century. Five centuries before that the territory of Brandenburg was built up by the Ascanian family in North Germany between the Elbe and the Oder Rivers. Though the territory was no larger than the state of Vermont, it was considerable for its place and time, and its rulers gained additional prestige from the fact that they were guardians of the German Empire's borders from attacks from the east. In the thirteenth century, the Ascanian rulers became electors, which is to say they were among the seven German political and religious leaders who had the responsibility for electing new emperors.

  During the fourteenth century, however, the dynasty died out and the territory passed first into the hands of a Bavarian family, then to the Luxembourgs. During this period the towns gained considerable control of their own destinies. Local administrators and judges, ruling in the name of the frequently absent Bavarian or Luxembourger margrave, gained more autonomy. As the power of the margrave declined, the towns purchased the right to their own jurisdiction, and even elected commissions whose sole function was to protect the rights of the town against the margrave.

  In the fifteenth century the Emperor Sigismund assigned the management of this inherited territory to one of his able supporters, Frederick of Hohenzollern, and a few years later named him Elector of Brandenburg. Frederick (1417-1440) and his sons Frederick II (1440-1470) and Albert Achilles (1470-1486)

28

set to work establishing control over the neglected margravate. It was not until the reign of Albert's successor, John Cicero (1486-1499) that peace was established throughout the land. It was maintained through the sixteenth century when constant civil wars among princes were rife through Germany, when the advent of professional mercenary armies meant an increase in maurauding, and when the Reformation brought the Knights' War, the destructive Peasants' Revolt, and the war of the Schmalkaldic League to various parts of the land. It was maintained during a period of administrative reform that saw the princely household transform itself into a central government at the same time the vanquished nobles were recovering their earlier independence. It was maintained into the seventeenth century while the Hohenzollerns acquired title to the Rhineland territories and the territories of the Teutonic Knights that were later to give them a basis for a powerful European kingdom that was never to match the modest Brandenburg state in providing peace for its subjects. It ended finally in the Thirty Years War, which engulfed the whole of Germany.

In a century of solid administrative reform, the early Hohenzollerns reorganized their state. Frederick I vigorously established his control over an unruly, brigandish rural nobility while conciliating the towns. He broke the power of the nobles in a series of campaigns against their castles, demonstrating the force of the newly developed cannon. He restored property to peasants and helped them protect it against their landlords. But then his desire to expand north toward the Baltic led him to seek alliance with Poland against Pomerania at a time when his emperor and patron was pushing policies opposing Polish interests. When the resulting conflict went badly, Frederick showed that his first loyalties were to the Empire, and returned to imperial affairs, leaving Brandenburg under the rule of his son, John the Alchemist.

John allowed the nobles to recover their power, and his tenacious younger brother Frederick (nicknamed "Iron Tooth") was sent to Brandenburg in 1437 to restore Hohenzollern control. Frederick, who succeeded his father in 1440, as John was given the older family territories, not only reasserted control over the nobility, but went on to begin reducing the independence of the towns. Taking advantage of a quarrel in Berlin in 1442, he supported the guilds against the patricians, obtaining veto power over the election of councillors and the right to nominate judges. He built a castle (called "coercion castle") in the center of town, from which he was able to quell a major revolt of Berlin's citizens in 1448. It required several decades, however, before he and Albert were able to complete the subjugation of all the towns within the territory. The process was expensive and Frederick Iron Tooth left a deficit that his brother, who seemed to take a larger view of administration and who, in any event, was left with only mopping-up operations, was able to pay off before the end of his reign. A policy of passing the entire margravate on to the eldest son was formally established by Albert and adhered to by all but one of his successors.

The Peace either began with suppressing a rebellion in 1488, the center of resistance being in Spandau, which had supported Frederick II 40 years before when he quelled the Berlin revolution, or it may have begun a few years later. Erving Beauregard says there were Pomeranian and Silesian incursions during the reign of John Cicero. It lasted until 1627, when the first of several invading armies crossed the Brandenburger frontier. The Peace included the 10,000 square miles of territory between the rivers, and an adjacent territory half that size, the New Mark, east of the Oder, acquired by Frederick II from the Teutonic Order.

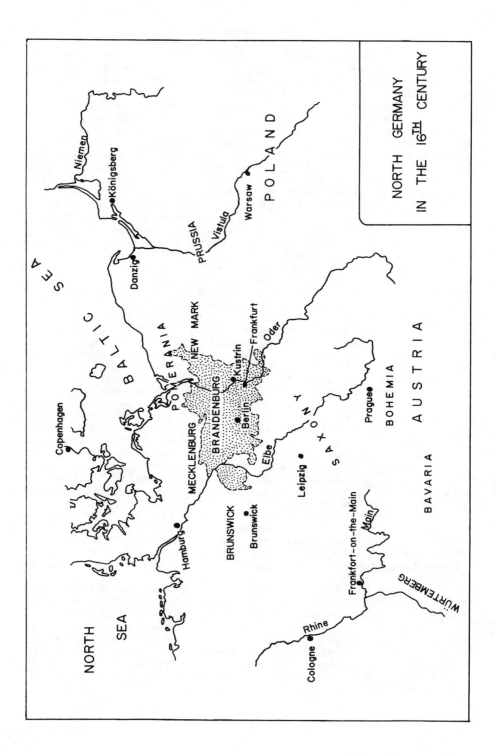

NORTH GERMANY IN THE 16TH CENTURY

Characterization

Throughout the Empire as a whole the revival of classical learning was leading to the employment of a precise, written, uniform, academic Roman law in place of a varying, verbal, local, traditional German law. The establishment of a university at Frankfurt by Joachim I (1499-1535) led to the training and employment of administrators who understood this law, a consequent centralization of law within the nation, and its more uniform application to nobles, townsmen and peasants.

The administrative reform that began with Frederick II and Albert continued under Joachim I who placed the towns directly under the surveillance of his government and reorganized a state-controlled police force. It culminated in the formalization of administration under Joachim II (1531-1571). Whereas under his predecessors the marshal might be in charge of both foreign policy and the royal kitchen, under Joachim four branches of government were established: administrative, financial, judicial and ecclesiastical. Thus the elector modeled his administration on that of a state rather than an estate. The process was completed under Joachim Frederick (1598-1608) by the creation of a privy council that became more influential than the Landtag, a diet of the estates.

This tidy picture of efficient consolidation of a state is completely upset, however, by the recovery of power by the nobility during the reign of this same Joachim II. For Joachim, unlike most Hohenzollerns, was recklessly extravagant. He could never balance his budget. As a result he several times asked the town and country estates to assume his debts, and this they did in return for the right to assess and collect their own taxes, raise their own troops and otherwise run their own domestic affairs. Thus the nobility, which had been politically suppressed, recovered privileges equivalent to that of the Polish and Hungarian nobility, except that the town patricians also shared in them. The losers in this transformation were the town guilds and the peasants.

The nobility did not, however, return to the intramural squabbling that had characterized Brandenburg before the Hohenzollerns. This pattern at least had been broken by several decades of peace and the identification among the town and country nobles of a common bond of interest. But the nobles did not oppress the peasants and lower classes as much as they might have because there were also conflicting interests between town and country, between greater and lesser rural nobles, and between merchants and guilds, so that they often checked one another.

Another reversal in pattern during the reign of Joachim II came about because his father dissented from the succession system established by Albert Achilles and left the New Mark to a younger son, John of Kustrin. This could have been a disaster, because John was a very different personality from his brother, much more like his father, and they disagreed not only in administrative style, but also in attitudes toward the Reformation where John was more inclined to support the Protestant cause. As it turned out, the brothers complemented one another, since John's more cautious fiscal policies provided a surplus to counterbalance the deficit accumulated by Joachim, while Joachim's religious caution tempered John's enthusiasm. Then they died within ten days of one another, John leaving no sons, so that the inheritance once again reverted intact to Joachim's son, John George (1571-1598).

There is little in the historical record to indicate that this was a time of general prosperity. The peasantry was relegated to serfdom and the land they worked was difficult to cultivate, much of it consisting of marsh and sand. Population was relatively thin and life was harsh. Nor were the artisans free to develop in the towns, and taxes must have been high and efficiently collected.

Nor was the peace anything like perfect. There are indications that there may have been border raids of some sort during the reign of John Cicero, as well as problems of highway robbery during the reign of Joachim I, and probably in other periods too. State justice, particularly during the time of Joachim I, was likely to be crude and violent, and on one occasion his administration had 38 Jews burned in the center of Berlin.

There are indications that the first half of the sixteenth century was a bad time for German agriculture in general. Overseas exploration was drawing farm labor from Europe, a population Brandenburg could ill afford to lose. This may have contributed to pressures for serfdom. Perhaps because of the imposition of serfdom there seems to have been considerable economic improvement in cultivation and commerce during the reign of John George, who came to be known as "The Economist." Still, his successor, Joachim Frederick (1598-1608) was forced to call the Landstag to pay further debts which, of course, helped restore the political and economic power of the nobility.

While these domestic transformations were taking place, the Reformation, whose winds were to be strongly felt in the peace of Poland, exploded in sixteenth-century Germany. Everywhere Germans responded to the nationalist, separatist implications of the doctrines of a Christian monk, Martin Luther. Luther was driven from the Church and in the 1520's his "Protestant" doctrines were winning widespread respect. This religious catalyst gave rise to the Peasants' Rebellion of 1524-1526 in which, at its height, 300,000 peasants and urban poor took up arms and much of Germany was devastated. But the Brandenburg of Joachim I, a bit removed from the main currents of culture, remained relatively undisturbed as its grim leader took a hard line against religious wavering, executing several dozen brigands, some of noble rank, to demonstrate he meant to keep order. The extent of his problem was subsequently demonstrated, however, when his wife turned Protestant and fled while his brother, a cardinal, showed strong liberal leanings.

By the time Joachim II came to the throne, the situation had changed. The advocates of Lutheranism and Romanism were almost equally balanced. After four years of walking on eggshells, Joachim finally decided to adopt a watered-down Lutheranism, but he kept much of the old Roman ceremony in it, allowed his wife to remain a Catholic, stayed in close touch with the emperor, and refused to join the Protestant Schmalkaldic League. He did not, however, permit religious freedom, as the Jagiellos were doing, but anticipating what was to become an accepted compromise for the Empire as a whole, he allowed those subjects who could not accept the state religion to emigrate to lands they found more congenial. Thus Joachim II managed to avoid the wars of religion that plagued so much of Germany in this period.

When, in the seventeenth century, John Sigismund (1608-1619) adopted Calvinism, he did not insist that his subjects, by then Lutherans, join him. If the rest of the German princes had been able to follow this example of tolerance, as they had that of Joachim II, there might never have been a Thirty Years War. Apparently tolerance did not extend to the Elector's family. His wife was a stern Lutheran, and in their disputes the royal couple were known to have tossed plates and crystal glasses at each other.

The picture of rising learning and rational resolution of political and religious reform should not be overdrawn. Even the hard-nosed Joachim I could be influenced by the mysticism and irrationality of the times. His addiction to astrology led him to take his entire court to the top of a 200-foot hill (mountains being hard to find around Berlin) to spend a long day sitting in a drizzle awaiting a predicted flood that never appeared. The fate of the grim Elector's astrologers has not been recorded.

Nor was Brandenburg in the vanguard of the intellectual ferment of the time. As Marriott and Robertson put it:

> The heroic and decisive personalities in the Germany of Erasmus, Luther, Charles V, and Maurice of Saxony are to be found elsewhere

than in Brandenburg, and neither the Hohenzollern electors nor their dominions can be proved to have contributed the capital formative forces that moulded thought or action between the days of Hus and the opening of the Thirty Years War [1946:51].

The foreign policies of the Hohenzollerns of those days were quiet and conservative. Frederick II bought New Mark, east of the Oder, from the Teutonic Knights, who needed money to carry on a last-ditch war against Poland. Through purchase, marriage and negotiations his successors added a number of towns and bishoprics. Finally John Sigismund fell heir to three small provinces on the Rhine and to the Dukedom of Prussia after a good deal of diplomatic maneuvering in which a number of his predecessors had an important hand. When his succession to Cleves was disputed by the Count Palatine of Neuburg, the Elector tried to work out a partition rather than risk involving his troops in a drawn out conflict. Military activity against other cities and provinces during the whole of the peace period seems to have been virtually absent for the Hohenzollern militia.

During the first century of the peace, when Brandenburg was strong enough to entertain foreign adventures, her leaders were either involved in watching for social rebellions or in trying to avoid religious conflict. During the last few decades when Brandenburg was weak, her German neighbors were either divided by succession and religious conflicts, as were Brunswick and Saxony, or simply not strong enough to take advantage of the situation, as were Mecklenburg and Pomerania.

There were also two neighboring great powers: Austria and Poland. Habsburg Austria had received continuous cooperation from Joachim II, who kept the Emperor Charles V apprised of the aims and methods of his religious policies, who refused to join the Schmalkaldic League or become involved in the resulting war against the emperor, and who cooperated in the Peace of Augsburg, which in 1555 brought about a compromise between Catholics and Protestants and a resulting reduction of hostilities. Austria had reason to be grateful to Brandenburg and to anticipate future cooperation. As for Poland, we have already seen that an attack on Pomerania or Brandenburg might have undermined the pro-Habsburg policy that the Jagiellos regarded as basic to the defense of their realm against the Ottoman empire.

Termination

The end of the Peace came with the devastating Thirty Years War. The Elector George William (1619-1640) first sided with the Protestants and his country was overrun by Catholics. He then tried switching alliances and his country was overrun by Protestants. The behavior of the invaders from both sides, who lived off the land, was atrocious. The invading armies remained fourteen years from 1627 to 1641. During that time the population of Brandenburg is believed to have fallen from 1,500,000 to 600,000.

The war was so violent and so widespread that not much of Germany escaped. It is difficult to see how Brandenburg could have avoided invasion. But if Brandenburg had a strong army, and if Joachim's policy of noninvolvement had been repeated, it is possible that the Imperial and Swedish armies would have preferred to fight on other territory.

It is possible. But Brandenburg had no such army. The nobles preferred to control their own, and the Elector's feudal army was no match for the standing armies of Albrecht Wallenstein of Bohemia or Gustavus Adolphus of Sweden. The Poles were to learn the same lesson in 1665.

The acquisition of East Prussia could have been a factor in the termination of the peace. With that acquisition the territory of Brandenburg doubled, but divided by Poland and Pomerania. There were more possibilities for conflict, and there was more territory to defend against external intervention.

Finally, but least important, George William seems to have been a well-intentioned but uninspiring, indecisive leader. Even if there had been a really able leader, as his son, Frederick William (1640-1688) later proved to be, it is difficult to see what he could have done. He might have put together an inferior army that would have been beaten anyway and brought the land even more damage than it actually suffered. Really, if any leader is to share the blame, it should not be the mediocre George William, but the ambiguously able Joachim II. His policies, after all, left George William without an army.

Reflections

It seems that a centralization of administration was necessary to end the internal squabbles that had characterized Brandenburg in the period of Bavarian and Luxembourg ownership. But once this had taken place, and a new pattern of relationships had been established, the loss of a central checking force did not mean a resumption of conflict. The recognition of a common bond among the nobles and patricians preserved the peace. The existence of some such spirit among a nobility seems to have been a common factor in all the European peace periods encountered thus far. Some bonding spirit among the elite of any culture is probably a factor found in most enduring peace periods.

If there must be reservations about the importance of centralization, so must there be about the system of succession. While it is true that Albert Achilles' system generally prevailed and may have prevented internal conflict, the one exception seems also to have contributed to the peace, with the financially prudent John of Kustrin balancing the religiously prudent Joachim II.

The Hohenzollerns seem to have done a masterful job of reacting to the difficult religious situation that confronted them. Joachim I suppressed when suppression was still possible and then died conveniently at 50. Joachim II performed a marvelous balancing act. His policies were avowedly, deliberately, painfully and elaborately directed toward maintaining internal peace. Finally John Sigismund foresaw the possibility of religious tolerance.

In both Poland and Brandenburg, a willingness to compromise and to tolerate served to prevent conflict that was taking place anywhere else in Europe in which the challenges to the Western Christian Church were allowed to take root.

Unlike the other examples from early Europe, the Electors of Brandenburg were in a situation in which they were not called upon to defend their territory from outside attack. Nor did they choose to commit themselves to attacks outside their own borders, which was not true of Poland, Hungary or Venice.

The Electors of Brandenburg were not attacked by neighboring great powers for reasons that were beyond their control, but they could recognize these reasons and at least not upset them. And, as is true in each of the other European peace periods, they were not in conflict with neighbors of comparable power, either because each had internal problems, because there were safer areas for external adventures, or possibly because there were feelings of empathy for fellow Germans or fellow Slavs of comparable rank and power.

At first glance, Frederick I would seem to be the founder of the peace as he was of the Brandenburg Hohenzollern line. But he withdrew from Brandenburg and by the time Frederick II came to power, he had virtually to begin from scratch, and this time with a forewarned nobility. Nor does Frederick

I, a reader of Petrarch and lover of books, have the image of a founder. But Iron Tooth, harsh and focused, filled the role perfectly.

In his management of finances, his arrangement of succession, and his completion of the taming of nobility and towns, Albert Achilles seems to have made a major contribution to reconciliation. Indeed, it is difficult to find a safe date for the beginning of the peace before the end of his reign.

Joachim II is a personality of a different sort. His weaknesses are qualities of humanity rather lacking in his family. He can't manage financial affairs because he is more interested in dealing with people. Yet only someone with his touch could have handled the delicate problem of personal relations which is his greatest triumph. So he is both the man who saved the peace and the man who can be blamed, if any can, for its ultimate loss. Joachim is also, in an odd way, a reformer, if we define the reformer as one who alters a structure to give it new life, this not by his administrative centralization, but for allowing the nobility to change the structure. But the first real reformer, Frederick William, came along too late to save the peace. Insofar as there is a magnificent monarch, Joachim II is also that. But magnificence and culture really weren't in the style of the Hohenzollerns.

The Hohenzollerns had their share of luck in the way in which leadership happened to emerge. Perhaps Iron Tooth's withdrawal from active rule in 1470 was timely, in that Albert Achilles' subtle talents were more appropriate for the situation that was then emerging. And Joachim I also died a timely death perhaps, leaving the scene when a compromiser was needed to preserve the peace. That compromiser, Joachim II, may not have had all the skills necessary to deal with the problems of his reign had his father not chosen to violate the succession principle and leave part of the rule to John of Kustrin. But if the very different brothers had fallen out, and it is amazing that they did not, would we historians not be blaming Joachim I for failing to perceive the wisdom of Albert Achilles? As it is we must concede the possibility that he really knew his sons along with the possibility that Brandenburg in this period was extremely lucky, as it was to be unlucky in the next century under George William.

Marriott and Robinson rate the monarchs between Frederick II and George William as "men of sound capacity, eminently practical, patient, and industrious" although "no single one of them reached the first rank in German still less European history" (1946:51). The monarchs who followed Joachim II were certainly not outstanding, but the problem they had to deal with was in some ways more difficult than that confronting Frederick I and his sons. They had to contend with a nobility united to defend its privileges, whereas their fifteenth century predecessors encountered a divided and feuding nobility.

There is certainly a tautological process in the evaluation of leadership. If they encounter and master a crisis we say they are great; if they fail, we judge them inept. If, like John Cicero they inherit a going concern and keep it running, we are not likely to say much about them. Probably they are like most of us, mediocre people who can more or less do a job they are trained to do so long as it doesn't change too much or pose problems for which they have no training. Probably George William, like John Cicero, was an ordinary man, as most men, even kings, are likely to be. In John Cicero's situation, we should never have heard of him. John Cicero, in George William's situation, would have been perceived as weak, indecisive, inept. Given the training monarchs ordinarily get, the really incompetent or irresponsible are likely to be even rarer than the really outstanding.

6

The Spanish Imperial Peace
(1492–1808)

The Permanent Sixteenth Century

"No other sixteenth- or seventeenth-century State was
faced with so vast a problem of administration, and few
succeeded in preserving over so long a period such a high
degree of public order in an age when revolts were endemic"
(Elliott 1963:376, on Spain proper).
  "Despite the relentless enmity of the strongest and ablest
European powers, the Empire lived three centuries which
count in History as one of the most creative, and certainly
the most peaceful [periods], a continent has ever known"
(Madariaga 1947a:281, on Spanish America).

Duration: 1492–1808 in Spain; 1535–1810 in New Spain; 1580–1780 in Peru.
Territory: Spain, excepting Catalonia; Spanish America, excepting the Caribbean
and certain Indian frontiers. Even the Philippines could be included, depending
on how one interprets the effect of Moro seaborne raids, from 1648 to 1896.

Origins

For the greater part of the fifteenth century the kingdoms of Spain
were at war. Not that this was a new phenomenon; with the effective completion
of the Reconquest in the early 1200's the last remaining Muslim outpost, Granada, became no more than a side issue, and the warlords of Spain turned their
very abundant energies mainly on each other. Occasionally the kings managed
to force some order on each regional version of this chaos, but these proved
to be thoroughly impermanent settlements. This was particularly the case
in Castile. Six civil wars during this one century served to outline the competing
interests well enough, and also to eliminate most of the competitors; when
the Peace was finally settled only one of the greatest families dated before
1400, and that only to 1398. The commanderships of the Crusading Orders
also went to the great lords, and archbishoprics and bishoprics to their younger
brothers, and both commanders and clerics felt as free as any other nobles
to lead their personal armies against each other or the king.
  In the 1460's these various competitions polarized around the question
of the succession to Henry IV (1454–1474). Henry began his reign with a program
of royalist consolidation not greatly different from that soon to be successfully
carried out by his successors, but he was not the man to accomplish it. Among
other failings he had the reputation of impotence, which meant a challenge

to the legitimacy of his daughter as successor. The opposition eventually gathered around Henry's half-sister Isabella, and Henry's death led to the last and most violent of the Castilian civil wars.

By this time the great lords themselves were tiring of the anarchy, and it was becoming apparent that Isabella and her husband Ferdinand, crown prince of Aragon, were the likely eventual winners. The decision still took six years (1474-1480), and had to be made largely in terms of compromises with one great lord at a time. Popular tradition suggests that the Catholic Sovereigns settled this affair in some kind of Spanish parallel to the solutions of the Tudors and some other European kings, forming an alliance with the cities and the rising merchant class against the aristocracy. But this impression seems to be a mixture of trying to force their actions into a standardized mold and of tracts issued by later polemicists who wanted to claim Ferdinand and Isabella as prophets of their own favored solutions. In actuality the victory of the Catholic Sovereigns was won by their own allies among the great nobles, who would not have favored any such program. Instead the lords were essentially bought off one by one, with confirmation of all their land-grabbings except the most recent and with award of almost the entirety of newly conquered Granada to replace what the Crown did reclaim. The result as of 1500 was that the nobles, less than two percent of the population, owned or had jurisdiction over 97% of the land of Castile.

Ferdinand and Isabella also created or modified various controls over the nobles. A kind of peacekeeping force, the **Hermandad,** was formed and approved by those aristocrats already on the royal side for use against those who were not; once the pacification was complete it was disbanded in turn as potentially dangerous. "Unnecessary" castles were destroyed. Private warfare was prohibited and Isabella even put on a great show of physical illness when this prohibition was violated. (Even this did not work in Aragon, and there the private wars continued for awhile.) When an heir to the throne was born, Ferdinand and Isabella began granting posts in his service to the nobles in hopes of detaching them from their country bases and beginning their transformation into a court. They also packed the aristocracy with their own supporters, more than doubling the number of dukes. The Crusading Orders were brought under control by the direct expedient of annexing them to the Crown, though this was not made formally permanent until the reign of Charles V. Control of the great prelates was only begun; not until the middle sixteenth century did the Crown acquire the right to appoint all religious officers in their realms. But the Catholic Sovereigns managed, under the doctrine of **pase regio,** to control religious actions. Decrees even by the pope had to be approved by the Crown before publication in Spain, and Ferdinand reprimanded his viceroy of Naples for not hanging a papal messenger who violated this edict.

But they did not limit their work to controlling obvious competitors. As rulers they also moved firmly toward creating a Crown-centered management system, particularly for Castile. The royal privy council was divided into three parts: State, Treasury, and Justice. State was made a decorative nonentity suitable for keeping its aristocratic members out of more serious mischief. Justice, with its membership an absolute majority of trained jurists not necessarily aristocrats, became the major instrument of government within Castile. Other councils were added as opportune. From Aragon they imported the Inquisition, modifying it in favor of their own complete control and placing it under its own council. The cities were brought under control by successful general application of an old individual remedy. For centuries the Crown had sent officials, **corregidores,** to manage the affairs of cities in a state of confusion, and previous kings had tried to expand their powers by making these officials permanent. The Catholic Sovereigns succeeded, regardless of the wishes of the cities, which acquiesced on grounds of temporary need. The Crown created

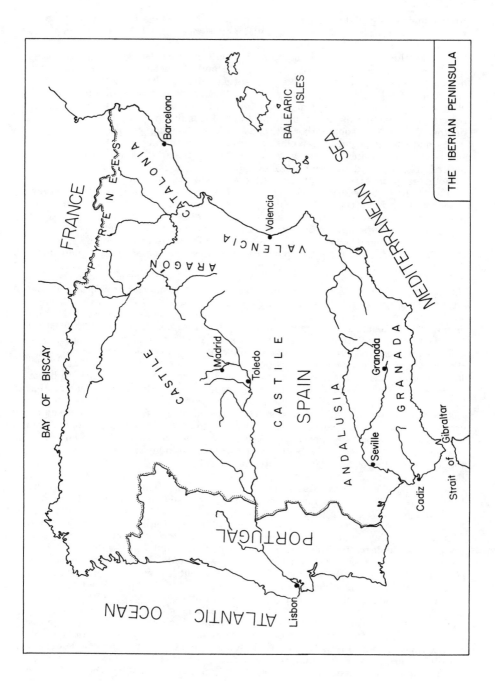

THE IBERIAN PENINSULA

FRANCE

BAY OF BISCAY

PYRENEES

CATALONIA

Barcelona

BALEARIC
ISLES

MEDITERRANEAN SEA

ARAGON

VALENCIA

Valencia

CASTILE

CASTILE

Madrid

Toledo

SPAIN

ANDALUSIA

GRANADA

Granada

Seville

Gibraltar

Strait of

Cadiz

PORTUGAL

ATLANTIC OCEAN

Lisbon

an internal information service reporting on the efficiency of local and regional governments. Finally there was the problem of public relations. Here they had the good fortune of a Crusade not of their making. In 1482 raids and counter-raids reopened the war with Granada; the Catholic Sovereigns assumed control of this and in 1492 cleared the last non-Christian kingdom from the soil of Spain. The Reconquest was complete, and the glory of its completion went to Ferdinand and Isabella. For this and for the ordering of Castile they were perceived even centuries later as the greatest monarchs of Spanish history, whose names were sufficient to hallow any cause. When Isabella died in 1504 the basic conditions and institutions of the Spanish Imperial Peace were all in place.

Characterization

The Spanish Imperial Peace was over three centuries long, and it is hardly to be expected that conditions remained the same all through such a long period. Nevertheless for more than two of these three centuries remarkably little institutional development occurred; one might even argue that only the competence with which the institutions were managed was changed. After Ferdinand and Isabella, the Peace saw ten more kings. The best, Philip II (1556–1598), has some claim to greatness, and may be described as the absolutely consummate bureaucrat in both the good and the bad implications of the label: a total and highly methodical workaholic, but equally jealous, suspicious, professionally self-righteous and autocratic without any great creativity. His father Charles V (1517–1556) was next best, a careful if not highly intelligent spend-thrift and heavily involved with events outside Spain, to the ruin of the royal finances. The ninth, Charles III (1759–1788), at least rose to a mediocrity that seems genuine competence in comparison with the rest of the lot. Looking at the others, it is perhaps the greatest testimonial to the work of the Catholic Sovereigns that the system survived under their successors.

Therefore with Ferdinand and Isabella gone, the Spanish Imperial Peace becomes the institutions and attitudes they left behind. Castile included seven-eighths of the population and the most vital part of the economy of the united realms, and its institutional influence was overwhelming. The realms of Aragon remained separate, indeed fanatically so, but Castile was so predominant that the contributions of the others may in this brief study be largely ignored.

Most important is the basic Spanish-Castilian understanding of the nature of government and society. On this there was so much agreement that the boundaries of individual realms (possibly excepting Catalonia) made no difference at all. Four words are key: Christianity, justice, **nobleza**, and **fuero.**

Imperial Spain was **Christian.** This cannot be too strongly emphasized. To separate Spanish from Christian life at the time would be to separate ice from cold, heat from fire. The **Reyes Catolicos** were the Christian universal rulers of the realms of the Spains. This is regardless of the Moorish and Jewish populations, both of them large and greatly contributory to earlier Spanish development. By the time of the Catholic Sovereigns the old **convivencia,** living together, of the three religious communities was a thing of the past. The Christian religion was to be a foundation of state, with no dilatory compromises considered. The characteristic Spanish attitude that stability lies in community of belief was formed in this period. This accounts, for example, for the popularity of the Inquisition, especially among the "Old Christians." Feared as it was, the "heaven-sent remedy" was respected as a necessary tool to maintain the Spanishness of Spain, and one of the sources of outcry against the liberals of the 1800's was their abolition of it. And the community of belief did in fact work; even at the depth of decline, when rags and starvation were the common lot of most of Spain, the basic orientations and institutions, even the social positions and problems of individuals, remained unquestioned. Moreover, this sweeping agreement led to a remarkable freedom of speech and print; censorship of a sort existed, but books and pamphlets circulated freely in Spain that were burned by the public hangman farther north. Galileo considered fleeing to Spain and perhaps to America to escape the harassment of Italy, but was confined before his inquiries on the subject were answered. This unquestioning acceptance of a particular value system as being the single legitimate Christian way of life had unpleasant consequences for Spain's later ability to keep technical pace with Europe, but more than anything else it was responsible for the stability that made the Spanish Imperial Peace.

It is, however, noteworthy that it was also directly responsible for two of the greatest interruptions of the Peace. Spain had non-Christians: Jews and Muslims. Under the ethos of Christianity, these groups by definition did not fit. The Jews were therefore converted or expelled as early as 1492, and an attempt was made to forcibly convert the Muslims, who formed a large part of the population of Granada and Valencia. The conversions were very shallow in many cases and were the occasion for founding the Castilian Inquisition. Moreover, both government and aristocracy tried to continue exploitation of the new Christians as if they were still old pagans; moreover again, the Muslim threat, from Turkey, was reaching a new height. Ottoman soldiers were even landed in Spain to support the Spanish ex-Muslims. The result was civil war and in 1565 expulsion, and it was a very popular result.

The second key word is justice, and specifically Christian justice. If the Anglo-American political system be broadly considered as a development around the legislative branch, then the Spanish political tradition is equally a creature of the judiciary. Overwhelmingly the single most important attribute of office in the Spanish realms was judicial authority, the rendering of justice. This does not mean that laws were always obeyed or that the system was always just; by proper Christian doctrine this had become impossible as of the fall from grace in Eden, and perfection was not to be expected. But it emphatically was to be aimed for. Thus when the Americas were conquered there was a prolonged debate, at times agonized and causing one convulsive constitutional crisis, on the nature of the Castilian Crown's claim and authority in the New World (religious, of course: Castile would Christianize the Indies) and consequent proper treatment of the natives. And if the Americas were not managed in so Christian a way as would be desirable, the Philippines provided a second chance. When the conquest of the Philippines proved drastically unprofitable, it was decided not to abandon them precisely because it would be unjust to abandon Christian colonists and converts.

This orientation resulted in an institutional arrangement quite different from current constitutional ideas. The principal differences were two. First, by definition an important office was a judicial office. There were officials without essential rights of jurisdiction, such as military commanders and tax collectors, but they are nowhere considered important to Spanish evolution until the end of the Peace. Otherwise, with all offices having essentially the same function, there was a very vague and overlapping delineation of authority, making for permanent conflict which had to be resolved.

The other difference in judicial orientation is the peculiarly Hispanic concept of the **poder moderador**, the moderating power. Since in all offices jurisdiction was the highest attribute, it was considered quite normal for an order issued by an official in his administrative capacity to be rejected and appealed back to the same official in his judicial capacity. Since, moreover, justice was peculiarly seated in the Crown, the Crown was the focus of such appeals, even against its own orders. This practice ameliorated the Spanish tendency to issue laws framed in terms of a very abstract justice far away from their actual area of application; the right of the king to issue such orders was accepted as was his right as lord of justice to have final say in such enactments, but the enactment itself was vitiated pending reconsideration. The doctrine is called **se acata pero no se cumple,** "[the order] is respected but is not obeyed," with the additional qualification that it was "impossible to put His Majesty's command into practice without great ruin and detriment to the republic." This practice was particularly common in the colonies, where such orders were popularly called unconsecrated (communion) Hosts. Even the absolutist Bourbon regime of the 1700's accepted the practice, if reluctantly.

The third word was **nobleza,** the recognized aristocratic value system and code of conduct, so to speak the actual behavior code where Christianity was the theory. This was a heritage from those days of old when knights indeed were bold; boldness, self-assertiveness, brash independence of any and every authority but the king's was its overriding characteristic. Although aristocracy was technically a distinct estate, in Spain nobleza was not just for aristocrats. The proper Castilian of any rank literally lived his life as if it were a book of chivalry, as if he were Amadis of Gaul posturing before history. A day laborer would work as long as was absolutely necessary to keep body and soul together and then walk away from his job, put on such cloak and sword as he could manage, and play the lordly **hidalgo** (lit.: son of somebody) until starvation forced him very reluctantly back to the workbench. To be a proper Spaniard was to be an aristocrat, other factors notwithstanding, and the aristocrat in rags was very much a stable figure of Spanish life. The rags were tolerable because of the aristocracy, and this was no small factor in keeping the Peace when much too much of Spain began to find itself in rags.

Fourth was **fuero.** The word is roughly translatable as charter, either a law or a privilege, and it concerned practically every institution of any kind in Spain. It was essentially a declaration of existence validated by custom or the king, and individual cities, professions, and many other things each had their own. The Spanish realms were a vast accretion of overlapping fueros. Particularly well-known or well-liked ones would be adopted elsewhere, with or without modifications. The result was an incredible tangle of conflicting practice. Castile, the most unified realm, had eight separate legal codes in 1492. The Crown would at times try to enact a single overriding code, but without success. The Catholic Sovereigns themselves knew better than to try to revoke this chaos; even centuries later the fueros were a war cry. But they could firmly establish the beginnings of a general civil law, in the Laws of Toro of 1505, and more important they established the right of the Crown to interpret the application of each fuero in any disputed circumstance. This was the "pre-eminent monarchy": The Crown recognized the existing welter of local regimes, but asserted its own right as lords of justice to settle problems henceforth. Moreover every official, every institution, even every person had the right to appeal to the Crown to resolve such disputes. The royal justice became very active and overwhelming indeed.

So with these basic orientations, Castile and the other Spanish realms entered a future without the Catholic Sovereigns.

This was a rather long transition. Isabella died in 1504, Ferdinand not until 1516. For some years it was rather problematic whether Spain would stay together. The great nobles of Castile had accepted Ferdinand and Isabella's preponderant position with very bad grace; with Isabella's hand gone they claimed the succession for her daughter Joanna and evicted Ferdinand. There are suggestions that some of them used this short period of instability to settle accounts with each other. But the new queen went mad with grief when her husband died in 1506 and Ferdinand was back in power in Castile again, and the instability came to nothing for the moment.

The transition on his death proved much more difficult. The mad queen was still alive (for forty more years); her heir, now heir to all Spain, was her elder son Carlos (Charles V, 1517-1556), a foreigner who obviously intended to retain his foreign ways, and worse to rule Spain as a kind of colonial dependency of his foreign interests. There were grievances aplenty already among the great nobles and the cities that had been reined in by the Catholic Sovereigns; this upstart foreigner proved just the emotionally satisfying focal point around which they could coalesce and act. Charles compounded his follies by demanding Spanish money to buy the crown of the Holy Roman Empire and promptly left the country to complete the purchase. He was not over the border before the country was rising in rebellion.

But as matters developed this too came to nothing. It began well enough. The cities of northern and central Castile convoked the Cortes, parliament, on their own initiative and declared that if dynastic legitimacy had forced a foreign king on Castile, then the realm at least deserved to have actual rule vested in Castilians, to wit themselves. In Valencia the resistance turned into a social revolution against the aristocracy, and in Castile a slow radicalization was putting fear of similar developments into the minds of the aristocrats. When after almost a year Cortes and royalists met for battle, most of the Cortes' former supporters had either turned neutral or deserted to the Crown. The single battle which occurred was more in the nature of riot dispersal, with fifteen or twenty wounded on the royal side and some 500 mixed casualties among the rebels. The Crown was merciful to individuals, but this was the end for Castilian parliamentarism and, effectively, Castilian pluralism.

As the sixteenth century wore on royal absolutism was increasingly recognized, and subordination to the king became so ingrained that even the greatest nobles, well able to revolt had they thought of it, submitted calmly to arrest (in New Spain, even to a pogrom) at the king's orders. The nobles increasingly sought their fortunes in the royal service, which by the end of the century was somewhat an aristocratic preserve. Philip II established a fixed capital for the first time, and as center of influence and patronage it became a magnet. The nobles found themselves, however reluctantly, establishing residences in Madrid, and in the next reign under much weaker rule they flocked in. By the late 1600's they were living off royal grants and had practically abandoned their estates and independence. Castile had become a dependency of the king.

The reigns of Charles V and Philip II are the development of this absolutism. Under Charles V it may be described as passive; he remained an absentee monarch, ruling through lowborn secretaries of high loyalty and low initiative, avoiding any further conflicts. Philip II was an active autocrat; one might argue whether he ever left his office other than for rest, dinner, and court. The Councils of government continued to exist, in a purely advisory capacity and knowing only what he wanted them to know. Philip even overruled established constitutional procedure, disallowing the right of the Cortes to pass on all revocations of existing law. This extreme centralization made for problems. When literally everything had to be approved by the king, nothing could happen at all quickly. Philip II's government was said to be staffed by "ministers of Eternity;" "if Death came from Spain we should all live a long time." Moreover he was so jealous and suspicious that he never appointed capable lieutenants, which caused such disasters as the Armada.

Nevertheless, Philip II was an extremely popular king, in some ways the embodiment of an ideal. He was the incarnation of benevolent despotism living strictly by the law. His sense of justice was such that in law cases in which he had an interest as a private party the courts were under standing orders to decide against him should there be any doubt.

The decline of Spain is a debate of massive proportions among Hispanic historiographers. The analyses show a wide range of alternatives, including one (Kamen 1980 **et al.**) that, if one considers decline primarily an economic phenomenon, then it never happened. What did happen was rather a mixture of failure to achieve inflated expectations, relocation of resources away from traditional centers, and a major over-valuation of the resources available in the first place. However this may be, it had become quite evident to everyone that enormous problems were in train.

The Catholic Sovereigns had recovered vast quantities of the royal patrimony and taxes, but even they on occasion had to subsist on loans. These were made not against the royal patrimony but against future tax receipts, and were secured by bonds, **juros,** pledging redemption in so much time at so much interest. Charles V had magnificent plans and to pay for them he ran up magnificent debts. At the end of his reign he could not even afford to abdicate properly, and Philip II began his reign with almost every source of revenue pledged for years in advance. He responded by confiscating the private revenue, both costs and profits, in the fleets returning from the Indies, for three years running. Even that was not enough, and the result was bankruptcy, declared in 1557.

Now the famous Spanish freedom of speech came into action: It was the Spanish citizen's bounden duty to advise his monarch, and of course to be rewarded for his advice. Such an effort was an **arbitrio,** made by an **arbitrista,** and already in Philip II's reign the arbitristas were beginning to flourish. The advice the Crown wanted was of one specific kind: how better to soak yet more money out of the economy of Spain to support the Crown. The invention of new taxes became something of a creative art form.

One such in particular may have had especially drastic results. Castile like all contemporary countries was essentially dependent on grain farming, but the Crown looked on these farmers only as potential soldiers and revenue producers, and as a source of problems when not enough grain was produced to feed the rest of the population. Such occasions meant rising prices and rising discontent, and the Crown's answer was typically not to encourage greater production but to freeze prices and force deliveries at the frozen price. Such price fixing was likely to drive the small farmer out of business or into the hands of moneylenders.

The Crown accelerated this process. One series of edicts stated that all land for which no royal grant could be shown was to be put up for sale, proceeds to the Crown. Suddenly quite a few large and small landholders had to find money to buy their own land, and then to borrow either to pay for their initial investment or to find capital to improve their crops. This was possible during good years, but bad years meant non-payment of debts and consequent foreclosure. The close of the sixteenth century saw enough bad years to produce a flood of ex-farmers moving into the cities and the monasteries. With the beginning of this process southern Spain went into a permanent grain deficit, and by 1583 this condition had spread over the whole country.

Such ruinous exploitation soon affected the treasury. A second bankruptcy in 1575 ruined Philip II's credit as well as many merchants and bankers. Still the exactions continued, with such money as remained increasingly being swallowed by government bonds. Even so, a third bankruptcy in 1597 astounded everyone.

Philip began the practice of selling state offices as producers of private revenue and status, though carefully avoiding those with the hallowed right of jurisdiction. Under the later Habsburgs all of this was carried much further. The top ranks of the nobility, seats on the councils, even vice royalties were sold at auction; new offices were created specifically for sale; old and new offices were sold two or more times over as supernumerary positions or expectancies of a future vacancy. Silver was replaced by copper, which was clipped, recalled to be stamped at a higher value, and clipped again; counterfeits arrived by whole boatloads, and six pounds of money by weight bought ten pounds of cheese. The economy reacted with wild inflations and depressions; the collapse of 1680 produced a deflation of prices (45%) worse than in the United States in the Great Depression (38%). Even the wealthy and powerful found their estates papered with mortgages, partly because of conspicuous consumption paid for by borrowing. It was said that the only lucrative professions left in the seventeenth century were the Church, the bureaucracy, and begging, and none of these was productive even of taxes.

This was occurring while gold was pouring into Spain from the New World. The country itself was impoverished, and the government was bankrupt. The gold brought in from America was flowing into the banks of Antwerp and Genoa, many of the bankers being the Jews who had been expelled by the Catholic Sovereigns.

Nor did all this pass unnoticed by the Castilians themselves. Philip II's first bankruptcy produced the first forecast of doom ahead, and by 1600 the word **desengano,** meaning both disillusionment and unvarnished truth, was becoming a commonplace description of the future. The funeral of the old magnificent expectations may be dated to 1605, when Amadis of Gaul became Don Quijote.

Such was the situation inherited by Philip III. And if the financial situation was horrible, the political situation was worse. Of Philip II it was said that he never slept; of Philip III (1598-1621) it might rather be asked whether he ever awoke. As of 1598 Spain had a ruler who sought more than any other a reign conducted without the necessity of his presence. And by this time Spain was facing a flood of problems that even Philip II had been unable to stem. After forty years each of the passive absolutism of Charles V and the active absolutism of Philip II, there was no longer any institution in Castile that could assume an initiative independent of the king. Such entrenched bureaucracies as the Councils might obstruct, so long as they did not directly flout royal orders, but no more. The reign of Philip III particularly shows this; his sole act of policy beyond an openhanded prodigality with what remained of the royal revenues was to resign absolute power to a personal favorite, the Duke of Lerma. Lerma was no better; almost his only policy was to receive as much as possible of what Philip was handing out. Yet this ridiculous pair held absolute power for twenty years against no opposition worth specific discussion, to a backdrop of increasing assertion of the divine right not only of the king but also of the favorite.

The next ruler was personally no better; Philip IV (1621-1665) had his favorite picked in advance. But this one was entirely different from Lerma. In the Count-Duke of Olivares, Spain had a master with all the energy, resolution and sense of autocracy of Philip II, who aspired to solve all the problems which even that king's formidable application could not handle. He taxed the aristocracy and they hated him accordingly but could do nothing; in all Castile, Aragon and Valencia nothing more is mentioned than general discontent and a single abortive conspiracy.

If Castile could no longer support the imperial enterprise, Olivares' answer was equally intensive exploitation of the other realms, in spite of the exemptions granted by their fueros. Even this was no longer enough, and the discontent turned to revolution. Embattled Catalonia revolted and France moved in to support it, and the ensuing war lasted 25 years. There was also a milder rebellion in Portugal, which had been acquired dynastically in 1580. Eventually, from sheer exhaustion combined with Catalan disillusionment with French rule, the war faded. Portugal also regained independence and Spain was more bankrupt than ever.

The last third of the seventeenth century was not entirely without history, but it seems rather in the nature of a tragic joke. Charles II (1665-1700) was both physically and mentally incompetent, without even the intelligence and strength of will to choose a favorite. Even the aristocracy was in decay by this time, and the bureaucracy became somewhat a hereditary elite, with sons, nephews and in-laws using their family connections to enter the administrative colleges and then the government. It does not seem to have been entirely closed; all through this period the public impression remained that the man who had no office obviously had no talent either, so one would expect some penetration by outsiders into officialdom. But very seldom was anyone able to secure personal rule well enough to carry out a policy. It is again a testament to the work of the Catholic Sovereigns that, in spite of everything, their settlement of affairs remained in force and the Peace continued. Indeed in spite of the exposed position of Catalonia and the continuing need for trained soldiers for wars abroad, the Crown felt almost no need for soldiers in Spain itself. When revolt broke out in Granada and later when an occupation force was needed to settle the position of Portugal, Philip II could find only a decorative royal guard and some frontier garrisons in all Spain, and had to depend on what was left of the aristocratic military levies, in deplorable condition. Even after the experience of the 25-year war in Catalonia, by the late 1600's all Spain had no more than 10,000 infantry and 4,000 cavalry, almost half of it in Catalonia. The need for an army to maintain order simply did not exist.

The foreign policy of the Spanish monarchs was extremely complex, but for various reasons it did protect the mainland from invasion. The main competing land power through the entire period of peace was France. In the sixteenth century, when Spain was strong, it was difficult enough for France to deal with Spanish forces in Italy. But certainly there was plenty of opportunity for conflict there. In the seventeenth century when Spain had weakened, the most attractive opportunities for France were in the Spanish Netherlands and Franche Comte. By the eighteenth century Spain may have been vulnerable to an attack from France, but the War of Spanish Succession foreclosed that possibility when a Bourbon monarch succeeded to the Spanish throne. The Bourbons of France fell in 1793, and so did Spanish immunity to French invasion.

As it turned out, Charles V was the only Spanish monarch to carry the imperial title. On his abdication, the imperial lands in Germany went to his brother Ferdinand. Spanish territories, including those in Italy, Western Europe and the overseas empire, went to Philip. Spanish commitments were still very extensive, but they had been truly overwhelming for Charles.

While the Spanish mainland remained at peace, Spanish military forces were perpetually busy, but with decreasing success. They were successful in the sixteenth century in maintaining their Italian holdings against the French and in stemming the Turks in the Mediterranean. But even in this century they eventually failed at sea against the British and on land against chronic rebellion in Flanders. In the seventeenth and eighteenth centuries Spanish forces were recurrently involved in the Thirty Years War, conflicts with Louis XIV and various wars of succession. Except for some victories in the Thirty Years War, these campaigns too were notably unsuccessful. Small armies were involved in most of these European conflicts, though total casualties mounted each century, with a notable jump in the seventeenth century, the century of the Thirty Years War, over the sixteenth, the period of wars between France and Spain in Italy. Even in the eighteenth century, relative casualty figures compared to population were considerably lower for Spain than for any other major European power. Spain, during modern history, however, was involved in more years of war than any of eight other major European powers (Sorokin, 1937, III:335–352).

Spain was also vulnerable to attack from the sea. In the sixteenth century the main danger came from the Ottomans, and Spain met the danger by capturing key ports along the Barbary Coast and with a decisive naval defeat of the Turks at Lepanto in 1571. Lepanto did not end conflict with the Turks, but it did reduce the likelihood of Turkish incursions into the Western Mediterranean. Lepanto, however, was followed by the defeat of the Armada, and after that there was a danger of British raids, one of which did occur at Cadiz. The British, however, who were not given to land invasions, were beginning far-flung enterprises of their own. So a land invasion of Spain never became attractive.

The period of the Imperial Peace coincided with a great period of aesthetic and literary florescence. The peak of this period, epitomized in the painting of El Greco and Velasquez and the writing of Cervantes, came in the seventeenth century, when political power and economy were already declining. This was a period of epic and literary poetry, of imaginative drama, notably by Lope de Vega; of realist novelists and short story writers. Perhaps the greatest architecture of Spain had already been produced in the earlier Moorish period, but a number of magnificent baroque cathedrals were produced along with civil buildings such as the Escorial of Philip II. There were a legion of painters imitating Italian and Flemish styles, but with their own vitality and nuance. If the Iberian Peninsula were a land base from which the talented adventurer emigrated to perform great deeds, there seems nevertheless to have been a great deal of talent left over at home, drawing on subjects who were themselves very lively if the realistic paintings and stories are to be believed. It may be that while in the sixteenth century the Iberian Peninsula was the population source for the great adventure of the Americas, by the seventeenth, with the Americas becoming settled and the Spanish aristocracy reasserting itself at home, a patronage had become available that propelled a tremendous creativity.

Consideration now turns to the overseas realms. These are partly mirrors of the metropolis; both the imperial government and the colonists took pains to identify the colonies with the homeland in every possible way, and even after ten generations the colonials still thought of themselves as Spaniards. But indigenous populations and a separation of thousands of miles did make the differences. The Spanish Empire was the largest the world has ever known; by 1600 it included, besides possessions spread over most of western Europe, the entire Western Hemisphere. Time was also a great separator: From the Philippines to Madrid and back always by way of New Spain, took four years, and that not counting the built-in delays of Philip II's ministers of Eternity. Nevertheless for over a hundred years no European power mounted a successful challenge to the Iberian monopoly of America and the East Indies, until the English finally managed a permanent settlement far away from the Spanish centers, at Jamestown. The sixteenth century is spoken of in a slightly different context as the age of the Spanish Atlantic, and one might add the Spanish Pacific as well. In so vast a collection of realms the existence of local situations is a foregone conclusion. Necessarily only the overall situation and a single particular example can be addressed in this chapter.

The overseas empire was considered important to Spain primarily as a source of bullion; it was the difference between Charles V and bankruptcy on a couple of occasions. But possibly much more important in actuality, it was a pressure valve. Half a world lay open to the restless knights errant of imperial Spain, and nobleza was an open statement that only the weakhearted would let such an opportunity slip by. The migration began almost immediately. Cortes, departing Castile one step ahead of a young lady's outraged father, arrived in Hispaniola in 1508 and had worked his way up to secretary to the governor of Cuba when offered the opportunity to command the expedition to Mexico, if he would assume 2/3 of the costs. Pizarro, illiterate bastard of an—at best—poor gentleman of Extremadura, arrived not later than 1509, and was a rich gentleman of Panama when he organized the expedition to explore rumors of a southern empire. Even after the golden years of the **conquistadores,** in the seventeenth century a Spanish soldier on the frontier could still (in some violation of the prohibition on trade) accumulate an estate of 50,000 pesos, and Spaniards living in Manila off the China trade were said to be universally clothed in silks and jewels. It was hardly a safe bet, of course; the dangers involved "weeded out the timid and even the prudent" (Dominguez Ortiz 1971:288), but these were precisely the people who would not start trouble at home anyway. A writer of 1521 reported, probably with vast exaggeration but nonetheless reflecting popular conceptions, that 40,000 emigrants per year were leaving for America. Current estimates, and they are no more than that, suggest anywhere from one to three hundred thousand emigrants during the sixteenth century, mostly young men. The numbers are even more debatable for later centuries, but even strict estimates grant 52,000 during the 1700's. It is impossible to say how much the adventure overseas contributed to the stability at home, but one would expect the contribution to have been considerable.

For the first few decades, through 1535 in New Spain (Mexico) and 1551 in Peru, one could hardly say that the new lands were at peace. In Peru the situation remained unquiet even then; not until the mass resettlement programs of the 1570's did the local Indian lords lose the will to resist. But the problems of building a supposedly absolute monarchy two years away from the king were all being addressed by the 1530's.

It was no easy task. The restless adventurers, now become rich and powerful, were not to be easily subjected to the organized routine of an increasingly bureaucratic government. The Crown first appointed governors, who worked well enough in the confined spaces of the West Indies. But in New Spain they were confronted by what amounted to feudal lords, **encomenderos**, recipients from the hand of Cortes of the king's right to the tribute and services of hundreds, sometimes thousands, of people. To control this new crop of prospective great lords the Crown appointed an (of course) judiciary with executive powers, the first **Audiencia** of New Spain. This was a horrible mistake; the first **Audiencia** was composed of glorified hoodlums who eventually had to be hunted down and arrested. The second solution tried was that already in place in the separate realms of Spain proper: New Spain, and soon Peru, were erected into separate kingdoms attached to the Habsburg Crown and given viceroys. Some further elaboration occurred through the 1570's, but this basically established the forms of government for the Spanish colonies for the next 200 years.

At the center was the king. This was even more the case than in Castile. The American realms were the personal property of the Crown, and the Crown's authority was not bounded by centuries of fueros as in Spain. At first Hispaniola sent **procuradores** to Castile as representatives, and there were some vague beginnings toward a Cortes here and there, but the dynasty was not about to encourage developments in America that it was busy curbing in Spain itself. The colonist at first reproduced in America the basic political unit they knew in Spain, the city-state (**municipio**) governed by a **cabildo**, but the royal officers quickly superseded any independence the cabildos had started to develop. What was left was the king, and this complete centralization of authority was very carefully and successfully maintained. Until the early nineteenth century even rebellion was conducted in the name of the king: **Viva el rey! Muera el mal gobierno!** and there were not many of these, beyond tribal affairs on the periphery, and one major but isolated uprising in Paraguay.

Presumably this attitude could fray rather quickly in a political system run by a self-consciously absolute monarch thousands of miles removed from local realities. But the Spanish system provided a specific remedy for this problem, the already-mentioned formula se acata pero no se cumple. There is effectively no mention of this principle during the imperial period in Spain itself, but in the Americas and even more in the Philippines one hears very

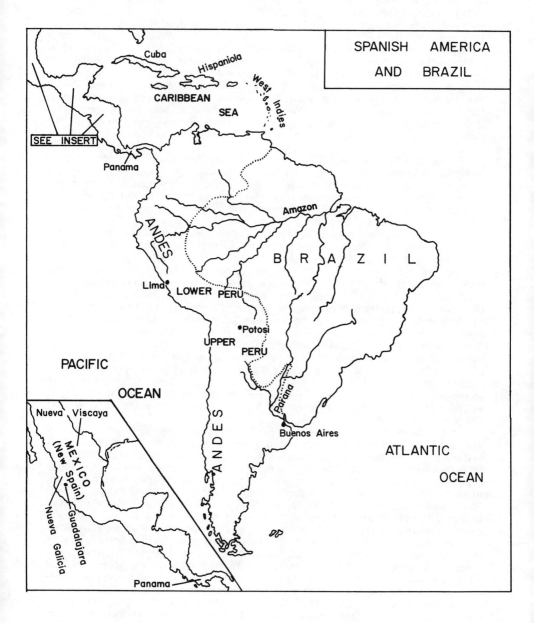

SPANISH AMERICA AND BRAZIL

Cuba

Hispaniola

CARIBBEAN

SEA

West Indies

SEE INSERT

Panama

ANDES

Amazon

B R A Z I L

Lima

LOWER PERU

•Potosi

UPPER PERU

PACIFIC

OCEAN

ANDES

Parana

Buenos Aires

ATLANTIC

OCEAN

Nueva Viscaya

M E X I C O (New Spain)

Nueva Galicia

Guadalajara

Panama

little else. This was determined by probably the single most important development in the Empire before 1700, the constitutional crisis of 1542-1551.

Encomienda, as mentioned, smacked strongly of feudalism, of a system
of commendation not unlike that which founded the unruly great lordships
of Castile itself. Obviously the **encomenderos** would want this to persist through
their heirs to the last generation, and moreover to use it to exercise the same
political rights in the colonies which the aristocrats had in Spain. Ferdinand
had confirmed encomienda in the West Indies in 1509 and Charles V had added
his approval for New Spain as recently as 1536. But besides political considerations there were strong arguments against it on Christian humanitarian grounds.
In 1542 Charles decreed the New Laws for the Government of the Indies, among
other things abolishing encomienda, and even worse he sent officials to the
Indies specifically charged with enforcing them, implying cancellation of the
review privilege of se acata. . . . The result was, to put it mildly, consternation.
In New Spain the official in charge of enforcement consulted with the viceroy
and the audiencia, realized where events were going, and invoked **se acata...**
anyway. But in Peru the official in charge was also the first viceroy to be
inflicted on Pizarro's turbulent assassins, and he consulted nobody. The result
was a rebellion which killed him and was not extinguished until another official
arrived who did invoke se acata. . . . Moreover, the Crown, seeing what had
happened, confirmed the validity of the practice, adding that the first Peruvian
viceroy had erred in not consulting officials on the spot before deciding whether
to enforce the royal order. Whatever might be the practice in Spain itself,
henceforth se acata. . . was very much a legitimate practice in the colonies,
giving the Spanish centralized absolutism a mechanism to reconcile the theoretical requirements of abstract justice to everyday local realities.

For the next two hundred years very little happened. The government
was in place: viceroy and governors, audiencia, Church—as much an arm of
government as any other—and **fiscales** (tax collectors), all with enough overlap
in their jurisdictions to guarantee that none would be able to act without the
consent of the others. Within the Church this was further complicated by running
conflict between the regular and secular clergy, and almost anyone could appeal
directly to the Crown **por la via reservada** whenever anyone else disagreed.
Moreover, after 1563 all new laws, even those promulgated by the viceroy
and audiencia, had in theory to be confirmed by the Crown before acquiring
legal status. (In practice many were promulgated and acted upon at all levels
without this formality.) The result was in some measure exactly the opposite
of the Crown's intention. The idea was to give no official more than the absolute
minimum of authority with which to be barely effective, so that no official
could establish a local domain independent of the Crown. In fact the officials
remained highly dependent on the Crown, but at the price of the Crown's equally
fervent desire to regulate absolutely everything that happened in the colonies.
The government by lack of consensus meant not that the Crown decided all,
but that nothing was decided. Spanish America became a highly voluntaristic
society, in which laws and regimes were effective only when there was in fact
a consensus behind them. With acceptance of the now far-removed theory
of absolute royal right and very near to hand practice of consensus, people
felt their government was right and so accepted it as well, and Spanish America
could remain very stable for a very long time.

Beneath this general stability there lay a multitude of differentiations.
The most important was that between Spaniard and Indian. At first the Crown
had wanted to integrate the conquered Indians into the Empire on the same
basis as all other subjects, but this hope ran hard aground on the reefs of
encomienda and other similar exploitations of the Indian by the colonists. The
theory came to be that Spaniard and Indian were two different peoples,
"republics," each to its own place in society, each with its own hierarchy of

government. For the Crown this had the desired result of separating the Indians from government by colonials and thereby not allowing that feudal base to take hold; the colonists accepted it on grounds that exploitation could continue, if in a rather more convoluted fashion than they preferred; the Indians retained their autonomy and so also accepted it.

One of the most studied regional evolutions involves the interaction or urbanized Spaniard and nomadic Indian on the northern frontier of New Spain. To some extent this great attention comes of the special interest attached to its results. On 8 September 1546, generations before Englishmen ever scratched dirt at Plymouth Plantation or Jamestown, or even Roanoke, there was born to the Spanish conquistadores and the open range country of northern Mexico, the Old West.

The occasion was the standard expedition in search of souls and silver. A troop of cavalry and friars made camp that evening and managed to open communications with some rather suspicious local Indians. The Spaniards traded trinkets; the Indians traded silver; the Spaniards rapidly found they had made camp on nearly a whole mountain of the stuff, the first of the great silver strikes that reached north eventually to the Comstock Lode. The great Zacatecan silver rush was on, and within a decade a series of strikes was drawing a flood of Spaniards and Indians north.

But New Spain north of Guadalajara was different. Unlike the old Aztec civilized areas, it did not have a settled Indian population to exploit, only nomads, the Chichimeca. Moreover it was too dry to support much in the way of agriculture without extensive irrigation. But somehow the new mining frontier had to be fed. At first this meant imports from the settled south, at fantastic prices. But the solution happened to be already at hand. Spain had learned the art of the open range as of the thirteenth century, with the conquest of Andalucia; in the 1500's Andalucian cattle were shipped first to Hispaniola and Cuba and thence to New Spain. Here on virgin pasture they began doubling every few years, to the point that Indian hoe agriculture was being driven out. With the population explosion in the dry north the cattle could be driven to a brand new market, with no competing agriculture. Soon the cattle herds of Nueva Galicia and Nueva Viscaya numbered up to a quarter million head (herds of forty or fifty thousand were considered rather commonplace), and with them moved the Andalucian cattle culture. Here it developed nearly its final form, to be annexed wholesale by the United States and Canada with little more than a change of accent (**corral, rancho, la reata, bronco, pinto** ...) or, even in fields not strictly cowboy, a dropped letter or two (**des[es]perado, bandit[o], jusga[d]o. . .**).

This was fine for the miners and landowners, but the nomadic Indians formed a different opinion as their lands and ways of life began disappearing into civilization. And when the cattle arrived they found that this was an intrusion which brought with it a supply of easily hunted meat vastly more plentiful than anything in the deserts, apparently available to the first taker. The result was a fifty-year war. Cargo wagons had to travel in convoy, with cavalry guards and sometimes a primitive tank (a travelling fort with firing embrasures). Towns were founded as military settlements along the wagon routes, and when these various defensive measures proved fruitless and the attacks if anything increased, a war "of fire and blood" was carried to the Chichimeca themselves, in spite of formal Church denunciation of the practice. This too failed, and by 1585 the Chichimec War had become the most serious problem in the whole of New Spain.

In 1590 a solution was formulated. Since the Indians were being dispossessed of their hunting grounds and responded by going elsewhere for their food and clothing, why not give it to them, with presents besides? After this policy began to turn the tide, and the Indians formed the habit of receiving these goods at fixed places, a group of friars would establish a mission in the vicinity to teach them the ways of civilization. Additionally civilized Indians were brought up from long-settled areas wherever agricultural conditions permitted. By 1600 this was almost completely successful; some warfare continued along the northeastern and northwestern frontiers, but peace had come to the mining areas of interior northern Mexico. And so was founded the mission system which by the late 1700's had spread as far north as San Francisco.

Finally as regards the Habsburg period, the colonies did develop an economic life of their own. As far as the Crown was concerned the Americas were a source of gold and silver, and any increase in other matters was likely to interfere with the flow of bullion. At first this was no problem; during the age of the **conquistadores** the colonists' dreams were not directed at mundane business activities. "Population centers" meant mining towns; Potosi, the mining center of Upper Peru, was for some time the largest city in the Americas (population 120,000), two-thirds of the Europeans being floaters and vagrants. But by mid-century a new generation was finding a more settled situation, and not only did local production begin but intra-American trade began displacing trade with Spain. By 1590 the trade between New Spain and Peru was already prosperous, and during the seventeenth century out of fifty vessels operating from Peru only four or five dealt (officially, at any rate) with the regular shipments from Spain. To no small extent this was the Spanish merchants' own fault. By keeping volume down they hoped to keep prices up, and indeed profits on a single cargo from Spain could run 300 or 400%, but this meant that the market was never satisfied. Waiting time for an order from Peru averaged five years. Necessarily the colonies had to turn elsewhere. To some extent colonial manufactures made up the deficit, but transportation costs within America, away from the coast, were tremendous—in bad times the freight charges by donkey-back from the coast ten miles to Lima could be as much as the whole shipping cost from Spain to Peru. Accordingly trade began shifting elsewhere, to northern Europe (which came to provide the vast majority even of cargoes from Spain), and to China by way of the Manila galleon. Smuggling probably accounted for more than half the traffic; Buenos Aires is recorded to have ordered passing ships into port there to trade, and in Peru everyone, churchmen and officials included, participated in the illegal exchange. Thus the result of Crown attempts to close the colonies and manipulate the market was rather a shift toward self-sufficiency and other sources. By controlling America as thoroughly as possible politically, Spain was already losing the economic basis of that political connection.

In most descriptions of peace there are both external and internal considerations. The Spaniards in Europe continually fought the French, Dutch and British, but generally outside of Spain. The same seems to have been true in the New World. There were battles over Atlantic Islands, and the British and French encountered each other in North America, but except in the Caribbean, the vast Spanish holdings during the sixteenth and seventeenth century were free of French or British incursions.

Termination

During the last twenty years of the seventeenth century, Charles II was dying. He had already proved incapable of fathering an heir, so the extended death watch was equally an extended debate on a question of European importance. Which of the competing dynasties was suddenly going to find its patrimony enriched by the largest of the European empires? The Spanish court itself

was seriously divided on the question, with different factions putting forward
different possibilities and keeping their options open.

The decision was made by war. In Spain (excluding permanently wartorn
Catalonia) the battles lasted from 1705 to 1710, in a strange mirror image
of a civil war: in this case the contenders were careful to do as little damage
as possible to their potential property while fighting about the ownership.
The eventual winner, the candidate of the Bourbon dynasty, even recognized
all promotions made by his competitor during the war. In terms of our criteria,
early Bourbon Spain does not quite qualify as an addition to the Peace, since
the peace period lasted only 98 years, through 1808. But the recovery of peace
for so long a period is worth noting. Some of the magic of the Catholic Sovereigns seemed still to prevail.

It should be noted, however, that while this peace covered a very large
area and lasted two centuries overseas and more than three centuries on the
Iberian Peninsula, it also suffered a number of disturbances. There were probably
episodes of violence during the Jewish expulsion at the beginning of the peace,
possibly again at the death of Isabella and then also at the accession of Charles
V, and certainly with the Morisco expulsion and the accompanying landing
by the Ottomans. Then there was the major conflict during the war of Spanish
Succession, and finally, just under a century later, the terminating Peninsular
Campaign, part of the larger Napoleonic Wars.

In this Bourbon period, there were changes. If Castile (with quite a
few exceptions among the great nobles) had held to the Bourbon succession,
the realms of Aragon had (partly) held otherwise, and the new king considered
this a very good excuse to accomplish Olivares' program of unification. The
fueros of the realms of Aragon were abolished and henceforth the laws and
customs of Castile ruled all Spain. Second, if the various nobles of both sides
had emerged with their titles intact and their fortunes in some reasonable
state of preservation, their political position was thoroughly undermined. Even
such unity as the **grandes** had maintained under the later Habsburgs had vanished.
The first rulers of the new dynasty were nothing like vigorous, but the nobles
were in no position to argue.

Meanwhile an entirely separate revolution was busy creeping across
Europe. Something thoroughly unexpected had happened in the War of the
Spanish Succession: England, a realm with one-quarter the population of France,
far less wealth and a political system twice disrupted by revolution within
living memory, and still apparently spending most of its energy on internal
argument, had beaten France. England emerged not only triumphant but rich;
le roi soleil ended his imperial designs not only defeated but financially ruined.
Moreover, the English Revolution had created a new outlook in the exploration
of knowledge itself, which proved its worth as quickly as the other innovations.
France was most closely and so most heavily affected by these changes, but
with the publication in 1726 of the first essay of Fr. Benito Feyjoo the Enlightenment entered Spain, and with it intellectual justification for new ways of
thinking. But for the moment this too had only begun.

The crucial turning point was the Seven Years War (1756-1763). Spain
entered late and proved in such poor condition as to be beaten quickly and
decisively. The humiliation, and more important the lesson as to future dangers,
was enough finally to convince the government that some changes had to be
made. By coincidence Spain had just acquired another foreign king, a junior
Bourbon from Italy, therefore again not attached to old Spanish ways. Charles
III (1759-1788) was hardly a vigorous ruler, but he was willing to appoint and
back up deputies who were.

The actual degree of accomplishment, especially within Spain itself,
is debatable. Charles decided, for example, to encourage production by making

it official policy that industry in no way contaminated the social status of its practitioners, but when the proto-industrialists actually attempted noble status he reversed himself to the extent of giving them no more than privileges short of nobility. But economic activity did improve to some extent, and talk of improvement spread rapidly. A group of independent societies for economic development spread across both Spain and the colonies, making proposals for changes. Their proposals tended strongly toward existence only on paper, but again they did suggest the possibility of change.

In the colonies the reorganization was much greater. In themselves the reforms were reasonably effective here and there, the cause of great dispute elsewhere, and certainly productive of much more tax money and (at least officially) much more trade. They were in particular relevant to future developments in these ways: the revival of the Spanish colonial military, the centralization of the imperial administration, and the forced imprint on the colonies' consciousness of not just the possibility but the actuality of change.

By and large the Spanish colonies had no great previous need, much less desire, for a home army. The military collapse of seventeenth-century Spain was matched if not overmatched in the colonies. When during the Seven Years War some need for armed force was felt the official comment on available soldiers was that they were a distinct threat to the public safety, more of a danger to their commanders than to the enemy, incapable of defending their own barracks, and so forth. This was the result of a long peace; foreign visitors were astounded at the lack of defenses in America. The military skills of the **conquistadores** were long forgotten, and new recruits deserted as quickly as possible so as to pawn their uniforms on the way to the nearest bar.

Despite the threat from Britain, little was done about military weakness during the fifteen years of peace following the Seven Years War. The imperial government concluded that although it wanted a better army, it did not want to spend money to get one. It therefore decided instead to grant status and privileges, to make the new soldiery a self-consciously separate group under its own **fuero.** This was not immediately effective; recruiting sergeants continued to be greeted by riots for some years. But gradually the desired local militia did become a self-conscious military force, and when after 1808 the Peace dissolved, organized army competition was ready to take its place.

Centralization was the byword of the later eighteenth century. The War of the Spanish Succession and various administrative experiments had brought "one king, one law" to Spain; it was now also to be the rule of the Indies. In part this involved a restructuring of administration; more important it meant a recovery of lost influence.

Under the later Habsburgs the imperial system had lost considerable control of its colonial administration. This was particularly the rule after 1687, when the royal penury meant sale of any office to anyone with the price of it. In the early empire it had been the rule both that no official should serve in his home locality, to avoid conflict of interest and the building of local power bases, and that Americans should not be appointed to colonial office at all, because of a definite partiality in the American mind toward overuse of the se acata ... doctrine. But as early as 1585 there were exceptions, and when offices began to be sold openly the best-paying buyers were those with local attachments. The late seventeenth century saw a major expansion of Americans in high American colonial office. Moreover, with offices going for sale there was no longer room for the regular promotion system in the bureaucracy, so an office once gotten tended to be kept for a very long time. The incumbents would become rooted in each locality, marrying into local families and otherwise establishing contacts which the government had previously been at pains to avoid.

In the later eighteenth century Madrid both stopped sales and reestablished the regular rotation and promotion system, and from the point of view of the Americans this meant closure of the only way to high office. Regional self-identification had stabilized to the point, particularly after the American Revolution, that while the colonies still accepted the authority of the king they had also come to think of each region as a distinct entity, their own home. They wanted home appointment, and this was precisely what the government was again very reluctant, while not entirely refusing, to do. In New Spain, for example, the saying became current that "the Spaniards [! sic] let us take no part in the government of our own country and they carry off all our money to Spain." When finally the Peace collapsed and a desperate interim government called an assembly including representatives from the colonies, this anticipation of dominion status was first and foremost among colonial demands.

Moreover there were forerunners, primarily in South America, especially in the viceroyalty of Peru. With the division of the colonies into republics of Spaniards and natives came exploitation of the natives, and in Peru this seems to have been particularly thorough. The **obrajes,** in effect workhouses, are an example. Travellers' reports at the end of the colonial period suggest that even in New Spain they had hardly the best working conditions, but while in New Spain an Indian forced to work in an obraje would often stay on after his forced term, in Peru the Indians drafted for **obraje** would request assignment to the mercury mines instead, and already by 1600 it was known that the vapors in those mines were a death sentence. One attempted reform in 1750 backfired, making conditions much worse than before. So all during the 1700's there were isolated tribal revolts, put down easily enough that no military reform was needed. The Tupac Amaru revolt of 1780-1781, however, threatened the vice-royalty itself: For the first time the Indians had a leader who understood and used Spanish tactics, rather than staying alive simply by avoiding contact with Spanish patrols. The viceroy later reported that that revolt and the Spanish scorched-earth tactics used in reprisal had cost 100,000 lives, and while this seems a gross over-estimate if population figures are to be trusted, certainly the revolt did disrupt the peace of highland Peru.

Finally there were the problems created by the fact that even for the overseas realms there was a world beyond Spain. Except for the Caribbean this had made very little difference before 1763, but in that year the first touch of the Enlightenment appeared in New Spain, in the form of a refutation of Rousseau. It rapidly became evident in the colonies that the traditional Spanish claim to a monopoly of worthwhile knowledge and virtue could no longer be sustained. Then came the French Revolution, soon followed by a reluctant Spanish alliance with France and the arrival of revolutionary French-men with revolutionary ideas in the colonies. Even as late as 1808 these various disturbing factors were not considered insoluble problems, but they were powder barrels ready to explode. In 1808 the fuse was lit.

Whatever may be said of more recent scions of the dynasty, the Bourbon kings following Charles III did not qualify even as mediocre. Charles IV (1788-1808) was at best another Henry IV. His son Ferdinand VII (1808-1833) was much worse, arguably a traitor to everything he touched and inarguably a total bungler even at his treasons. He conspired with Napoleon to dethrone Charles IV, an effort so ludicrously executed that Charles IV ended up abdicating twice, Ferdinand VII once, and a Bonaparte was placed on the thrones of Spain against opposition from competing Bourbon loyalist groups that promptly proclaimed themselves interim governments. In the colonies the appointments of incumbents, particularly unpopular ones, suddenly became of doubtful legitimacy; New Spain even saw a major popular uprising and the first military coup against a seated viceroy. With conflicting programs all over the place, some viceroys and governors instituted regimes of naked force and terror. In Spain the interim government in Cadiz assumed some degree of legitimacy and passed a constitution far removed from the absolutism of Charles III and very unwelcome to the terrorist regimes trying to restore order in the colonies.

Since Spanish political theory, regardless of interim formulations, did still place final authority in the king, possibly the situation could have been retrieved by a competent king. This was no description of Ferdinand VII. On assuming power in 1814 he instituted terror and armed repression against all possible opponents, including those in the colonies, and with the old consensus already coming under question and the king a visible traitor, this no longer worked. Even the Spanish people lost interest; soldiers destined for the colonies rebelled both in Spain and on the way over, and once there they deserted "in flocks." Finally in 1820 one unit about to embark rebelled as a unit, and their commander used the opportunity to overthrow the royal dictatorship and reinstate the interim constitution. Thus the government was turned topsy-turvy yet again. The restored constitutional government lasted through three years that saw 122 local revolts and continued intrigue by the king to bring in a foreign army against his own. When in 1823 the foreign army arrived the royal repression was worse than before, and chaos became total. Spain dissolved into twenty more years of civil war, and in Spanish America the confusion was such as to engender Simon Bolivar's famous remark, the recognized epitaph on the Spanish Empire in America, that he who served the revolution plowed the sea.

Why, after more than 300 years, with everyone still believing as late as 1808 that the problems could be solved, did the situation collapse so quickly and totally? By consensus the answer lies in the failure of the central assumption of the system. The king was Chief Executive; the king was Justice; **everything** depended on the king. When an incompetent king ruled, the system could blame problems on subordinates and continue to operate on the basis of royal legitimacy; Justice would be deferred, but was still there. If the functioning was not perfect, still even the rebels saw this system as the only way to go. Ferdinand VII destroyed this. Even the strongest belief has problems justifying the rule of a public traitor, and Ferdinand's treasons were so obvious, in a period when the nature and conduct of government were coming under increasing scrutiny anyway, that the monarchy itself was discredited. Nor could anyone find and establish any fulcrum to replace it; Justice itself fell with the king. There were attempts to resurrect the **poder moderador** in republican format, but these were assessed "political monstrosities" (Thomas 1956:264-265) and did not survive. They were not the king; they had no legitimacy; people did not believe in them. The Spanish world, Spain and the colonies alike, dissolved into a government by armed force in which the only legitimacy was supplied by the personal charisma of the individual leader, and changes of government, "revolutions," became little more than changes in who was holding the bayonet. Paper constitutions continue to promulgate a justice recognized by nobody, and the search for justice continues.

Reflections

This is the only imperial Peace in Western history, and even as such must be qualified. The Spanish realms, like the western Roman Empire, were a mixed imperium, part conquest state and part colonial expansion. Spain, like east Rome, also had some purely alien sections, with no Spanish colonies and no Spaniards outside the ruling groups, in the old Burgundian realms and over much of Italy. But the former were in permanent war and the latter were an extraordinarily complex mix of owned, dependent and allied states with little relation to Spain, which must be reserved for a future study. In this section they come under the heading "foreign policy."

The mixed conquest/colonial realms, on the other hand, also present problems. Any attempt to draw the boundaries of the Spanish Empire in America, or even in the Philippines, would be ridiculous. Spain was quite happy ruling the cities and mines closely, their agricultural support areas less closely, the cattle frontiers and outside farms very little, the non-tributary Indians hardly at all—Spanish expeditions penetrated to Wyoming or Nebraska; Spain claimed even Manitoba and Mackenzie. To map all the fluctuations, variations and interpenetrations of these categories is beyond the capacity of this study. As a geographic entity the Spanish Empire was unique to itself, and must for the moment be left at that.

While this is the only imperial peace in Western history, there have been other Western empires, but none both sufficiently Western and sufficiently peaceful to qualify for this study. Quite evidently Spain accomplished something unique. The examination in these pages has emphasized these proposed differences. All medieval Europe emphasized the judicial function of the Crown, which has been called the police department of the medieval polity, but the Hispanic realms kept this orientation after the more northern monarchies had been drastically modified by the Protestant revolution. Moreover, Spain developed it through the theory of the moderating power into a uniquely Spanish set of institutions, with such highly successful—but, from the northern point of view, weirdly self-contradictory—adaptions as the se acata doctrine. Likewise Spain had the same aristocratic estate as the rest of Europe, but the Reconquest, the permanent crusade, insured that the Spanish aristocratic ethos never became a monopoly of the aristocracy. Anyone could and should go off to become an aristocrat, and since America was a wonderful opportunity for this orientation, quite a few anyones did. Finally a pair of exceptional monarchs, Ferdinand and Isabella, applied the finishing touches to the amalgam of these ingredients, and Spain became a uniquely interconnected web of belief and practice that applies in almost any circumstances. Its mesh with physical and especially economic reality left much to be desired, but the Spaniards seem to have considered this an easily tolerable shortcoming. This may be a lesson for those students who emphasize the importance of economic factors above all.

Physical factors certainly also helped Spain. Spain itself was on the periphery of Europe, protected by a mountain range from the only state powerful enough to be a real threat, and the one area where the mountains could easily be breached was also outside the Peace, a permanent war zone. The Spanish American Peace was even a double periphery. The Caribbean pivot was the normal landfall of sailing ships using the northeast tradewinds and so was a permanent war zone; within the Americas Spain quickly seized and concentrated on the civilized areas, and the peripheral nomads seldom constituted more than a nuisance, never threatening the central areas. Such miniature Indian revolts as occurred before the Tupac Amaru rebellion were so small a problem that the Spanish American lack of a military force excited the wonder of visitors and the disgust of visiting Spanish officials.

The Spanish Empire (exactly contradicting its Brazilian counterpart) also emphasizes the permanent usefulness of good institutions. Only the first rulers may be called anything better than mediocre, yet the system and the Peace survived quite well under some outstanding incompetents. Only when one of them betrayed the basic assumptions of the system, at a time when these assumptions were coming under increasing question, did the Peace collapse. Considering that this was a Peace maintained over planetary distances with only pre-industrial resources, it must certainly be assessed one of the outstanding accomplishments of the type.

7

The British Peace
(1485-1940)

Origins

The British Isles lie 20 miles off the coast of Europe. This coast was usually dominated by, if not occupied by, a power much greater than Britain in size and population. The British response to this situation was a major factor in the long period of domestic peace that the islands experienced.

The Peace began, however, in 1485 with the ending of the last and greatest of a series of domestic feudal power struggles. It continued with one major interruption—a civil war in which fighting lasted for almost a decade—until it was ended more than four centuries later by German bombing and rocketing in 1940-1944.

The British Isles consist of two major islands with an area of 94,000 square miles. The full Peace was procured only for England, which occupied the southern two-thirds of the island nearer Europe. It was extended to Scotland, which occupied the northern third, after 1746. Ireland, the other island, was more or less included from 1691 to 1916.

Characterization

Though England was certainly affected by European patterns, she seems to have been sufficiently divorced to have modified these patterns in several ways. For instance the nobility of England was powerful, as it was in Eastern Europe, but early on it shared this power with lesser classes. The king was advised by an assembly called Parliament, which consisted of the great lords and clergy in one body, and the lesser lords and townsmen in another body. England, like other European powers, went through a long period of struggle between the monarch and the great lords which culminated in three decades of feudal civil war in the fifteenth century, the Wars of the Roses.

The peace began with the emergence of a dominant monarch, Henry VII (1485-1509), following a final battle at Bosworth Field between two dominant houses, Lancaster and York. The prolonged war had greatly weakened the nobility, and a general desire for respite probably prevailed. Henry Tudor, a Lancastrian, set about founding a new dynasty and establishing order. He married Elizabeth of York as a gesture of future solidarity between what was left of the rival houses. He forbade the battered nobility from keeping private armies or from interfering with royal justice, and he enforced these measures through the creation of a special court to deal swiftly with provincial injustice charged to the nobility. He increased revenues by effective collection of taxes, by raising levies for wars that he didn't fight, by encouraging the resumption of commerce, and by frugality.

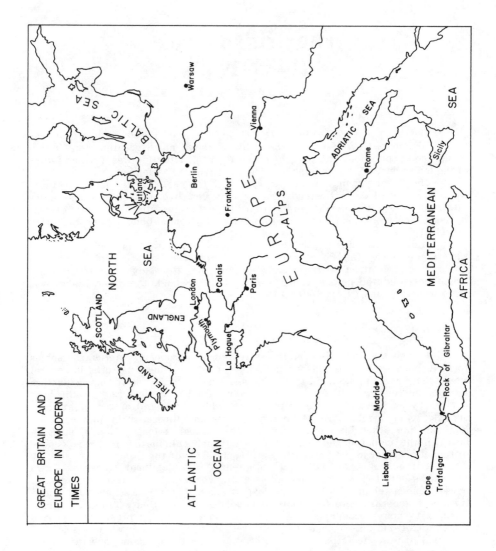

GREAT BRITAIN AND EUROPE IN MODERN TIMES

To his son Henry VIII (1509-1547) and granddaughter Elizabeth (1558-1603) was left the problem of dealing with the European Reformation. Henry broke from the Catholic Church and brought Parliament into the process, which led also to Parliamentary participation in succession questions. After brief reigns of Protestant and Catholic successors, Elizabeth presided over the development of Parliamentary acts ending papal jurisdiction and establishing a common prayer book and a definitive set of doctrines for an Anglican Church. The negotiations throughout the century were prolonged and tortuous, the times particularly during the reign of Henry VIII were often fearful, and there was a great deal of compromise and bargaining along the way.

The religious transformation helped Henry VIII financially, since he was able to confiscate the considerable wealth of the Catholic monasteries. This was necessary because he tended to be extravagant. But in return he presented the aspect of a magnificent monarch which probably strengthened his position in the eyes of his subjects. Elizabeth was helped financially by a return to her grandfather's frugality plus the revenues that were coming to the country from increased commerce and raids on Spanish ships bringing silver back from South and Central America. The influx of silver, in turn, raised prices and further encouraged commerce.

In the seventeenth century a new dynasty, that of the Scottish Stuarts, came to power, and Britain went through a critical stage in domestic and foreign affairs. The Stuarts had a continental outlook toward their position, feeling that Parliament should be subservient to their wishes. They aroused the opposition of Parliament, which defended its right to control finances, to meet regularly, and to advise the king on foreign policy. The conflict for final authority in England between king and Parliament involved a civil war ending in the execution of one king and, when a successor tried to reverse his verdict, the expulsion of another. Parliament finally emerged victorious by engineering a coup d'etat against the Catholic Stuart King, James II (1685-1688). Few Englishmen wanted to fight another war by the end of the seventeenth century, at least not one over religion. Few wanted religious excesses of any kind. James II, like other Stuarts devout and shortsighted, had misjudged his times and lost his crown. He was replaced by William of Orange (1688-1702), the Dutch son of James' sister Mary and husband of his daughter, also Mary. William III accepted the crown on Parliament's terms, insuring its regular elections and meetings, control of taxes, and participation in foreign policy. Moreover Parliament also decided upon William's successors, since he had no children.

Parliament had won more than a partnership. German-speaking kings of the Hanoverian dynasty, which succeeded the Stuarts in the eighteenth century, found that they could get political results only if they had a minister who could control a majority of votes in Parliament. Gradually the power was passed from the king to the minister, whose appointment, by the nineteenth century, was determined not by the king but by Parliament. This prime minister in turn appointed his own cabinet, which was responsible to Parliament, not the king.

By the nineteenth century, however, Parliament was no longer dominated by the great nobles, who now shared power with country squires and a growing urban middle class. Thus a new instrument was forged that met the needs of a changing society, and the changes were made with relatively little conflict. Lower classes were also provided for. Small farmers were always free in England, and many of them became landowners and as such had influence in the lower house. When nineteenth-century mass production brought an urban working class into existence, the franchise was widened so that the new class could also be represented in Parliament. As for Queen Victoria, who gave her name to the entire age, she was much loved and revered for her longevity and as a royal symbol uncontaminated by public political involvement.

Subsequent legislation, creating public education and a sequence of welfare laws (hours and wages regulation, compensation for injury, health and unemployment insurance) was consistent with a general pattern of nineteenth and twentieth century legislation that was gradually spreading through Europe.

All of this was not accomplished without social unrest and occasional violence. In 1780 there was a week-long riot in London, nominally aimed at the houses of wealthy Catholic citizens. More than 300 persons were killed. Social conditions in the nineteenth century among the working classes were a scandal, and there were a number of instances of rural and urban violence.

On the other hand, the British often showed a spirit of comradeship that transcended volatile situations, a perception that violence is not an acceptable means of behavior. When a police force was developed in the nineteenth century, its members carried a club, but no pistol. (But so did many ordinary citizens, the truncheons being called "life preservers".) In 1926, when a general strike was called, middle-class people ran public services for a week and the only conflict that occurred was a soccer match between the police and the strikers.

During these many centuries, England experienced several periods of aesthetic creativity, with literature predominating over music or painting. The reign of Elizabeth marked a great period of writing for the stage, but this was in part a response to the European Renaissance as much as it was to peace. There were other particularly creative periods in the late seventeenth century, in the middle of the eighteenth and in the latter part of the nineteenth, each of these also relating to general European culture. A brief list of names, from Shakespeare to Shaw, would be filled in differently by each Western reader, but few would suggest that the long peace was not a period of repeatedly renewed aesthetic achievement.

Within her islands England had to contend with two other powers, Scotland and Ireland. Both countries were economically less developed than England, and inclined to feudal war long after England had been united. Though England sometimes participated in these conflicts, often in Ireland, the Irish were never strong enough to invade England, nor were the Scots, except during the period of the English Civil War and again in 1745. Conflict with Scotland was reduced by the Union of Crowns under the Stuarts, and finally resolved by an act of union in 1707, in which both countries accepted the Hanoverian succession, though there were subsequent pro-Stuart rebellions in Scotland in 1715 and 1745. The last conflict with Ireland was an outgrowth of the coup against James II. Relations with Ireland were tense and ambiguous through the eighteenth and nineteenth centuries. A union comparable to that with Scotland was not concluded until 1800, and before and after this union there was much underlying hostility and a smattering of violence. This included a rising that coincided with a threatened French invasion in 1798 which provoked a month's fighting with several hundred killed, along with smaller outbreaks against enclosure in the 1760's and 1770's and against tithing in the 1830's, as well as two farcical independence risings in 1848 and 1867. But when World War I failed to bring separation and independence to Ireland, as it did for so many European states, the Irish rebelled, and the British were obliged to allow them to go their own way. The rebellion lasted intermittently from 1916 to 1924, involving first a conflict between Irish and British, then between Irish radicals and moderates.

Britain was involved frequently in continental affairs. Until the fifteenth century, this often involved acquiring and holding continental territory. But the Tudors were gradually forced to relinquish their desire for continental land; Henry VIII continued to act as if he were interested, but he never committed forces sufficient for a reinvasion of France. Calais, the last English holding in Europe, was not finally lost until the middle of the sixteenth century. In no subsequent settlement of major wars did the English acquire any territory on the mainland except, in the War of Spanish Succession, the Spanish Rock of Gibraltar, which they wanted for control of the entrance to the Mediterranean, not for a foothold on the mainland. When they chose kings from the Hanoverian line in Germany, their monarchs were also rulers over mainland territory, and this may have involved them in an unwise switch of alliances from Austria to Prussia in 1756.

But though they generally refused land commitments they soon began a policy of opposing the acquisition of the Lowlands—Belgium and Holland—since control of this territory would provide a landing stage for an invasion of Britain. Thus the British, with energy, imagination, and persistent determination, opposed Spain in the sixteenth century, France in the late seventeenth and eighteenth, and Russia and Germany in the nineteenth and twentieth.

Generally the British would not commit many troops to the mainland. They would rely instead on raising alliances among continental powers with common interests, on diplomacy to buy off or divert a threatening great power, on subsidies to allies and on naval power. Only in the most serious situations did they allow their own troops to fight in Europe: in the eighteenth century against the French Monarch Louis XIV, when he threatened to acquire the throne of Spain, in the nineteenth century against Napoleon's bid to dominate Europe, and against Germany in the twentieth-century World Wars.

Once the dominant power was weakened, England did not hesitate to withdraw her opposition. She made a separate peace with Louis XIV in the war of Spanish Succession once it became apparent that her Austrian allies might emerge stronger than France. She supported the Bourbons and the restoration of France's old frontiers after the Napoleonic Wars.

Her one major deviation from this policy was supporting Louis XIV against the Dutch, at the outset of the French monarch's aggressive policy. This came about because the Stuart king Charles II (1660-1685) was more concerned with getting French subsidies and avoiding conflict with Parliament. British interests in this case were saved by the Dutch who, led by William of Orange, breached their dikes to stop the French by land and managed to check the French and British at sea as well. The British soon came to their senses and had Dutch naval support to help them prevent a French invasion of Britain in 1691.

In retrospect, the need for naval power to defend an insular peace is obvious. But the British Peace was well under way before English seapower developed. The sixteenth-century Spaniards had a superior navy but the English, under Sir John Hawkins, equalized the situation by converting merchant ships into part-time warships and by introducing a new tactic of warfare. The Spaniards fought by grappling and boarding, relying on their numbers and abilities at close fighting. But the British nullified this by concentrating on developing rapid vessels with high, long-range, firepower. These could stay out of reach of the Spanish vessels and yet sink them.

In the seventeenth century, under the Stuarts, the Navy was at first neglected, but it revived under the threat of Dutch competition and French power. In the eighteenth century it came into its own. Except for a period in the latter eighteenth century, they managed to maintain a navy as large as those of France and Spain combined, since the two Bourbon nations might always unite against Britain. In addition they had the advantage of superior seamanship which came from greater access to the sea and a tradition that made the navy an attractive field for younger sons of good families. France, as a land power, stressed army careers.

In the nineteenth century the British were challenged by changes in naval technology, with wooden ships giving way to iron. This made the old fleet obsolescent, but still the British were able to maintain their lead because of a strong industrial base and the prevalence of coal and iron. In the twentieth century the introduction of the dreadnought, a ship with such superior firepower and protection that it rendered all others obsolescent, again threatened the British. Still they were able to stay two years ahead of the Germans in the subsequent arms race, and maintained a three-two ratio of superiority in capital ships.

Britain's continental opponents attempted to overcome her in two ways: by invasion or by cutting off her supplies. Invasions were attempted by the Spaniards, Louis XIV, Napoleon and Hitler. The first three invasions were repulsed as the result of single naval battles, the Spanish Armada routed off Plymouth in 1588, the French defeated off La Hogue in 1691 and again off Cape Trafalgar in 1805. Each victory meant the British had retained control of the sea, and that the invaders could not negotiate the channel with troops they had ready. Hitler's attempt was defeated in a series of air battles lasting for three months, but in which the British again maintained control and were able to prevent a crossing.

Attempts to cut off British supplies were made by Napoleon and the Germans. Napoleon attempted to cut off British trade with the mainland, a kind of inverse blockade he called the continental system, but the British were able to make up the deficit in non-European areas. The Germans in the World Wars attempted to cut off British supplies from overseas by using submarines, and they came close to success, although the British with American help managed to survive. In World War I the Germans hoped to use their fleet of dreadnoughts to help, but the British kept them bottled up in the North Sea. The only naval encounter, the battle of Jutland, while indecisive in terms of casualties, was possibly more decisive than Trafalgar in defense of Britain.

One other factor that may have helped the naval defense of Britain was the alleged weakness of the British army. Both Napoleon and Hitler, frustrated in their attempts to invade Britain, were able to turn and fight Russia instead without fear of a British counter-invasion. In the end they miscalculated because the British were able to recreate alliances, and their own army did in fact play a major part each time in defeating their adversaries. But their reputation was distinctly helpful in allowing the world conquerors to remove the pressure.

The question arises: if the British naval power was so successful, why didn't larger powers like France and Germany build larger navies? The answer is that they had greater land commitments than Britain and they lacked the naval tradition and perhaps colonial wealth. For the British, by virtue of controlling the seas, were the most successful world colonists in history, their building of a world colonial empire made them wealthy, and this wealth could be used for building ships, for paying crews, and for subsidizing continental allies.

It appeared in the eighteenth century, however, that the colonial policy might backfire. The British so effectively defeated the French in colonial warfare that their American colonists no longer needed their protection. On the contrary they used the support of other European powers, particularly France, in a successful revolution against British control. The British were then faced with a hostile power on their flank, and American opposition during the Napoleonic Wars showed what a potential threat this might involve.

But as it happened, the Americans developed their interior instead of their navy. That being the case, they were content to rely on British naval protection while the British, so long as they were assured of American friendship, usually had no need to protect their holdings in Canada (see Chapter 12).

By the twentieth century, however, the relation was changing. The Americans developed a stronger navy and concentrated it in the Pacific, while the British concentrated on the Atlantic. In both wars American merchant fleets helped the British overcome the threat of starvation as the result of sinkings by German submarines. And then, with World War II, the Americans developed an air force and by this time their superior technology and larger

population made them one of the great powers of the world. Britain by comparison declined in relation to the Americans as the Dutch had declined in relation
to their British allies in the eighteenth century.

We have mentioned the British colonial policy just in passing in since
we were focusing on British relations with European neighbors. But the British
were the leaders among European powers in a world expansion that was going
on for almost the entire peace period. This expansion involved exploration
and conquest of vast areas of the globe and leadership in the industrial revolution
beginning in the eighteenth century supported by a continual influx of raw
materials from the colonies. Whether this was an exploitative or symbiotic
process is the subject of many volumes in Western socio-economic literature,
but in any event it made possible British power and continued intervention
in European affairs, provided opportunities for the middle classes and younger
sons of nobility, and made the British Isles prosperous, if unevenly so, from
the eighteenth through the twentieth centuries.

The social structure was volatile and to a degree mobile. The rural
population was free, unbound to the land, never had been peasants. As urbaniza-
tion and industrialization took place, rural workers moved to the cities, where
they sometimes were able to improve themselves and move into the middle
class, but often found themselves working long and dangerous hours to support
a precarious living standard. The social separation between even the rising
middle class and the upper class was perpetuated by a highly selective educational system through the end of the Peace.

Termination

The first phase of peace ended with the Civil War, fighting lasting from
about 1642-1651. The victory by Parliament, coupled with subsequent reforms
taken without war, enabled England to go on with a longer period of peace.
But even in this war, most of the casualties came on battlefields. There was
not much bloodshed otherwise, and though regicide was spectacular, it was
not accompanied by a violent reign of terror.

The second phase of the Peace ended in quite a different manner, as
part of another successful prevention of foreign invasion. But this time invasion
involved control of the air as well as control of the sea, and in attempting
to win control of the air the Germans bombed Britain often and severely. More
than 40,000 were killed in the raids of 1940-1941. The raids tapered off then,
but rocket raids resumed the destruction in 1944. The casualties and damage
caused by these raids seem sufficiently intense and prolonged to call this the
end of a peaceful period.

In the long run, of course, these raids may appear only as a second interruption, comparable to the decade of civil war, in a still longer British Peace.
But if that turned out to be so, it would be under different circumstances.
The advent of air power, not to mention rocket power, had reduced the insularity
of all states. In any future conflict, Britain would not be protected by the
English Channel. If she were protected, it would be more likely because she
no longer posed an important threat, nor would bombing or occupation produce
the advantages that would have accrued before 1940.

The leadership of British Prime Minister Neville Chamberlain was much
criticized in this period, and the pact he made with German Chancellor Hitler
in 1938 at Munich has become synonymous with foolish appeasement of an
uncompromisingly expansionist power. In retrospect it would seem that leaders
before Chamberlain might have intervened more strongly a few years earlier
to prevent German rearmament and mainland expansion. But it was not until
the invasion of France in 1940 that the true extent of German power became

evident. Then Britain played her usual role in rallying a successful coalition to defeat the dominant European power. It was the development of air power and rockets, not inferior diplomacy, that cost the English and the Scots their immunity to attack.

Once again, as in many other cases, we are confronted with the problem of casualties occurring outside the area of peace. The British Empire lost a million men in World War I, and suffered three million casualties. Yet Australia, New Zealand, South Africa, Canada, and Britain, which contributed these men, continued to enjoy peace at home. By comparison the British Peace ended because some 50,000 persons died at home instead of abroad. They died, of course, in what proved to be a successful defense of their independence. They might have lived if the British government had considered the situation hopeless and surrendered to Germany. So the defense of peace and the defense of sovereignty often involve a conflict. Sometimes one must be sacrificed for the other, and people are not in agreement about which is most worth having.

Reflections

This long British Peace demonstrates the advantages of insularity, properly exploited. Central for the British was keeping their continental opponents divided, switching alliances as the power structure changed. Poland, it is true, supported a strong power against a stronger power in backing the Habsburgs against the Turks, but the Poles did not switch alliances in the way the British did. The development of naval power closely followed the Venetian pattern, even to the extent of using that sea power both for defense and for economic prosperity, which in turn contributed to the building of the navy.

The great length of the British Peace may be attributed to insularity also in the sense that this insularity permitted the development of a different internal pattern of government and social relations from that developed on the Continent. This would not have been meaningful in itself, except that this pattern proved to be particularly concerned with means, with the way processes were carried out. The parliamentary system proved to be admirably adapted for handling the transition from personal to constitutional monarchy. It served as a model for other progressive countries in this period. For rapid economic changes from rural to industrial economies were taking place throughout the world, partly as the result of worldwide exploration by the Western Europeans in the sixteenth and seventeenth centuries.

The British had long shown a capacity to create patterns of compromise. Henry VII had sealed his victory by marriage into the family of his rivals. Henry VIII and Elizabeth were only the earliest of British leaders who demonstrated a remarkable capacity for religious compromise. Always institutions were developed that would partially and often irrationally resolve seemingly irresolvable differences.

Prosperity helped oil these peaceful transformations. It was Tudor prosperity, brought about by domestic peace, Spanish windfalls, and disengagement from European affairs, that made possible the building of a navy and the development of overseas commerce. This commerce, in turn, created a world empire offering scope to those dissatisfied at home, and maintained a level of prosperity in England which at least kept economic grievances below the level of desperation. But this was less important than the internal pattern itself, since economic rebellions did take place in other countries where prosperity was probably not markedly below the British level.

It is difficult to find individual heroes in parliamentary states. Many ministers, military leaders, intellectuals and even gentlemen farmers made contributions at one time or another that defended the nation or contributed to solving problems that could have led to conflict. But certainly Henry VII, like Charles Robert of Anjou, stands out as a typical founder-consolidator, healing wounds, suppressing opposition, restoring finances. Henry VIII and Elizabeth completed the consolidation, though Henry could also be seen in the role of Magnificent Monarch. And William of Orange stands out less as a reformer than as a leader who understood the reform and made it work, and moreover put Britain back on what in retrospect proved to be its most effective type of foreign policy: opposing the strongest continental power. Leaders of the nineteenth century, like Lord Grey, William Gladstone and Benjamin Disraeli were reformers too, tinkering with and modifying laws to fit changes in the social system. But the British had a great capacity for such tinkering, and this is rare. Generally, however, one finds not single heroes, but a long list of names of men and women who performed important and often unexpected roles. The British Peace was the product of a nation, not of a man.

Of all the cases presented here, this one has drawn the most criticism from readers. It is not that the case is not valid by the criteria, but that the criteria themselves seem to be flawed by the case. It is not only that many of the British were killed overseas, fighting one war or another, but that the British were perceived to be exploitative in amassing their Empire. It has seemed to several readers that there is something wrong with describing the home society of a people as peaceful, when representatives of that society were out acquiring the world. Even if they did, as Alice Vines points out, it was not the result of a military plan in the fashion of Napoleon, or even a pragmatic crusade of the kind engineered by the Venetians, but a slow growth of trade and influence followed by a "need to control and make the area peaceful for profit."

At any rate, the society of Johnson and Boswell as well as that of Dickens was peaceful, whatever the government of George III or Queen Victoria may have been doing in the rest of the world. Whether the society could have been peaceful if the government were not carrying out these activities is another question. As it happens we have a case of another insulated society that was not imperialistic, but which maintained peace for a much larger area than the British Isles for more than two centuries, and continues peaceful today. This is the Scandinavian Peace, to be considered in the next chapter.

8

The Scandinavian Peace
(1262-   )

"By Law Shall the Land Be Built"

"It seems advisable to me that we do not let their will
prevail who are most strongly opposed to one another, but
so compromise between them that each side may win part
of its case, and let us all have one law and one faith. [For
it] will prove true that if we divide the law we will also divide the peace."--
Thorgeirr Thorkelsson, Lawspeaker of Iceland, A.D. 1000,
in his decision whether Iceland should accept Christianity,
as reported by Ari Thorgilsson the Learned in the **Islending-
abok** (Johannesson 1974:135).

Area/Duration: Iceland, 1262- ; Norway, 1371-1612, 1814-1940; Denmark,
1660-1801; Sweden, 1721- ; Finland, 1809-1918.

Peaceful Scandinavia: Nowadays these two words couple so readily
that the Scandinavian states have become the automatic example when an
advanced war-free society is needed for citation. Yet the observer of Scandinavian beginnings would hardly have expected such an outcome. The Scandinavians
first appeared in history in their own right as the Vikings, and the Northmen's
fury was followed by some centuries of assorted other wars. When peace did
come it came in so many fragments that it seems odd to speak of a single
Peace. Only the Kalmar Union created anything approaching a common government, and at no time did the Peace embrace all five Scandinavian states at
once. Yet there has been a shared background of ideas, experiences and geography, such that the individual fragments of peace show definite similarities.

Origins

Peace, as just stated, came in fragments. In Iceland it began when regional gatherings of 1262-1264 commended the island to the Crown of Norway
to end an increasingly serious civil war. In Norway the last royal war occurred
in 1371, but wars between Denmark and Sweden spilled over into Norway during
1612-1814. Denmark saw peace after the successful Swedish invasion of 1658-
1660; Sweden likewise began peace after losing a major war. Finland, a permanent war zone while contested by Sweden and Russia, became peaceful because
of the definitive Russian victory of 1809. In all these cases peace was not
so much achieved as regretfully accepted, a passing of glory rather than an

end of troubles. Yet if it seemed somewhat the best of a bad bargain, it came to be a highly beneficial and desired best.

The Scandinavian Peace involved separate components in internal and foreign affairs that recurrently coincided to support long periods of peace. At the core, however, was an interaction between constitutional and geographic factors.

Constitutionally, the Scandinavians have at least since Viking times, and arguably even then, enjoyed a consensus amounting to serenity on the forms and purposes of community, while at the same time taking an almost Viking pleasure in resorting to arms over the question of who was actually going to rule. This problem was settled only very gradually. In Iceland and Norway it was settled early by removal of the kingship somewhere else. Iceland being almost completely isolated immediately became almost completely peaceful (an occasional pirate disturbed the island); Norway being somewhat less geographically isolated still had occasional problems with Sweden. Denmark and Sweden being somewhat isolated from Europe proper could enjoy peace when they wanted to, until European development ended this peripheral status. The Scandinavian Peace occurred, therefore, whenever geographic isolation and constitutional development interacted properly. In Denmark the last civil war occurred in 1534-1536, in Sweden in 1598. Since then internal peace has been disturbed by the occasional coup d'etat, but never again by armed seizure of the throne. Finally the last, so to speak, "Scandinavian civil" war occurred in 1814, over the ownership of Norway, and since then warfare has not been considered a legitimate means of establishing possession of territory in that area.

The development of this rule of peace is a distinctly Scandinavian phenomenon. Scandinavia is a culturally distinct region on the northern periphery of Europe. European involvements have been a major cause of Scandinavian warfare, but always certain crucial points of individuality were maintained. While England, France, Germany, Italy, and Spain were developing as successor states of the Roman Empire, organized in principle around the monolithic theocratic heirarchism of Roman Catholic thought, the Scandinavian peoples were busy first with a warlike localism testified by many ruined fortifications and buried treasures and then with the equally exciting age of the Vikings. Neither of these involved any concept of a generalized right to rule. Instead each locality cohered around a rough-edged consensus in the locality, expressed in a general assembly called a **thing.** It is important to remember that not only was consensus thus the basis of authority but also this was a locally developed concept, not at all beholden to old Roman ideas of the proper purview of community effort. One would search in vain in old Scandinavian concepts for anything approaching a "state."

Iceland presents both the best chronicled and least contaminated such development. There was a single basic official, the **godi** (pl. **godar),** a more or less priest (in the sense of officiating at sacrifices) who was also a more or less chieftain. The office, **godord,** could be inherited, bought or sold; one person could hold two or more such offices; or one could be exercised jointly by several people. The nature of authority of a godi is just as vague as the nature of its transmission. It certainly involved law; godar and their liegemen were bound to support each other in lawsuits, and the godar sat with the single elected official, the lawspeaker, as the legislative committee of the Icelandic Althing. Each freeman chose his own godi and could change his choice every year if he felt like it and could find a new godi to accept him.

The Icelandic **Althing,** the various regional **things** all over Scandinavia and the local **things** all had consultative authority bordering on lawmaking; the Icelanders even referred to their political arrangements as not "our state" but "our laws." The **thing,** in the person of the lawspeaker, could state the

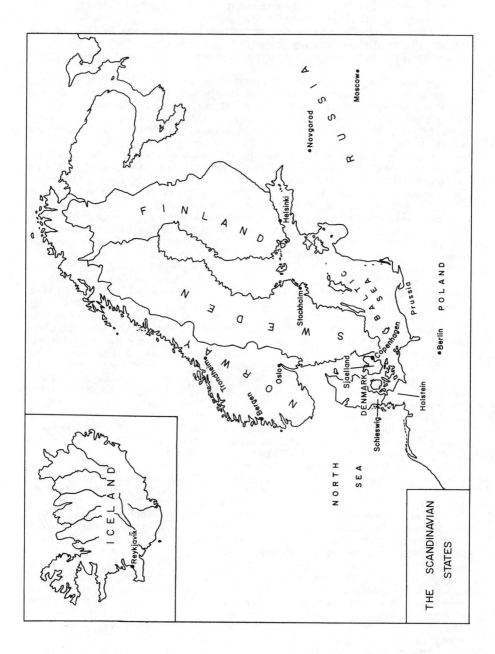

THE SCANDINAVIAN STATES

law and could make changes or deletions by the simple expedient of stating them without challenge. They could arbitrate disputes or call for such arbitration. Their statement certainly amounted to recognition of law-in-being and arguably to creation of new law. And this law was very much the cultural focus of Scandinavia. Concerning Sweden for example it can be said with only pardonable exaggeration that every freeholder house could be counted on to contain two books, the lawbook and the Bible—and the former gathered rather less dust. Yet however important a concept law was, it remained for centuries very incomplete.

Law was made by the community, but Scandinavian constitutional concepts did not recognize the right of the community to enforce its own agreements. Indeed to a certain extent reliance on community action was actively discouraged in favor of individual private enforcement; for example, the **Gulathinglag**—the law around Bergen and Stavanger—states in so many words (title 186) that "no one, either man or woman, has a right to claim atonement [monetary compensation, **wergeld**] more than three times, unless he has taken revenge in the meantime" (Larson 1935:140). An appeal from lawcourt to axe was held quite proper and acceptable, and as late as the thirteenth century the **Frostathinglag** (around Trondhjem) still provided for settlement by revenge. However much community consensus might lie behind any particular law, enforcement of legal rights was essentially a personal and kin matter.

But outside Iceland, which was not subject to the usual raids and counter-raids of Viking times, another institutional nucleus was developing. In most of Scandinavia, the local warlord, **jarl** (earl) or **konung** (king), was a very necessary part of the local organization. Traditionally this was an elective office, though possibly from particular high-status lines. The Viking Age both introduced Scandinavia to European concepts of kingship and, since local raiding could be just as enticingly profitable as the more long-distance variety, gave good reason for the construction of a broader local authority. Towards 1000 the local warlords began claiming something like European kingship, and gradually three separate crowns, Denmark, Norway, and Sweden, established prescriptive rights to some kind of overlordship among groups of tribes. In practice each crown had a habit of being grabbed by the strongest lord in the vicinity, but said lord, once recognized, would nevertheless be required in return to recognize each regional law, and was subject to deposition when this was neglected. This unstable throne-right led to two modifications: The kings gathered as much lawmaking authority as possible, and rights of appointment to regional offices wherever possible, into their own hands, and they tried to assert the Catholic theory that state power was a gift of God rather than a grant by election on terms amounting to a social contract. The three kingdoms produced three different resolutions of this problem.

Norway went the farthest toward continental European practices, receiving a single royally promulgated law (with the local laws continuing in place locally), granting divine right and binding the king only to a coronation oath to uphold the law, and confirming a fixed hereditary succession. But as in many continental cases this cost Norway its independence. Beginning in 1319, with finality in 1450, the kingdom became dynastically subordinate to Denmark, and whatever may have developed from this European-style concentration of powers in the Crown lost its chance.

Denmark took a middle course, confirming succession within a single dynasty and electing a new one when the old one failed, promulgating at least one royal law (of Jutland, 1241), but with the Crown remaining elective within the dynasty. Moreover as of 1282 the kings were bound not just by oath but by a coronation contract, the terms of which became more and more onerous over the centuries. In Denmark the theory of the social contract was firmly established, and remained the case even when absolutism was finally achieved in 1660.

The Swedish tribal ("folk-land") laws were written down in the 1200's, and two general codes, one each for country and city, were promulgated about 1350 and recognized in the later 1400's. But the monarchy remained elective with no single dynasty recognized, and the law codes continued to provide for deposition as well as recognition of a king. Indeed Swedish history continues to have a distinct flavor of anarchy right into the sixteenth century.

Iceland was somewhat anomalous, and for that reason provides a particularly good illustration of the requirements of the situation. Iceland, as noted, had no warlords to become kings, but nevertheless found kingship so necessary that eventually it recognized a foreign lordship rather than remain without it. Originally Iceland had had only local **things** as political instruments, but already by 930 the island had grown together sufficiently that an island-wide Althing was considered advisable. The conversion to Christianity accelerated this interaction, because Catholic tithes went not to the Church but to the owners of each individual church under Icelandic law, thereby providing them with the resources for more effective competition. As of the twelfth century this competition began threatening the rather loose peace established by the law. Warring families would come to the Althing with their private armies; in 1163 there was armed conflict even in the legislative committee. By the thirteenth century three or four families had gained primacy over all the others. The bishops, claiming the primacy of the universal church over any such local considerations as Icelandic law, also entered the fray; Jon Johanesson holds one bishop, Gudmundr Arason (1203-1237), primarily responsible for wrecking the old Icelandic consensus by his uncompromising pursuit of Church prerogatives (1974:200-211). In 1207 Icelanders for the first time had to refer an island dispute to a foreign tribunal for settlement; in 1242 they went for the first time to the king of Norway. Moreover the Norwegian kings were actively trying to establish their rule over Iceland, collecting liege oaths from Icelanders who had come to Norway to seek their fortunes and then enforcing them back in Iceland as well. Finally, no other solution being visible to what seemed to be becoming a permanent state of conflict, the Icelanders commended themselves to the crown of Norway. It was by no means unconditional; by terms of the commendation treaty of 1262 the Crown was bound to respect Icelandic law, to create no new laws without the consent of the Althing, and to keep Iceland in peace. The effort to maintain a purely Scandinavian system had failed.

This should not be taken as simply a failure of consensus. There were other problems, most notably the end of the warm climate of the settlement age. Its name regardless, Iceland had been free of coastal ice earlier, but in the 1100's coastal winter drift ice began returning and in the 1200's the island was entirely surrounded. It is noteworthy that the agreement of commendation also required Norway to keep the supply ships running to Iceland; evidently their profitability and arrival had become increasingly uncertain.

Thus by 1300 all of Scandinavia had established royal regimes of varying degrees of authority. For the next few centuries breaches of the peace would focus on the balance between Crown, aristocracy and people.

Iceland had already settled this. By 1262 the locally great families had long since achieved primacy over the people, and with the removal of sovereignty to foreign shores the power question was settled permanently. Such few officials as were appointed, whether of local families or Norwegians or Danes, intrigued with the Crown for position rather than carrying disputes to the old method of pitched battle, and no one seems to have felt able or constrained to challenge the final sovereignty of the Crown. The Crown in turn usually treated the island with disinterested neglect, giving very little cause for offense. Iceland enters a period very nearly without stimulus of any kind; even the tremendous burst of creativity that produced most of the Scandinavian saga literature died out shortly after 1300.

In the fourteenth century Norway also lost its resident Crown, but followed a different path from Iceland's. The Black Death hit Norway very hard indeed. Of some 300 aristocratic Norwegian families in 1300 fewer than 60 survived in 1400, and other effects of the Plague had so reduced the national wealth (by about 2/3) that even the surviving nobles sank rapidly into standard freeholder status. Moreover the Norwegian freeholders lived not in towns or even villages. By 1400 Norway had become a geographical expression, a few towns amounting to foreign colonies in a sea of disconnected farmsteads. The last Norwegian royal war, involving Haakon of Norway and his father-in-law, Valdemar of Denmark, was against the Hanseatic League. In the course of the war, which ended in 1371, the shores of Norway were raided a number of times. After that, for more than two centuries, such breaches of the peace as occurred were of the kind of Amund Bolt's rebellion (1436), which would nowadays be called a protest march. From 1612 to 1814 there were occasional spillovers into Norway of the Danish-Swedish wars, but excepting Charles XII's attacks in 1716 and 1718 and Charles XIV's in 1814, these seem to have been on a very small scale, in one case seeing the invading force destroyed simply by joint action of the local Norwegian farmers. Whether they were of sufficient magnitude to count as breaking the Peace is a decision that must await further study, but for now, it will be assumed they were.

Denmark had an elective monarchy, though within one dynasty; indeed the realm seems to have been less firmly established than the dynasty. Under King Niels Svensson (1104-1134) Denmark had begun a serious program of Europeanization in order to resist German conquest, creating the standard European mounted knighthood with aristocratic privileges. By 1200, though these aristocrats often still worked their own fields, they also began traveling in Europe and learning the ways of European aristocracy. It was they who in 1282 forced the Crown into the first of the increasingly onerous coronation charters, and who also increasingly made Denmark away from the capital into a collection of local lordships and, concomitantly, local power bases. At the same time they degraded the position of the freeholders, and between 1200 and 1400 the proportion of freehold landownership shrank from 50% to 15%. In late medieval Denmark the king remained head of government in a Europe increasingly emphasizing royal prerogative, among an aristocracy with no intention of allowing any such emphasis. This tension remained to be settled.

Sweden was on the far periphery, as much involved with Russia as with Europe. There was a Crown of Sweden, but it seems almost irrelevant until the thirteenth century and very unstable even into the sixteenth. Magnus Ladulas (1275-1290), 150 years after the same events in Denmark, imported various German forms to strengthen his rule, but one such (1279) was tax exemption for armored cavalrymen, on which basis the Swedish aristocracy was built. On the other hand the freeholders remained an important part of Swedish society, in 1400 still owning 50% of the land. Where Denmark had a Crown-nobles axis of conflict, Sweden still had a balance among three foci. For the moment this produced even more instability than in Denmark.

Such conditions do not appear a very fertile ground for peace, or even for law. And on occasion one will find such comments as were made during the Swedish civil war of 1388, that "no one asked after law or right." But these conditions were held not just evil but exceptional, and even in strongly monarchical Norway the ideal of the rule of law was maintained. Everywhere, kings could be and were (at least in popular story) forced to bow to the law. "Change had first to be sanctified by legislative agreement, and it was not forgotten that kings might be thrown into the well" (Scott 1977:65).

So by the end of the Middle Ages Scandinavia was divided between two realms, Denmark-Norway-Iceland and Sweden with Finland. In Denmark the peasantry was becoming more and more closely bound to the soil and to the interests of aristocracy and state, and even in Sweden there were signs of the beginning of such a process. The chain of events which reversed this course began in 1397.

In 1397 dynastic considerations united both realms under a single dynasty, in what came to be called the Union of Kalmar. It was not a strong union; indeed it is hard to say that Sweden was much less independent under it than formerly. But the aristocracies of Scandinavia were becoming more and more intermarried, with a rising Scandinavian rather than local outlook, and the Church of course was very much a multi-realm affair, so the Union was by no means predestined stillborn. But if the crowns and nobilities were beginning to merge, Sweden, unlike Denmark, still had a peasantry that counted. The firestorm was set off by a combination of a foreign policy that injured important Swedish local interests and peasant discontent with the royally-appointed bailiffs. The usual remedy in the latter situation was simply to massacre the offending bailiffs, which usually communicated discontent to the Crown well enough. But in the event the protests got out of hand, the result was a national revolt in which freeholders' armies sprang up spontaneously in several areas, and since they won, the freeholders were definitely recertified as a force to be dealt with in Sweden. The same freeholder sentiments were appealed to again and again in the next century, and when eventually Sweden seceded from the Union, the crown-aristocracy-freeholder triangle of power was well established.

The sixteenth century saw the last of the Danish and Swedish civil wars, which were involved with the more general issue of Protestantism. Every step in this rather tangled evolution was carried forward with careful attention to the letter (hardly always the spirit) of the law. When Gustavus I Vasa (1523-1560) rebelled against Copenhagen, dispossessed the Church, established hereditary succession, he legitimated each move by consultation with the nobles' council, the Swedish Parliament (Riksdag), or such other assembly as seemed necessary, convenient and pliable, backtracking whenever a freeholders' revolt or aristocratic resistance became too dangerous. Indeed Gustavus moved so cautiously and correctly and managed so ambiguous a Reformation that for decades it did not even involve breaking with the Pope.

His son Erik XIV (1560-1568) attempted a more roughshod royalism about equally tainted by lowborn secretaries and his personal insanity, and so the hereditary monarch was deposed in favor of an "elected hereditary" monarch. In 1589 the Royal Council established the precedent that it could force the king to change his stated policy.

The reign of Gustavus II Adolphus (1611-1632) added a key development: Under a written Form of Government the Crown was to rule only in consultation with the representative bodies, at this time primarily still the Royal Council (of high nobles) rather than the Riksdag, with the highest positions reserved for the nobles. Since Gustavus was overseas much of the time he also appointed a chancellor with wide powers, specifically answerable "to God, to Us, and to every honorable Swedish man" (Masson 1968:12). This also held in the reign of Queen Kristina (1632-1654) even though she stayed at home until abdicating. In the short run the position of the nobles was also improved by Gustavus' intense need for money to finance his wars. Sale or other alienation of royal property was a traditional method, mostly going to the nobles, to the great future detriment of the Crown revenues and equally great future discontent of the tax-paying burghers and freeholders from whose pockets the deficits had to be made up. At the same time another change began a reorientation of much longer term: The nobles' service obligation was transferred from that of armored knight to the broader field of government service in general. Henceforth not just the great offices but a much larger part of the government were a legitimate opportunity for noble advancement and enrichment. Indeed it quickly became the badge of nobility to have such an office.

It was the alienation of royal property and consequent ruin of the royal finances that sealed this development. Somehow the Crown had to find more money, and the burghers and freeholders grew increasingly strident over attempts to designate them the sources. Only reclamation of some of the alienated property appeared as a feasible alternative, and the nobles fought this tooth and nail. During 1655-1680 the Crown managed a very limited reclamation; finally in 1682 the king appealed to the Riksdag-at-large against the great nobles and received recognition of his sole authority in any questions concerning former royal property. The proportion of land held by nobles then dropped from 72% to 33%, with much of the reclaimed land being resold, but to tax-paying freeholders this time. The nobles were so thoroughly dispossessed that for many government service became the only source not just of advancement but of the ability to make a living, and at the same time the supremacy of the Crown-in-Riksdag was established.

There remained the problem of the balance between these two. The lower orders had joined with the Crown to override the great nobles, but in doing so gave the Crown powers which in the next decades increasingly resembled a blank check. As the hazards of this arrangement became evident there was increasing sentiment to revoke the check, but since the kings were careful to remain within the letter of the law, no concerted opposition existed. But the reign of the autocratic Charles XII (1697-1718) ended in almost total disaster, discrediting the autocracy. Moreover Charles had spent almost all of his reign outside Sweden, five consecutive years of it in Turkey, an absolute monarch as much as a year's communication-time away from his government. Increasingly the government was run on a day-to-day basis by the Royal Council, the Riksdag, and the bureaucracy. When Charles was killed these assumed in the open the policy-making power they had been gathering behind the scenes, forcing the Crown to accept whatever limitations the Riksdag chose to impose, and the Crown found it had no force available to counter this imposition. Henceforth the internal development of Sweden was to revolve essentially around each faction's ability to sway the Riksdag, and this was not to be a matter for the weapons of war.

Meanwhile Denmark saw its own internal shifts. During the later Middle Ages the king had assumed in Denmark a position only debatably better than that of first aristocrat of the realm, and such attempted absolutism as the reign of Christian II (1513-1523) served only to emphasize this. But the Danish aristocracy seems to have been so anxious to gain privileges and lose responsibilities as in the end to lose control of the shifting power bases of the society. Closing its ranks against newcomers was particularly damaging, since that removed the incentive for aspiring talents to defend privileges they could hope one day to enjoy. In 1658-1660 one of the monotonously frequent wars with Sweden ended in almost total disaster; Copenhagen itself was saved only by the heroism of its citizens. The south Swedish provinces, the granary of Copenhagen for centuries, were lost with no foreseeable chance of recovery. As in Sweden the disaster was used to unseat the system in power at the time. The nobles were blamed for everything that had gone wrong within living memory, but they still refused to abandon any of their cherished fiscal privileges to help pay the crushing debts left from the war. In the ensuing prolonged dispute the estates of clergy and burghers decided as a panacea to ask the king to settle matters, fully expecting him to create a balance of the estates in the Rigsdag in place of aristocratic domination. The nobles would not countenance this, and the king resolved the stalemate by sealing the city and calling the people to arms. This overawed the nobles; the Rigsdag returned to the king his coronation charter, to revise as he would. Only after the Rigsdag adjourned did the king put forth his revised plan of government: absolute hereditary monarchy, with the Rigsdag permanently out of session and all authority concentrated in the Crown. The France of Louis XIV was suddenly to blossom from the soil of Denmark.

So at least was the theory. In practice the change was considerably less. The new absolutism required an administration; this was modelled directly on Sweden's system, which if it did not positively require that aristocrats do everything, was certainly practiced along those lines. Indeed by virtue of their much greater opportunity for education if nothing else, the aristocracy developed to be just as primary a recruiting ground for the Danish bureaucracy as for the Swedish. The aristocratic local governments were swept away in favor of a strong centralization: which consisted now of appointed aristocrats. The aristocracy was opened to talent, and the new entries became just as fervent defenders of their new privileges as any of the old-line nobles. The subjection of the peasants continued and even increased, though gradually under new forms of state requirements instead of feudal obligations. For the next 140 years, excepting the occasional Crown-centered political intrigue, the evolution of Denmark was thoroughly placid.

Characterization

Thus in the later seventeenth century both Denmark and Sweden had achieved the basic formulation which was to ensure domestic peace within each realm henceforth. It has been called in recent discussions of possible reforms in the American university system, participatory bureaucracy, and may in its simplest form be characterized by the statement that policy-making positions should be filled primarily by the people who will have to implement the policies. The characteristic attitudes of this system are rather different from those behind American political life; again for example, government is assumed to be not a necessary evil and constriction of freedom but a constructive and distinctly paternalistic guide. The Scandinavian countries have nothing like the American intrinsic distrust of the state. In the seventeenth and eighteenth centuries this was expressed through the aristocracy, which was primary recruiting ground for the bureaucracy and for which the bureaucracy served as the principle channel of advancement. But later development would show class aristocracy to be unnecessary, and it was gradually replaced as a status indicator by simple membership in the system.

There were differences. In Sweden during the Age of Freedom, as the non-royalist period 1721-72 is called, the final responsibility of the bureaucracy was to the Riksdag, not to the Crown. But the Riksdag developed in practice to represent mainly the bureaucracy. Of the four estates, the Riddarhus—the nobility—were by definition in government service, and dominated the proceedings. The clergy were appointed as members of a state church and so were state employees, although they did not think of themselves as such; the burghers tended strongly to be represented by mayors and members of town councils. Only the peasants were not in government service, and the Riksdag also left them as far as possible out of Riksdag proceedings. Developments in Sweden during the Age of Freedom were largely the products of faction fights within the bureaucracy, and (within the realm, that is) that was the only fighting allowed.

In Denmark on the other hand there was no Riksdag, and the bureaucracy was responsible to the king. This might be expected to lead to tyranny, but it did not. The rule of law, of precedent, procedure and consensus, had become so strongly institutionalized that in spite of theoretical absolutism, Denmark saw neither mass purges of warring factions in the bureaucracy nor risings of the governed against the possible tyrants. The kings/regents seem to have acted as benevolent governors and referees, not as autocrats, and if the royal signature could and did topple governments, it was expected and almost always observed that some very considerable consensus would be established before that signature was applied. The key to the peace of Denmark was not a balance of power among competing interests but more a matter of morale: The law was there, recognized and respected, consensus was not abused, and that was that.

Externally developments were otherwise. If the Viking pleasure in armed competition had been institutionalized out of existence within the states, a touch of imperialism in foreign relations was still quite manly and heroic. Until 1720 the wars between Denmark and Sweden constitute almost a single recurrent Hundred-and-Fifty Years' War, and neither power was at all reluctant to assault other neighbors as well. Denmark began a peace in 1660 purely because the central realm had become isolated from most warfare, which would be conducted in the adjunct realms of Slesvig and Holstein or across the Sound in southern Sweden. When in 1700 Charles XII managed a surprise landing near Copenhagen, this though it incurred no casualties did end a war.

In Sweden a fragile peace began in 1721. It was fragile partly for being incomplete—Swedish Finland was still subject to recurrent wars with Russia—and partly for being somewhat involuntary. Denmark and Sweden were not entirely reconciled to the idea of peace, but by this time their international position had evolved to the point of demanding it.

First, war was an expensive business, and Denmark and especially Sweden remained distinctly underdeveloped for a very long time. The Viking interest in commerce had been rather casual, and by 1300 the more organized commercial system of the Hanseatic League had driven even the seafaring Norwegians from competition. Because of this underdevelopment the Scandinavian realms were inveterate subsidy hunters. Even the glories of Gustavus Adolphus in the Thirty Years War had depended considerably on French money. Moreover this relative underdevelopment continued for a very long time; Sweden remained so underpopulated that as late as 1840 wolves were a common sight in Stockholm itself. So necessarily even at their most powerful the Scandinavian states were somewhat dependent on foreign powers.

Second, by 1720 the Scandinavian states were no longer at their most powerful. As early as 1660 and 1679 Denmark, even when theoretically on the winning side in a war, was forced by the great powers into making unwelcome concessions. Sweden's power relative to the rest of Europe had shrunk enough that in 1672 it agreed with Denmark for a joint convoy system for their ships in hostile waters, and in 1691 formed the first league of armed neutrality. But this did not mean the Scandinavian states had already recognized themselves to be brothers in adversity: In 1769 Denmark signed a treaty with Prussia and Russia for the partitioning of Sweden, like that of Poland shortly to occur; in 1789 Denmark attacked Sweden from both Denmark and Norway, and only great power insistence forced withdrawal before the situation came to actual fighting. Likewise in 1786 Gustavus III of Sweden (1771-1792) planned to attack Denmark and only because of Russian non-cooperation attacked Russia instead; in 1813 Sweden wanted both Norway and Sjaelland as the price of cooperation with Russia, and did attack both Denmark and Norway to ensure possession of the latter. One may argue whether these consitute significant violations of the peace. Certainly the Swedish invasion of Norway was significant enough to enforce transfer of Norway.

But these Scandinavian conflicts seem to have been the tailing off of an old conquest tradition, in spite of the growing imperialism of Europe itself at the time. After 1814 there were occasional threats of war, particularly of a Swedish attack on Russia during the Crimean War to recover Finland, but these came to nothing. The Scandinavian states had become too involved in a Europe ruled by much greater powers that could enforce on Scandinavia whatever they felt like enforcing. The possible gains no longer balanced the definite hazards from war.

Post-Napoleonic Europe also developed a positive reinforcement of this intra-Scandinavian peace. The Romantic nationalism sweeping Europe also affected Scandinavia, creating a sense of joint Scandinavian nationality. This remained mostly an intellectual movement, a cause of much talking and quite a few good parties, but it did mean public expressions that war among Scandinavians was henceforth unthinkable. It also led to some talk of federation, but since everyone realized that any such federation would be dominated by Sweden, nobody but the Swedes was much interested. When eventually Sweden and Norway did not join Denmark in the final Slesvig-Holstein war against Prussia and Austria in 1864, political Scandinavianism was dead. But the Peace continued.

Internally, the establishment of participatory bureaucracy governed the forms which competition could in future take, and in Sweden the existence of occasional shifts in the balance of power provides convenient dates for monitoring the expansion of participation to new groups. Initially "participatory" referred just to the high nobles, who had even a formal monopoly of power: Until 1720 the Riddarhus was formally divided into upper, middle, and lower nobles, which in 1626 numbered 12, 23 and 92 families respectively. Each section had one vote as a group, so the upper third of the nobles had absolute control of the Riddarhus for any program on which they could agree. New royal appointments increased participation to some 2000 noble families by the end of the eighteenth century. Since there were three other estates and the nobles generally depended on the cooperation of clergy and burghers for a majority in the Riksdag, and since the mercantilism of the eighteenth century increasingly involved the government in economic questions, the achievement of full participation by all the nobles proved to be only the prelude to the extension of participation to members of the two middle estates. The influence of the freeholders remained more theoretical than actual, but the two middle groups were clearly breaking down old noble preserves.

The precise details of the parliamentary party system (and it was that) achieved in eighteenth-century Sweden are beside the present point; suffice for the moment that it did successfully provide for an alternation of power among elected representatives controlling government policy, even at that early date. But by the later eighteenth century Swedish politics were becoming polarized around the question of aristocratic privilege. The nobles had in their favor the letter of the law, always a powerful point in Scandinavia, while clergy and burghers expressed a presumably much wider consensus that the law needed changing.

Matters came to a head in 1772. The first partition of Poland momentarily made a tremendous issue of the need for unity against foreign dangers, while the party system specialized in factional strife; there had been two consecutive crop failures and consequent starvation; the privilege question had so split the Riksdag that neither party was willing to trust the other with the government. Accordingly the focus of power shifted again, with all sides deciding that the matter should be settled by the king.

This did not mean a Danish absolutism. In effect the old government was continued, but with neither of the two parties holding power, each expecting the king eventually to decide in its favor. This state of suspense continued for seventeen years, with various royal reforms and adventures standing at least as temporarily successful diversions.

Finally the king, Gustavus III, had to decide, and in spite of his personal aristocratic predilections, he chose the commoners. In 1789 by what amounts to an act of sheer bravado he faced down the Riddarhus and secured from the other three estates almost absolute personal power in return for sweeping cancellation of the essential political and economic rights of the nobility. Since by any interpretation the consent of the Riddarhus was needed for this, his action was technically unconstitutional, and earned him the violent hatred of most of the nobility. Only three years later a noble conspiracy murdered him, but so deep had respect for formally correct procedures become that this assassination shocked the country into maintaining the greatest continuity possible, passing on the same absolute powers to the crown prince. Only when the new king proved another Erik XIV was he in turn, this time quietly and bloodlessly, deposed in favor of a king chosen by the Riksdag, on its own terms. It is noteworthy that the Riksdag did not choose to re-establish the discredited party system of the 1700's but rather only re-adjusted the balance between Crown and Parliament, arguably more in the Crown's favor that its own. The care for equity is also visible in the creation of the office of ombudsman and the provision (in 1809!) for a variable income tax (at the time, 0.25 to 10%). Only one major structural change remained, the abolition of the old system of four estates, which had become hopelessly inflexible in reflecting the much more complex professionalism of the modern world, in favor of the standard bicameral parliament.

If the position of Sweden is considered vis-a-vis Europe, what is immediately striking is that the Swedish Peace begins with the ending of the Great Northern War, the same war that marks the end of Sweden as a great European power. Sweden had emerged as a great power at the beginning of the seventeenth century in spite of the limited development of her resources.

But by the eighteenth century, England, France and Prussia had caught up in administrative development with Sweden, and Russia, under Peter I, was learning rapidly during the exhausting Northern War. Moreover the neighbors of Sweden, having the advantage of more usable territory and warmer climates, were much larger. Sweden's population was under two million while Brandenburg, even before it had been united with Prussia, exceeded two million. The great continental powers were much larger. Thus circumstances were making participation in power struggles more difficult for Sweden. The spectacular military leadership of Charles XII for a time masked Sweden's relative decline, but ultimately the war left Russia in control of Swedish possessions on the South Baltic coast, while Sweden retained only Finland. Sweden tried twice again in the eighteenth century to retaliate against Russia, but, despite a decisive naval victory at Svensksund in 1790, her offensive military weakness on land was only made more apparent.

Thus if Sweden could no longer participate effectively in European conflicts, she could defend herself against her two most dangerous neighbors, Russia and Prussia, since they had to devote a good part of their energies to other wars. In the eighteenth century any invasion of Sweden would have involved a great effort for these powers, and would have put both the invading force and the depleted home front in an exposed position.

When France dominated the continent at the beginning of the nineteenth century, however, Sweden was in a more difficult position. The Swedes had to agree to join the continental system, refusing to trade with England, and then actually to declare war on England. But by agreement with the British Baltic commander, the Swedes permitted the British to trade under neutral flags, and the declaration of war went no further than words. Meanwhile the Russians, protected by agreement with the French, attacked Finland and took it from Sweden.

But the elected heir to the Swedish throne, the French Prince Bernadotte, foreseeing Napoleon's fall, aligned Sweden with the anti-French alliance, albeit with as little actual military commitment as possible until the balance really had turned, and then mostly against Napoleon's ally, Denmark. Hence the Swedes worked their way through a very difficult situation, avoiding invasion that might easily have come from France, Russia, Britain or Denmark, and receiving compensation (Norway) for lost territory in the bargain.

Between the Napoleonic Wars and World War II Sweden was again protected by a combination of naval power and European division. But in World War II a central power, this time Germany, once again dominated Europe. And once again Sweden cooperated, supplying the Germans with iron ore and allowing them to use Swedish railroads for passage from Norway to Germany and Finland. But as soon as Germany became well involved in a war with Russia, the Swedes reduced their supplies to Germany and provided shelter for refugees. Once again the Swedes had carried on a difficult balancing act to become the only European nation to avoid invasion and bombardment in all three great European wars of the nineteenth and twentieth centuries.

Actually the control of central Europe by a single power did lead to invasions of Scandinavia. In both centuries Finland was invaded by Russia, after agreement with the central power had been reached, and in both centuries, the central power acquired control of Denmark and Norway, Napoleon by political threat, Hitler by invasion.

Norway thus re-enters the equation at this point. Since the fifteenth century most of its developmental history had centered on events in Denmark. During the eighteenth century this began to change. The peace continued: The two great disturbances of the times are called the Striler War and the Lofthus Rebellion, but the first consisted of a group of peasants and townsmen roughing up the governor and sheriff of Bergen in protest against a new tax, which was accordingly not only repealed but repaid; the second involved some 800 armed men but no reported conflicts or casualties, being rather a large-scale protest against presumed collusion between local merchants and Danish officials, ending with the arrest of its leader. Meanwhile the Norwegian towns continued as isolated as before; Oslo, Bergen, and Trondhjem would only reluctantly admit they were in the same country. But Norwegians were serving in Danish officialdom, especially as clergy, and in position in Norway—the governor of Bergen in the Striler War was a Norwegian—and Norway was in effect a semi-detached part of Denmark. Its peculiar emphasis on shipping was growing again, and during the wars of the eighteenth century Norwegian neutral carriers began bringing prosperity back. In a very low-level, very quiet way, through local societies and local consciousness, Norway was finding its identity again. When in the country-shuffling of the Napoleonic period Norway ended up being dealt to Sweden, it developed that Norway had no taste for this at all. The Norwegian alternative was almost unique: A constitutional convention (mostly bureaucrats, of course) gathered on its own initiative, discussed Scandinavian practice and current political theory, wrote a constitution, and it worked. It is arguable how much of this success should be credited to the varying need for unity against the varying danger of absorption.

For Norway and Sweden, the period of developing separation marked the beginning of a very productive period of aesthetic development. There were a number of outstanding scholars and scientists, at least four of whom have gained world fame: the composer Edvard Grieg, the playwrights Henrik Ibsen and August Strindberg and more recently, the film director Ingmar Bergman. The turn of the century also marked the beginning of a series of annual prizes, provided for in the will of Alfred Nobel, Swedish scientist and inventor, including one for fostering fraternity among nations, abolishing armies and holding peace congresses: the Nobel Peace Prize. The eighteenth century, at the beginning of the Swedish Peace Period, was productive particularly in philosophy and science, with the mixed religious, astronomical and geological speculations of Emanuel Swedenborg, the development of the thermometer by Anders Celsius, and the biological classification system of Carl Linnaeus.

There remained only the evolutions toward peaceful independence of peripheral Scandinavia, and in the nineteenth century both Iceland and Finland regained active separate development.

Sweden began occupying Finland not later than the 1200's, and organized Finnish society existed as a frontier of organized Swedish society. But it was also a frontier of Russia, so war was a regular condition, with bits and pieces of Finland being passed back and forth as spoils. Finally in 1808 Russia conquered the whole country. But for the moment Finland remained Scandinavian; the strongly monarchic Swedish constitution of 1789 acquired a Russian monarch, who carefully went through all the proper formalities of legitimate power, and excepting a governor-general who seldom spoke the local language and so had to depend on local help, everything remained as it was. Finland remained not only Scandinavian but Swedish in all essential internal respects.

But Finland was ruled by a very strong monarchy, and if violations of autonomy were rare, tendencies toward parliamentarism were even rarer. And there was considerable danger that the constitution would be violated. The governor-general of 1823-1825 already wanted to treat Finland as a Russian dependency, but the new Grand Duke Nicholas I ended that. The danger remained only potential, and Finland had a much more immediate problem to worry about.

Finland had been Swedish, and by consensus it had no intention of becoming Russian. On the other hand the Swedish population of the autonomous grand duchy was only 15% of the total, and the rest saw little point in acquiring a culture which had become foreign. The Swedish population saw this situation as a threat to its own identity and resisted change; the Finnish population did not yet have enough identity to enforce change; neither by itself could hope for an independent country. So for several decades peace was the only feasible program for every side.

There were some advantages to the situation. Under Russian rule, the Finns not only maintained nominal political autonomy, but also received their own tax revenues instead of sharing them with Sweden. More, they had protection against military invasion from the country that had most frequently invaded—Russia. They did, however suffer a few British coastal raids during the Crimean War.

The growth of Finnish identity took some time. Only in 1824 was the Finnish language a requirement even for clergymen with Finnish congregations. In 1861 Finnish was first recognized as **an** official language in Finland and only as of 1902 did it achieve an equal position in all fields. Finnish Sagas were rediscovered, Finnish language newspapers gradually replaced Swedish, and a great national composer, Jean Sibelius, appeared. The Swedish rear-guard action after 1863 was particularly acrimonious, but any opportunity for a return to Swedish control seemed to have been lost with the end of the Crimean War.

By the end of the 1800's the Finns were essentially victorious in Finland. It was just at this time that the Russian overlordship began turning into more of a problem. Russia felt very threatened after the Crimean War, and one response was a policy of "Russification," reduction of the many national minorities to a single Russian standard. In 1890 Russia annexed the Finnish postal service, a small and tentative step but still the first time the imperial government consciously and without excuses violated the Finnish constitution. In 1899 Nicholas II decided the time had come to forget such niceties as constitutions, acting in such manner as to be called henceforth in Finland, Nicholas the Perjurer. But this meant not a united resistance but a division of Finland between advocates of opposition and those of cooperation in order to forestall future losses, hoping for a return of better conditions later. The 1905 revolution in Russia produced the hoped-for better conditions; the much-weakened imperial government restored the Finnish constitution and even allowed a new meeting of the Estates to re-write it radically. The four estates were combined into a unicameral legislature elected by proportional representation by an electorate ten times as large as before.

Iceland resumed its independence much less quickly and spectacularly. The island had been under benign neglect by its Norwegian and Danish overlords at least until the Reformation, and the economy continued at least productive enough for the wealthy families to grow more so, primarily by an increasing emphasis on fishing instead of farming. But with the Reformation the Danish Crown became increasingly interested in using Iceland as a money farm, and since the fishing business depended mostly on export the Crown had an easy time controlling it. In 1602 Icelandic commerce became a royal monopoly.

There was no native Icelandic authority system during this period to legitimate this oppression. The Althing continued to exist as a formality and to some degree as a law-court, and some of the appointed officials were native Icelanders, but any relation of these to popular approval is not mentioned. Yet in this society always remarked for its individualism and lack of respect for supposed authority, there were no revolts. There were very seldom even any assaults considered worth reporting, unlike the cases in Norway and Sweden with their protest lynchings. In at least some ways Iceland seems to have survived as a self-aware entity not only in ways that have little if anything to do with economics or politics but arguably by dissociation from or even abolition of the formal institutions of both. The urban nucleus considered necessary to civilization elsewhere was totally missing in Iceland. In 1751 Reykjavik like virtually everywhere in Iceland was a single isolated farm; in 1801 when it became the "capital" (seat of the high court which replaced the abolishing Althing) it had barely 300 people, and nowhere else was as large. Even in 1880, 92.6% of the population lived in units of fewer than 300 people. Yet the country had quite possibly the highest literacy rate in Europe. Reading (not writing) was taught in the monasteries until the Reformation, in schools or the private home afterwards. One incident put forth as typical involved a literary historian out tramping the countryside and, passing by a farm, hearing two farmers in lengthy discussion over a tragic death: It developed that the incident occurred in the Saga Age, and they were discussing in detail lives and situations of most of a thousand years before. At least on superficial inspection, Iceland maintained its identity not by practice but by, second only to Confucianism, possibly the single most powerful and pervasive apotheosis in world history of an old-time situation and its associated personalities. Iceland lived in the sagas, whatever plague, disaster and oppression might have brought in the following centuries.

In the nineteenth century Romantic nationalism was introduced to Iceland as to all the rest of Europe, and Iceland had no problem finding a national identity to assert. The problem lay rather in convincing people that national identity was the kind of thing which required a separate government for purposes of assertion. Such island-wide institutions as existed were more or less controlled by the many branches of the powerful Stephensen-Finsen family in conjunction with an intrigue-prone but very small number (full-time, no more than 25) of Danish officials. The initial impetus came from a single man, Jon Sigurdsson, an Icelander settled in Copenhagen, who combined Icelandic nationalism with the most punctilious Scandinavian use of every legal nicety available. There followed eighty years of consuming argument over the proper interpretation of the annexation treaty of 1262, all of it peaceable if noisy, as autonomy came in stages.

But however much Iceland valued its ancient heritage, the world had changed since saga times, and Iceland had not been changing nearly as much. The established professional orientations simply did not exist there as in the central Scandinavian realms; rather there were those widely spread family connections and a group of small, limited electorates with a distinctly proprietary attitude toward local power. The twentieth century exploded onto Iceland almost as much as it has on some more recent postcolonial societies. The island has had to face these problems all at once, with little prior experience, and the result was a much greater and stronger factionalism than in the continuously evolved central realms. This was alleviated by consensus at least on which institutions were proper.

In the 1830's and 1840's a strictly advisory body was created and blessed with the hallowed name Althing. In 1854 the Danish trade monopoly was lifted. Home rule was gradually obtained between 1874 and 1903, and independence under the Danish Crown in 1918. During World War II, while Denmark was occupied by Germany, Iceland became a republic, with a ceremonial president and a cabinet responsible to the Althing.

Other internal changes that took place paralleled developments in progressive, peaceful countries of Western Europe. Prosperity developed over a varied economy that stressed agriculture, fishing and light industries. Population rose rapidly, passing 120,000 in 1940, 180,000 in 1960. Religious freedom existed, but in fact there was little to contest among an essentially white, Scandinavian, Christian population. Compulsory free public education was initiated. A corresponding cultural revival took place, beginning with the novel in the nineteenth century and extending to poetry, theater and art in the twentieth. The tradition of peaceful consensus served Iceland very well during this period, and by 1950 the standard interlocking professionalism of Scandinavia had become established to the point of stability. Political evolution has continued within this standard format since.

Of foreign affairs there is little to say. English naval power defended the island through the three great European wars, intervening twice to nip a rebellion in 1809 and actually to occupy the island in 1940 to circumvent German invasion. After World War II Iceland joined the United Nations and the North Atlantic Treaty Alliance, an American-dominated organization. Thus Iceland, having no military forces of its own, was switching its dependence from the great sea power, Britain, to the great air power, the United States.

Internally, then, threats to the Scandinavian Peace are no longer in prospect. External relations are, however, something else entirely. Arguably as Scandinavia adopted a more civilized attitude to peaceful coexistence the surrounding countries moved just the other way; certainly the technology of both war and economics has exploded to the point of ending Scandinavia's cherished isolation.

The nineteenth century was a transition. It saw the last quarrel that seems really to have threatened the peace within Scandinavia itself: the union between Norway and Sweden. And it saw Scandinavia, specifically Denmark, dragged very much against its will into continental conflict.

Norway had fought against annexation to Sweden, and had accepted it mainly because the great powers had said point-blank that they would enforce it. Sweden, on the other hand, was also very disturbed about the possible results of great power interference and so gave Norway the best terms possible, in effect recognizing the constitution which Norway had drawn up as an independent state. Sweden then tried four times (1824, 1839, 1855, and 1856) to make the union tighter, all unsuccessfully, and with the Norwegian nationalist defeat in 1871 of a last effort at redefinition, the union became something of a corpse walking. There were various reasons for the failure, not least that the two countries were so similar that their peoples assumed a competitive rather than complementary relationship. But more to the point, beyond the occasional political efforts, almost nothing was done to create common interests. The banking systems were separate; the foreign interests remained not only different (Norway toward Britain, Sweden toward Germany) but competitive; a common tariff was established only in 1874 and was then abolished by Sweden in 1897 when Sweden decided on protectionism. Even socially there was very little mixing, with Swedes snubbing Norwegians in Sweden and vice versa. Almost no one was interested in preservation of the union for any other reason than Swedish prestige. This was enough to abort one ill-prepared Norwegian attempt at secession in 1895; it was not enough to abort a well-prepared one, with all the legal formalities carefully addressed, in 1905. The 1905 attempt caused much talk of war, but even the few Swedes who thought a union enforced by arms to be worth preserving realized that the great powers would not allow any such war. The matter was settled by negotiation, with a very long demilitarized frontier commemorating the degree of understanding involved.

The dissolution came about because of the development of the nineteenth-century concept of national self-rule, because the Norwegians felt they were losing control of foreign policy to the Swedish foreign ministry (whereas it had been controlled by the Swedish king, who was also their own king, in Bernadotte's time), and because since the Napoleonic War, neither Norway nor Sweden had been threatened by the danger of external attack. The dissolution was managed peacefully because there was sufficient sympathy for nationalist aspirations in the Swedish Riksdag, because moderates prevailed in both the Norwegian and Swedish Parliaments, and because the Norwegians agreed to accept a demilitarized border and an agreement to settle future disputes by arbitration. The representatives of both nations were accustomed to working problems out through committees, by compromise and without violence. Nor were there any strong divisive issues of religion, race, or doctrine.

The same domestic factors that kept internal peace in Sweden would also apply to Norway.

The maintenance of peace in Scandinavia became a complex problem in so tremendous a conflict as World War I. Neutrality in a continental war in a continental industrial age proved to be the proverbial tap dance on a slack wire. Sweden, with its background of wars with Russia and its German-educated upper class, was neutral in Germany's favor, to the point that it was "generally expected" to come in on Germany's side. Norway was neutral in favor of its British coal supply. Neutrality was not completely successful. Norway, for example, lost only 1500 lives in World War II in resistance to German occupation, including executions; it lost 2000 in World War I in ship sinkings. But Scandinavia at least avoided the meat-grinder battles and horrible casualty lists of the actual combatants. Then in World War II Norway and Iceland were both occupied, causing a resistance movement and casualties in Norway, but nothing like the situation on the battle fronts. Germany targeted but never got around to invading Sweden. These relatively light experiences with world war were presumably again the result of Scandinavia's peripheral status, but do clearly indicate that such status was no longer sufficiently peripheral to be a protection in itself. The internal peace of all five Scandinavian nations looks to be quite capable of lasting indefinitely, but the external peace looks less secure because of the vast increase in world technological complexity since World War II. By 1950 Scandinavia could in no sense be held any longer peripheral. The Scandinavian Peace may therefore be held to exist at the moment not at all by virtue of its former status as too peripheral to worry about.

Termination

For Denmark, the only continental Scandinavian nation, peace was ended by complications of the Napoleonic Wars. Britain raided Denmark twice during these wars, the first time in 1801. Denmark fought three times trying to keep the Crown's rights in Slesvig and Holstein; in the first two Prussian troops entered Jutland and were withdrawn only when Russia threatened to intervene if they were not; by 1864 the Crimean War had destroyed Russia's ability to make such threats and the conquest was carried through. Denmark was invaded again, though without heavy casualties, by Germany during World War II.

The Finnish Peace had its beginning in a settlement arising out of the Napoleonic Wars, and its ending in a settlement arising out of the World Wars. The crisis of World War I meant reassertion of a program of total Russification. This too ended suddenly. The collapse of 1917 meant another restoration. Finally with the October Revolution the Finnish legislature decided enough was enough and formed a new government and by a majority of only 100 to 88 declared independence.

But the narrowness of the vote for independence and the division between resisters and compliants earlier seem in retrospect to indicate just how deep was the lack of consensus in Finnish society. Like the rest of Europe, Scandinavia was swept by Marxism in the later 1800's. In Denmark, Norway and Sweden the revolutionary Marxists were absorbed by the moderates, in Norway after a taste of government. But Finland resembled more the Russian political spectrum. In 1905 there was already a close brush with violence between Red and White Guards. In 1918, less than two months after independence the Finnish Red Guards revolted against the elected government and a four-month civil war killed some 13,000 people, with almost 10,000 more of the defeated Red Guards dying afterwards in prison camps or hospitals. The Whites, in victory, had been aided by a German contingent that captured Helsinki. German influence, in turn, was conveniently removed by the outcome of World War I in the same year. That independence from Russia could mean the end of long periods of peace became evident when Finland was twice invaded by Russia during World War II.

The German invasion of Norway may be held responsible for the continued peace of Sweden, since it protected Sweden from British blockade. Sweden supplied two-thirds of Germany's iron ore, and the winter route for this vital wartime raw material was along the Norwegian coast. If Norway came under control of the British, the ore supplies would be cut off during the winter.

The Germans also believed, mistakenly as it turned out, that the invasion would be accompanied by a coup of the Norwegian Nazi party, thus reducing the commitment of German forces. But even so the invasion of undefended Norway was a much easier proposition than would have been the invasion of Sweden with its larger population and stronger navy. By invading Norway instead of Sweden the Germans got greater cooperation from the Swedes for a smaller commitment of troops, and control of the Baltic and Atlantic bases as an added dividend.

Sweden, having miraculously maintained peace through both the Napoleonic and the World Wars, continued at peace through the latter half of the twentieth century. She kept pace with other industrializing countries of Europe in passing legislation that averted dissatisfaction. Feudalism had disappeared, full political rights belonged to everyone, railroads and maritime services were developed for the encouragement of the middle class, welfare legislation protected the poor, constitutions existed before constitutional revolutions emerged and the monarchy gracefully accepted a less powerful and more ceremonial role. Religious discrimination was gradually eliminated. Industrialization made the country prosperous. As in Britain, leadership was multiple and often farsighted, a logical product of an effective system of education.

Iceland, at peace at least since 1262, has the honor of having maintained the longest peace in Western history.

Despite isolation, smallness, cold weather, an often depressed economy and soporific society, seven centuries of peace is an accomplishment for which Icelanders may take a great deal of pride.

Reflections

Scandinavia was excluded geographically from the main centers of European action. Being in that situation, a territory is less likely to be crucially necessary to the powers at the center of social and political activity. And peace ended in both Denmark and Norway when circumstances suddenly made their locations crucial.

The Scandinavian powers were not able to involve themselves effectively in the main centers of action after 1721. Gustavus III tried, but his failures only confirmed the futility of such a course. Sweden was thereafter not a military threat that must be dealt with before other projects could be safely undertaken.

When the usual European balance was overturned, as it was during the periods of dominance of Napoleon and Hitler, the Swedes resorted to what might be called appeasement. They cooperated in public and sabotaged privately in response to Napoleon. They supplied the Germans with their iron ore requirements but also traded with Britain and provided refuge for Norwegians and Danes. If appeasement means making concessions short of territorial surrender to a stronger enemy, it sometimes works.

A small country may have peace at the price of independence, itself to be protected by a larger power, at the cost of being able to run its own affairs. Norway, Finland and Iceland had peace under these conditions. In the case of Finland, it would appear that independence could be had only at the cost of losing peace.

Sweden was not a coalition-maker like Britain. But her interests generally coincided with those of Britain, particularly on the desirability of keeping Europe divided. Sweden almost always, tacitly, secretly or openly, supported British policies. But as a weaker power Sweden could depend on geography, where Britain had to defend itself. Neither Napoleon nor Hitler had to worry about trying to invade Sweden, as they would have liked to invade Britain, before they attacked Russia.

Internal peace was maintained during a period of transition from modified monarchy to representative government. The Scandinavian governments managed to make the transformation by absorbing the aristocracy into the state rather than making its members superfluous and discontented enemies and then by providing a gradually increasing distribution of power. The development of increasingly advanced governments provided meaningful alternatives to revolution, and the transition was made smoother by the advent of the industrial revolution supported by necessary educational and welfare programs, resulting in a general and widely distributed prosperity and the single best-known modern peace.

9

The Swiss Peace
(1856-   )

Origins

On the whole the past two centuries have not been peaceful for mainland Europe. We have seen that the famous Pax Britannica cannot be considered a period of peace even by our modest standards. Sweden and Iceland, on the outskirts of Europe, did maintain internal peace through both the Napoleonic and World Wars, but no other country was as fortunate. Others were involved in the frequent political rebellions of the nineteenth and twentieth centuries or caught up in one or both of the continental wars.

There was arguably a century of peace for the Netherlands, however, from the 1839 conflict that led to the British guarantee of Lowland neutrality, until the German invasion of 1940, just over a century later. The maintenance of peace by any small country in an international situation involving much conflict is worth studying, and there are some interesting questions about the importance of neutrality, willingness to defend, and just plain good luck involved in the situation. This Dutch Peace, though comparatively short and involving only a small country, would be well worth investigating.

But a more famous, complete and intriguing oasis of peace emerged in the landlocked, multilingual state of Switzerland. This state had its origin with an alliance of three tiny South German political entities at the end of the thirteenth century. More joined in subsequent centuries until, by the nineteenth, there were 22 leagued together, the group covering no more than 15,000 square miles, a territory the size of Brandenburg and the New Mark.

The problem of these 22 cantons, as these entities were called, was to maintain their collective independence from the two great European powers, Austria and France, while at the same time maintaining their league against internal strains brought about by the Reformation, differences in outlook between rural and urban areas, and class conflict between aristocrats and peasants and artisans.

Generally the Swiss were successful at keeping their territories free from external invasion after the Habsburgs were driven out in the fourteenth century. The major exception was a violently resisted occupation by the French during the Napoleonic Wars, between 1799 and 1813. Internally they were less successful. There were civil, religious, peasant and urban-rural wars among the cantons from the fourteenth through the seventeenth centuries and insurrections against patricians and landowners in almost every canton in the eighteenth. After the French had departed there were more uprisings in the uneasy period between 1815 and 1848, culminating in the Sonderbund war which arose when seven Catholic cantons attempted to secede from the Swiss League and form a league of their own.

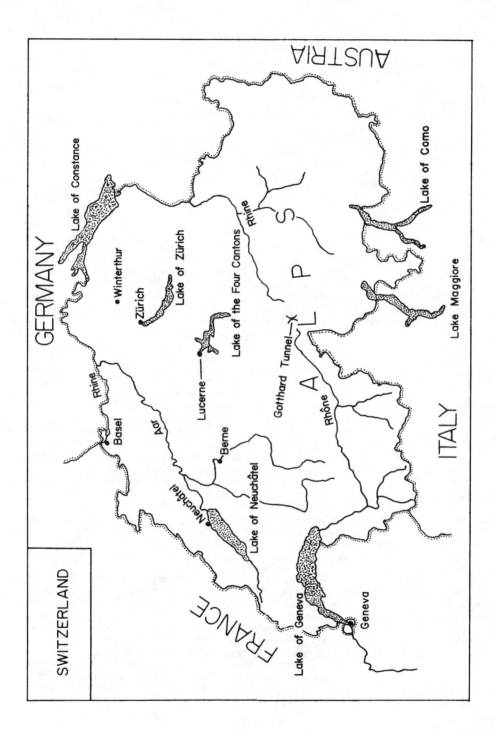

The defeat of the Sonderbund League, however, gave the Swiss cantons the opportunity to strengthen their confederation through the creation of a new constitution, and they did so successfully. The strength of the federal union was tested by a violent counter-revolution in Neuchatel in 1856. The international crisis that followed showed that the Swiss confederation had become a viable nation and marked the beginning of a period of peace that still continued in the 1980's.

Not only did the revamped federation maintain internal peace, but it managed to maintain peace through two great twentieth-century wars that engulfed the whole of the European continent. Considering its relatively small size, its central location in Europe, the general turbulence of the times and its previous history of domestic conflict, the century and a quarter of as yet uninterrupted peace achieved by the Swiss since 1856 constitute a considerable achievement.

Characterization

The individual cantons within the league had always maintained domestic independence and even conducted their own foreign policies. They did send representatives to a diet, but this was nothing more than a conference of diplomats. The French effected a stronger Swiss union during their occupation, and this provided a model for federation, but perhaps more important were the ideas that germinated in the French Revolution. One of these ideas—the concept of nationalism—professed that a people of similar language and culture should live together under the same government. This concept had already led to the unification of diverse provinces in North America, and it was now to lead to similar unifications in Italy and Germany. But the same idea also led to division. What constituted a nation? Could not a sub-culture within the main culture also consider itself a nation, and separate politically from the larger culture? This idea was also to be tested in Switzerland, America and the Habsburg Empire. It led to stronger unions in the first two, and the disintegration of the third. But in Switzerland the fate that overcame the Habsburgs seemed distinctly possible. The forces of nationalism could easily have led to the dissolution of the nation into German, French and Italian provinces.

One of the criteria for defining a culture is religion. Where religion, language and history coincided, the definition of the nation was obvious. The Scandinavians were Protestant, the Poles were Catholic. Not every Pole might be a strong believer, but the religious tradition was nonetheless in his background. But Switzerland was split. Seven cantons were predominantly Catholic, fifteen predominantly Protestant. By the nineteenth century, however, the religious differences in Switzerland were not great among moderates. The conflicts that led to the forming of the Sonderbund were primarily between militant Jesuits and radical atheists. Once the moderates did prevail, the religious differences among Christians in Switzerland were no greater than they were in other countries.

The Revolutions of 1848 and 1849, which were occurring throughout Europe, echoed the rhetoric of the American and French Revolutions. Guaranteed by the constitution were, not only religious freedom, but freedom of the press, of association, and specific assurances that freedoms applied to all minorities who were Swiss citizens.

Another criterion for defining culture is language. The Swedes spoke Swedish and the Poles, Polish. But Switzerland, by the nineteenth century, was multilingual. Two-thirds of the population spoke German, one-third French or Italian. Moreover each of the linguistic groups tended to live near the borders of their fellow Italian, French and German-speaking neighbors. This suggested to some alien nationalists, and to some Swiss, the logic of partitioning the cantons according to prevailing language in each, among the German, Italian and French-speaking states. This possibility was weakened when the Swiss federation preceded the unifications of Italy and Germany, but it remained a possibility in the event of civil or general European war.

Another factor in the atmosphere of nineteenth-century Europe was the idea, or related set of ideas, that were grouped under the heading of liberalism. Urban liberals favored equality of opportunity for the lower middle class and poorer farmers against the rural and urban aristocracy. But they were not making much progress so long as aristocrats and oligarchs maintained their autonomy as rulers of individual cantons.

The Sonderbund War gave liberals and nationalists their opportunity. The Sonderbund states chose to secede from the League in 1845 in order to be free from what their leaders considered to be encroachments on their religious preferences and their way of life. It was not until 1847 that the Protestant-dominated Diet responded, calling upon the Sonderbund to disband and appointing Henry Dufour as commander-in-chief to carry out the order. The fundamental issues at stake were the supremacy of the League as opposed to that of the individual cantons, the secular or religious control of public institutions, and the liberal-urban philosophy versus the conservative-rural philosophy of government.

Dufour, who possessed superiority in men and equipment, conducted a compact, efficient campaign. It lasted three weeks, involved only one major battle and a few hundred casualties. The Sonderbund was disbanded, but the defeated cantons were treated with great moderation and generosity. The victorious liberal federalists, aided by threats of outside intervention and anti-establishment revolutions taking place all over Europe in 1848, were able to draft and gain majority approval for a constitution that created a central executive authority.

The authority consisted of a seven-man Federal Council elected by a legislative body that in turn was composed of two houses, one giving equal representation to each canton, the other elected according to population. This legislature, the Bund, also elected judges to a newly established Federal Supreme Court. The Bund gradually increased areas of control, creating national postal, telegraphic and railway systems, unifying and standardizing weights, measures and currency and eliminating internal customs. Later the Bund gave the Federal Council the right to enforce social legislation, to unify central law and establish a national bank. The central government took charge of all foreign affairs and all male citizens of appropriate age were bound to perform military service for the federal government.

The drafting of the constitution, and the negotiating and persuading that went with it, was the work of many men. But in retrospect Jonas Furrer, a calm and rational lawyer from Winterthur, was perceived by many of his contemporaries as having contributed the most to converting contradictory and revolutionary ideas into a document that would be accepted by the majority of the Swiss. And so it was by a vote of nearly 2 million for, fewer than 300,000 against. Furrer became the first president of the Federal Council, the nearest a Swiss administrator could come to being the nominal head of state.

In the period following the inauguration of the new federation, Switzerland pursued an economic development similar to that of many progressive Western states of the nineteenth century. Lacking farmland, resources, navigable rivers or even a seacoast, the Swiss capitalized on their water power and concentrated on industries requiring highly developed technology and skilled labor. They imported coal, metals and fabric and exported manufactured goods, balancing trade by establishing a tourist industry and specializing in international banking.

To simply state all that was done is to understate the amount of conflict involved. The lack of rivers, for instance, could be made up by the development of railroads. But here there were difficult political and technological problems. The political problems involved an energetic conflict on the degree to which the state should be involved. In the 1850's a private enterprise viewpoint prevailed, and the railroads were built by individual companies. But there were countless battles for franchises and many bankruptcies culminating in the financial collapse of the Gotthard Railroad of tunnel fame. The railroad was bailed out by the government, but that brought about new laws giving the government a stronger role in the planning. Only then were resolved the technologically expensive problems of extending the system to mountainous areas.

The high technological level of the Swiss economy required a high level of education, which was met with the establishment of a system of universal, compulsory public education. An attempt to create a national university, however, met with strenuous opposition. The French feared Germanization, the Catholics feared atheist domination, and centers already having local universities feared that a federal university would sap their resources. Thus the linguistic, religious and cultural minorities became a majority, and higher education remained decentralized.

A bi-product of the educational system, or perhaps of prosperity and the general pattern of Europe as a whole, was a high-level general culture, the lively development of local musical societies and amateur theater, which included development of a number of scholars and artists of international renown, such as Gottfried Keller, Jacob Burckhardt, Charles Francis Ramus, Arthur Honegger, Alberto Giacometti and Le Corbusier. The Dadaist art movement was organized in Zurich by Tristan Tzara, and several Swiss have won Nobel prizes for peace and scientific achievement, including Jean Henri Dunant, founder of the International Red Cross (1864).

The Swiss Peace in its formative period lacked charismatic leaders. Henry Dufour and Jonas Furrer stand out for their mildness, competence and understanding of the larger issues, but they could not have prevailed if most provincial leaders had not shared their feelings. The seven-man Federal Council seemed to be a deliberate attempt to avoid placing any one man in a dominant position. The leader of the country was the president of this Council, but he was elected by his fellow members for one-year terms, and he could not succeed himself.

In the early years of government two leaders emerged who both supported and opposed each other, because of class origins rather than party. Alfred Escher of Zurich, a wealthy aristocrat, became president of the National Council, which was the dominant body of the Bund. He opposed Swiss intervention in foreign affairs and was a champion of **laissez-faire** principles, including private control of railroads. Jacob Stampfli of Berne, son of a peasant, was three times president of the Federal Council. He favored support of foreign revolutions and state intervention in economics, particularly railroads. Despite their differences in personality and background, and a rivalry between Zurich and Berne for the federal capital, the two men often collaborated. Their cooperation was helped, perhaps, by the sharp criticism of Philipp Segesser of Lucerne, who played the role of opposition leader for the former Sonderbund Cantons.

Critics of the Swiss system have felt that internal cooperation has become excessive, with industrialists and bankers too much involved in government, and management and labor too often in collaboration. Defenders of the system say that there is a great deal of interaction between industry and government in all modern countries, and that Switzerland is characterized by a large number of small and medium-sized industries, with other needs and interests, flourishing alongside the giants.

Strong external pressures and threats no doubt supported some of the internal consensus that has developed in twentieth century Switzerland. The country has needed unity to survive in a situation in which it was entirely surrounded by four powers commanding immeasurably greater population and resources. That unification of Italy in the 1850's and Germany by 1871 seemed so threatening to Swiss existence, not to mention peace, in retrospect can be seen as an important contributor to Swiss unity, and to policies that were to preserve the peace.

The very idea that it was not until 1848 that foreign policy became the domain of a central authority illustrates the problem of unity in Switzerland. Once there was a national identity, however, the spirit of nationalism seemed more and more to flow into it. When the conflict between Switzerland and Prussia over Neuchatel surfaced in 1856, there was a strong response in support of the national government everywhere, even from the Sonderbund cantons. And when the American Civil War followed, sentiment in Switzerland was overwhelming for the North, the side that was fighting for federal dominance. When Lincoln was assassinated, some 300 addresses of sympathy were drawn up by governments and associations. These were signed by more than 20,000 people, collected, and sent to the American government. This was certainly an unusual response to an event in a distant rimland nation.

In fending off the Habsburgs and the French, the Swiss had already developed two traditions. First the citizens of the cantons had been accustomed to serving in a voluntary militia, while Swiss mercenaries had developed a reputation throughout Europe as exceptionally capable fighters. Second, since the sixteenth century the Swiss had concentrated on defensive warfare and not intervened in foreign countries except to hire out mercenaries.

Under the new federation the tradition of the citizen soldier was continued and the mercenary was dropped. A standing army was practically non-existent, except for a minimum cadre. All men took four months' training supplemented by a three-week refresher course each year. All of them kept their arms at home. When external danger threatened, as it did in 1856, in 1870-1871, in 1914-1918 and 1939-1945, these men could be quickly organized into fighting units. Military training concentrated on defensive tactics, particularly on the holding of narrow passes in situations in which few men could fend off many.

A defensive foreign policy was also maintained. The country observed strict neutrality and avoided military alliances. The Swiss tried to be as just as they could, thus building up a reputation for justice and particularly for fair treatment of aliens. This meant that they were bound to grant asylum to all aliens--and there were a good many in this period--regardless of their political convictions.

This policy of neutrality did not come easily. Stampfli's view was shared by many radicals and liberals. He saw the Swiss struggle for liberty as part of the revolutions of the period and argued that it was immoral for the Swiss to refrain from intervention. Revolutionists like Mazzini in Italy created secret associations, including a "Young Switzerland," designed to support revolutionary planning within Switzerland and to gain volunteers when such revolutions should emerge. Refugees were always a problem in Switzerland, since they always included leaders who protested internment and tried continually to create new alliances against whatever they were refugees from. Ultimately the view of Escher prevailed here, and the Swiss government struggled to prevent such plots from developing, though inhibited by a reluctance to order expulsion if that would mean persecution of the person expelled. Over time, however, the Swiss government built an image of attempting to treat internees evenhandedly, and trying to prevent their using neutral territory as a staging ground for further participation in conflict.

The Swiss also built up the image of their country as a useful neutral ground. International organizations for treating the wounded in war, for establishing agreements of commercial usefulness, and for peaceful political settlement all found their headquarters in Switzerland. When major wars were going on, belligerents could maintain contact with one another, exchanging terms of settlement and so forth, through their embassies in Switzerland.

This combination of justice, usefulness and firmness worked. The Swiss succeeded in avoiding great power intervention during the Sonderbund crisis partly by the firmness, rapidity and mildness of its resolution. They managed a settlement of the crisis with Prussia over Neuchatel by demonstrating a consistency in policy, a willingness to fight, and a capacity for negotiation. They provided asylum for 85,000 French troops during the Franco-Prussian War of 1870-1871, but disarmed them and refused to allow them to participate further in the war. They stayed neutral through both World Wars, though the cost in standard-of-living and citizens' time was great. Since the French and Germans fought on opposite sides in each of these wars, the difference in opinion between French and German-speaking citizens might be expected to be great, but this also made the central government's task of enforcing neutrality somewhat easier. During World War II Switzerland admitted nearly 300,000 refugees. But Switzerland could not defend against the wave of anti-semitism that swept Europe, and there is considerable evidence, particularly in the earlier years of the war, that refugees were denied admission because they were Jewish. Between the two wars Switzerland was the center for an international political league designed to settle disputes peacefully, but the Swiss found their neutral policy disrupted in 1935 when the League of Nations, with the support of one of her neighbors, France, applied economic sanctions against another neighbor, Italy. When the League was reconstituted as the United Nations after World War II, the Swiss decided to stay out of it. But their determination to stay neutral was made more imperative by the situation in Europe, which after 1945 had two centers of power, one in Western Europe, one in Eastern Europe. Switzerland was almost on the border between them.

Certainly the maintenance of peace in the early decades was helped by the divisions that existed in Europe. Interference in the Sonderbund War was minimal because the great powers had to contend with revolutions at home. Prussia certainly would have intervened in the Neuchatel conflict, where she had a reasonable case. Neuchatel had rebelled against Prussian rule in 1848, when Prussia could do nothing about it, and Switzerland had accepted Neuchatel as a new canton. But when a violent counterrevolution occurred in 1856, Prussia had the opportunity to offer support to the proponents of reuniting the province with Prussia. That she did not intervene was partly attributable to the fact that the national militia put down the rebellion within 24 hours, so that there was no provincial government to appeal for Prussian aid, but also attributable to the fact that in subsequent negotiations, Louis Napoleon in France and Lord Palmerston in England strongly resisted Prussian claims to the province. But after the Franco-Prussian War, it is difficult to believe that any power could have effectively resisted intervention in Switzerland by a Bismarck, a Ludendorff or a Hitler.

Reflections

When we think of the problems of empires, we tend to look for internal divisions. When we think of the problems of small powers, we tend to think of external threats. Yet small size hardly forecloses troubling internal complexity, as witness Venice and Costa Rica elsewhere in these pages. But no country is better known for internal divisions, successfully handled, than Switzerland.

For some of its problems Switzerland created the same solution as other states of the time: Nationality division were partly submerged in a flood of increasing prosperity and state services. Here there was mutual interaction all across Europe, and Switzerland is hardly unique.

Switzerland's unique success seems to have come of a combination of geography and the very external threat which so endangers small countries. There is no more centrally located country in the world, but Switzerland has made of this great danger a shining virtue. The country had been a confederation for 565 years before the Peace began, precisely because unity was needed against potential foreign domination. In the course of that half millennium this country of very disparate languages and religions had made a nationality out of a common political culture, and the in-pressing European situation had made this evolution particularly rapid in the last sixty years before the Peace. "External threat" was an awareness passed with the mother's milk in Switzerland, and made any resort to sedition very difficult to sustain.

This also created important secondary effects.

No one canton was strong enough to establish and maintain its own rule, so joint action has been a necessity of continued existence. This applies throughout; such leaders as Furrer and Stampfli might become reconcilers, but not commanders. Compromise and negotiation are emphatically the rule.

And, the external threat could be appeased. Switzerland became an international clearing house of needed services, too small to threaten outside interests but offering too many needed benefits for disruption to be considered as a casual solution to other problems. And these services have been offered with the most careful neutrality possible; no external state, whatever its politics, would find Switzerland dangerously biased in an enemy's favor.

And, the external threat could be threatened back. Even here Switzerland is unique. A large standing army could defend the country, but might also be taken as an offensive threat. Therefore the Swiss standing armed forces are almost non-existent (in 1969, 0.38% of the population, lower than in any other west European country except Iceland, Luxembourg and Malta) and do not even have an active-duty commander (one is elected when needed). Yet Swiss military expenditures are as a percentage of the national budget (27.6%) third highest in western Europe (after Portugal and the United Kingdom, as of 1969). The defense force is militia; more than 10% of the population can be mobilized on 48 hours' notice. Without the need of a standing army, Switzerland has nevertheless become Europe's backyard wasp nest. Quite certainly it could be defeated, but the process is not likely to be enjoyable. And so the Peace continues.

10

The Brazilian Peace
(1654–   )

The Improvization of Tomorrow

"Brazil. . .is a world wonder. The country passed from
colony to independent nation with a gentleness and serenity
[almost unique in the Americas]. . . . The change–over gave
the people a reason for celebrating, the army a holiday,
and everyone an excuse to parade. Nothing was heard from
the armed forces, except band music. Sixty–seven years
went by; then the Brazilian empire made an equally smooth
transition to a republic. . .[which] was proclaimed in a box
in a newspaper. . . . In more recent Brazilian history. . .the
waters of the Amazon still run to the sea unstained by blood,
whereas elsewhere in the world, Amazons of blood have
been shed over changes of government" (Arciniegas 1967:
xxi–xxii).

Duration: 1654 to date. Area: Brazil, excepting the Indian frontiers and the
province/state of Rio Grande do Sul.

Among the peace periods, the Spanish American section of the Spanish
Imperial Peace and the Brazilian Peace make together a case study of heredity
vs. environment. Both were derived from an Iberian milieu very nearly the
same in both Portugal and Spain. Indeed the Portuguese poet Luis Vaz de Camoes
said in the middle 1500's that "Portuguese or Castilians, we are all Spaniards,"
and when Ferdinand and Isabella appropriated the label "Spain" for their union
of crowns, the king of Portugal protested the usurpation. Socially and juridically
what was said of the early Spanish Empire may stand for the Portuguese as
well, except that the "se acata. . ." doctrine, that a law could be "respected
but not obeyed," was specific to Spanish America and is not found in Brazil.

It may not have been necessary. One may question whether the royal
decree was obeyed, or respected, or even particularly noticed in most of Brazil.
And the Crown accepted this situation, so long as proper respects were tendered
and proper taxes were forthcoming. New Spain and Peru were two of the brighter
jewels in the Spanish Empire, with vast wealth in mines and civilized exploitable
Indians, and the Spanish Crown attended to America accordingly. Brazil was
an afterthought to a Portuguese Empire primarily interested in the spice trade
of India and Southeast Asia, and it was left in that state of benign neglect
on which British America was later congratulated. From this difference arose
a very different evolution.

The one permanent exception to the Brazilian Peace emphasizes this
difference. The southern boundary of old colonial Brazil lay north of the present

BRAZIL

Amazon

Pernambuco
Province

Salvador

Minas
Gerais

São Paulo   Province
Province

Rio de Janeiro
Province

Rio de Janeiro

São Paulo

Rio Grande do Sul
Province

boundary; Rio Grande do Sul was annexed only towards the end of the 1600's, well after Spanish culture was penetrating the area. Rio Grande do Sul like much else of Brazil is cattle country, but while in the north the cowboys (**vaqueiros**) worked on plantations (**fazendas**), Rio Grande like Argentina and Uruguay sported **gauchos** working on **estancias**. Though Portuguese did become the local language, the area did not share the north Brazilian development and so stayed as violent as its Spanish American neighbors. Indeed, once the northern colonial wars were over, and excepting a few problems with Britain over the slave trade and with worldwide ideological conflicts in the 1930's, Brazilian foreign policy can be written almost entirely in terms of wars on the southern border. The worst of them, the Paraguayan War of 1865-1870, killed 50,000 Brazilians, and it was only the last of many.

Origins

Brazil was discovered and allotted to Portugal at the beginning of the sixteenth century, by modification of the old treaty of Tordesillas. Since Portuguese interest lay elsewhere, the Crown did very little about this until towards 1530 when, as the British were to do later, the matter was turned over to private enterprise, which in Portuguese terms meant not the chartered company but the feudal lordship. Huge stretches of coastline and indefinite hinterland were granted out as hereditary captaincies, with the grantees having the rights both to sub-grant and to appoint their own local officials, including even those with the hallowed right of jurisdiction. Such grants were issued as late as the late seventeenth century and the centralizing policy of the Crown in the eighteenth century did not reclaim the last of them until 1791, only 32 years before independence. Moreover the sub-grants were themselves divided and further assigned, with ties so loose that the grantees were quite able to ignore or even fight over any claim conflicting with their own power to seize and hold. The result was formation of vast private domains, one of them reported larger than Portugal itself. This privatization of authority was further accentuated by Portugal's habit of using Brazil as a dumping ground for dissenters, criminals, and nonconformists, none of them particularly amenable to official authority. Finally the Spanish victory in the succession dispute of 1580 meant the arrival in Brazil of large numbers of relatively high-ranking immigrants who decided their futures would be much improved by putting some distance between themselves and the winner, and who by marriage or otherwise could grace real power with long-standing aristocratic privilege. By 1600 the pattern had been set. Brazil retained the official Portuguese organization into captaincies further divided into **municipios**, effectively city-states, but most of these theoretical cities became no more than central sites where the successful great lords of the countryside could repair for church and "town" meetings—when these did not interfere with managing their plantations. Below the rural lords were large numbers of free farmers, small ranchers, artisans and other free groups, below these a slave population which by independence was roughly half the total. The whole was organized in intricate familial ties, real or artificial, maintained by clientage and debt and forming a dependence hierarchy which became the basic political unit of Brazil. In some places it still is.

Thus the basic background of colonial Brazil. The first century and a half of this development was, however, deeply involved with foreign relations. The late sixteenth century saw Portugal and its empire annexed by the Spanish Habsburg dynasty, and while this made no great difference to Brazil proper—Portugal and its empire remained generally autonomous for most of the Habsburg period—it did involve the Portuguese domains in Spain's wars against France, Holland and England. For Brazil this meant both rampant piracy and outright invasion, not ended until in 1654 the Dutch were driven out of Pernambuco, largely by the Brazilians themselves. There were limited aftershocks, a brief loss of two Amazon fortresses to a French expedition in 1697 and two French attacks on Rio De Janeiro in 1710 and 1711, but for Brazil (always barring the frontier area in Rio Grande do Sul) the colonial wars were effectively over.

Characterization

In one way Brazil seems an unlikely candidate for a Peace. The Brazilians are commonly remarked for an aversion to settling problems by violence, but the traditional descriptions suggest that in the competitions between the rural great lords violence had about the same place as in the more mythicized versions of Tombstone, Arizona or the Chicago of Al Capone. Just how much of this Brazilian armed competition is equally mythical is an open question; just as in the world at large, the extant tales revolve around personal heroics, not around peaceful resolutions. Nevertheless in practice corruption rather than elimination seems to have been the standard fate of challengers to established lords; where at all possible, a strong newcomer would be bought or married into the establishment. It may also be indicative that most of the heroic tales involve the Robin Hood variety of outlaws rather than unruly great lords and retainers. There is never any hint of the generalized military anarchy that characterizes unbridled competition, nor is the term "warlord" ever used. While the question remains largely unstudied, the system seems to have quite successfully institutionalized limitations on accepted violence.

Meanwhile Brazil was growing. Settlement, at first purely coastal, began after the Dutch wars to reach into the interior, primarily as a cattle frontier with all the easing of social barriers found elsewhere under those conditions. But it also involved the gold and diamond frontier of Minas Gerais. Brazil sent some two million kilograms of gold to Portugal during the colonial period, providing in the eighteenth century some 80% of the world's supply. This upset the social equilibrium within Brazil and brought in a standard gold rush, but it also made the Crown decide to pay considerably more attention to its wayward Americans. During the eighteenth century government was considerably strengthened, especially in the mining area. This meant some reduction in the powers of the municipios, which in the seventeenth century had been able even to expel royal officials (including governors) who were not liked. But even in the later eighteenth century in the viceregal capital itself, an outgoing viceroy advised his successor simply to let the city council manage the city's affairs, in the name of peace and quiet. Unlike the case in Spanish America, the locally responsible governments maintained both legitimacy and a considerable degree of power to the very end of the colonial period.

Towards the end of the eighteenth century Brazil like the rest of the Western world was swept by the Enlightenment, and then by the even more practical examples of the American and French Revolutions. Then in 1807 Brazil had a stroke of purest good luck. The French invaded Portugal, and the Crown took refuge in Brazil. Whatever inconfidences might have been abuilding, suddenly the very focus of Brazilian as of Portuguese existence had come to settle in Brazil. It may be said that Brazil was born of this event; what beforehand was several more or less isolated groups of islands of settlement now had a common geographic center and a single ruling authority which the viceroys had never been able to provide.

Brazil discovered it did not entirely like this idea. The king brought a swarm of Portuguese notables who needed high-status positions providing the financial support to which they had been accustomed, and Brazil had to supply them. But for the short time involved this was only an annoyance, easily paid for in increased pride and royal grants of titles to the Brazilians. Indeed Brazil did entirely too good a job of supporting its Crown; when the French were chased out of Portugal the king decided to stay on anyway. Then in 1820 Portugal had its own liberal revolution, and the revolutionary Cortes recalled the king. The Cortes then further decided to cancel every privilege granted Brazil during the Crown's stay there, and objections by Brazilian delegates were simply howled down.

By the end of 1821 it was plain to the Brazilian ruling elite that unless they did something Brazil was going to revert completely to its former colonial status. But there were problems in gauging the proper reaction. Two were minor: There were Portuguese garrisons in the major cities and the Brazilian elite itself was not united, including both diehard loyalist and outright republican extremes. One, however, was major. The ruling elite was terrified of the very possibility of revolution. From the Terror in France to the massacre of whites in Haiti there were by 1821 plenty of examples of what revolutions could do to ruling elites, and even barring so drastic an outcome, revolutionary Argentina right next door had in the previous year had twelve governments in twelve months. Moreover Brazil was only very slightly yet Brazil. It remained quite possible, for example, for the delegates to the Cortes to speak of themselves as coming from the individual provinces, not from the country as a whole. Major change clearly carried the shadow of bloody anarchy.

The great majority of the politically active elite therefore strove as fervently as possible to dissociate Brazil from the rule of the Portuguese Cortes with an absolute minimum of other changes. Their hopes lay in the crown prince. When the king had left he had told the crown prince to stay and, if Brazil chose independence, to claim the crown for himself, possibly in hopes of a future reunion. When in late 1821 the Cortes recalled Crown Prince Pedro as well, the Brazilians put tremendous pressure on him to stay. When he agreed, this was in effect the Brazilian declaration of independence.

Brazil became independent under its legitimate dynasty with the Portuguese garrisons being expelled by street demonstrations or the cruise of a British naval squadron. But this once accomplished, there was considerably less agreement on the proper forms for the independent state. The great lords of the countryside had no more use for dictation by a ruler in Rio de Janeiro than one in Lisbon. Dispute quickly reached such a level that Pedro dissolved the assembly charged with writing a constitution and issued his own version, not as a contract with the people but as a gift from the throne. This Brazilian constitution of 1824 is one of the strangest ever issued, standing between worlds in a remarkable number of ways. It was granted by the emperor, but it specified Brazil to be a political association of its citizens, not a dynastic holding. The imperial and all other powers were specified to be delegations of the nation, not inherent divine rights of the Crown. Article 3 specified the "Government [to be] Monarchical, Hereditary [and also] Constitutional and Representative." Pedro himself called for division of powers according to Montesquieu's three branches, then added the old Hispanic **poder moderador**—a poder moderador defined as "the key to the entire political organization. . .delegated exclusively to the Emperor. . .so that he constantly can watch over the maintenance of the independence, equilibrium, and harmony of the other Political Powers" (Burns 1966:214). This was then spelled out, not in terms of Hispanic abstract justice and the final right of jurisdiction but of naming and dismissing ministers, members of the upper house and provincial presidents, calling and adjourning the legislature, and other quite modern functions. This bridge between the medieval and the modern might be considered an uneasy compromise, but if so it proved a very successful one.

Its first challenge came from the emperor himself. The constitution assumed the several branches of government would work in harmony, by his guidance if no way else, but Pedro I was not a man to appease opponents. Within a decade he had alienated almost everyone until finally, in 1831, rather than compromise either his principles or the constitution, he abdicated. Brazil was without the one focus of loyalty that had given the independent national government legitimacy.

Pedro abdicated in favor of his infant son. This meant a regency, and under the constitution a regency had only such power as the legislature chose to give it. In the event it was very limited; later on the Regency would be known as an experiment in republicanism. As such it was a disaster. The first four years saw numerous shortlived and very local tumults and a great increase in electoral fraud, but in 1835-1838 there began four major (for Brazil) provincial revolts. The worst, as might be expected, was in Rio Grande do Sul. The others, variously 1835-1841 and one aftershock in 1848-1850, seem to have been considerably less violent. The only one reporting even "hundreds" of casualties (dead plus wounded), mostly from street fighting, occurred in the old colonial capital of Salvador in 1837-1838. In terms of the five to seven million population of Brazil in the period this casualty rate seems quite negligible, but as compared to surrounding times it was shocking, and should be considered an interruption in the Peace.

Certainly it changed the minds of the ruling elite. "The experience was so overwhelming that the republican opinion of 1831 had disappeared in 1837 from the face of the country, as it disappeared in France after the Terror" (Nabuco 1975:71). Finally in 1841 the matter was settled, by what amounted to a coup d'etat by the entire legislature, declaring the young crown prince of legal age even though the constitution indicated he was still a minor. Any remaining sense of adventure was submerged in favor of peace, quiet and the safest possible way of doing things.

Pedro II (1841-1889) both reigned and ruled, and this was constant throughout his reign. But Brazil was changing. At independence it still had been several more or less isolated archipelagoes of settlement. Even in the early nineteenth century transportation was by mule train where it could not be by canoe; in the late eighteenth century the main road from Rio Grande do Sul to Sao Paulo was a footpath impassable even to mules. The middle 1800's saw the beginning of railroads in Brazil, and if it was a beginning that bankrupted some very rich people, it did initiate a high-density commerce system that could penetrate the interior without depending on the vagaries of rivers. At the same time the old export economy built around northeastern sugar was dying under the attacks of West Indian organization and European sugar beets. For the moment this did not mean any degree of industrialization; throughout the Empire and for decades afterward Brazil was almost 100% dependent on foreign manufacturers. Instead the country changed from sugar monoculture to coffee monoculture. Coffee had been introduced only in 1727 and became a low-quantity export almost immediately; with the decline of sugar, coffee reached 48.8% of total Brazilian exports in 1858/1860, and this while Sao Paulo was only beginning to enter the market. Thus there was a geographic shift of economic power within Brazil, and by the end of the Empire this created serious strains between the imperium and the new coffee-rich provinces. It did not, however, upset the system itself, which adapted to one kind of export monoculture as easily as another. The great landowners continued very much the ruling elite and almost autonomous on their holdings; when the imperium tried to intervene in and govern their land disputes, it failed miserably.

But there was evolution inside the system. At first the emperor appointed and dismissed each minister, etc., himself, but rather quickly this became choice by the Crown of the prime minister and choice by him of the others. The various partisan groups of the Regency resolved into a two-party system,

Conservatives based mostly on the landowners and so usually dominant and Liberals based on dissident landowners, merchants, miners and other outside groups. This two-party system in turn evolved into a patronage competition and remained quite stable throughout the reign, a record unmatched even in the United States of the time, much less elsewhere in Latin America. The stability was based on the nature of the system. Elections were thoroughly fixed. The party in power would, through its ministers and provincial presidents, confirm old deals and strike new ones with the lords of the local dependency hierarchies, who would then deliver the votes they controlled. Moreover the ruling party both validated and then counted the votes. Thus the party in office dependably won every election. Pedro II did not like this situation—he if anyone was the Philosopher King ruling a Republic of Virtue, somewhat fussy and fusty virtue but universally recognized. Despite his efforts to reform it, the system of central power by negotiation with local electoral machines was ultimately the political expression of the untouchable local lords, so here even the will of the throne could not prevail.

Rotation in power and flexibility of government therefore depended on the emperor's unchallenged right to designate the party in office, and so on his personal judgment of prevailing opinion at the time. For three decades this judgment was considered acceptable, even impartial, and the system worked well.

But a crisis began in 1868. At core it was no more than a dispute between emperor and prime minister over an appointment to the largely honorary upper house. The prime minister had his own candidate; the emperor, as was his right, decided to appoint an outstanding **litterateur** instead; the prime minister resigned and the government with him. By consensus the prime minister's party did have a stranglehold on public opinion at the time. But the emperor, instead of appointing another government from the same party, called in the opposition, which held new elections and of course won them. Henceforth the emperor's impartiality was permanently held in question, and with it his exercise of the very general poder moderador.

Also in 1868 Isabella II of Spain was overthrown in favor of some new arrangement, temporarily a republic; in 1870 the French Second Empire was overthrown definitely in favor of a republic. Brazil's (as all Latin America's) cultural connections were much stronger in Iberia and France than with any other countries, and these republics seemed to be official invitations to discontented Brazilians to begin charting a similar course. In 1870 the first Republican Club was founded in Brazil, and the emperor did nothing about it; later he even appointed the leading republican theorist to be official tutor to the royal grandchildren. Republicanism became an acceptable alternative and the emperor became dispensable.

In the remaining nineteen years of his rule the emperor continued to do as he thought best, and even the most obvious royalist props were left uncultivated. Of royal splendor and glamor there were none. The official aristocracy is even called "improvised" (Mario de Andrade, in **Prado** 1962:xv), being only a collection of honorary titles with no attached privileges and no rights of inheritance. The Brazilian Church was under the same tight control by the throne as had existed in the absolutist sixteenth century, in an age when the Vatican was demanding ever more autonomy and loyalty, and the emperor was as carefully impartial in religious disputes as (usually) elsewhere. The Church, if not actively against the Empire, had at least lost interest in its continuation. The great landowners had their own power base independent of the Empire. Only the military could be considered even largely imperialist, and its loyalty had been severely damaged by Pedro's impartiality in questions it saw as affecting military honor. Before the Paraguayan War of 1865-1870 it had been essentially an eighteenth-century organization, an employment service for impoverished aristocrats and status-hungry lower groups. The army in particular had low status, being looked on as a forced draft of rabble commanded by not much better, and was very sensitive about this image. Moreover the younger officers were subject to the usual infection of new and sweeping ideas, which among Brazilian junior officers became something of a tradition, called **tenentismo**, and republicanism was the new and sweeping solution of the day. Even the army's loyalties were therefore divided.

The battle over slavery was decisive. The emperor was convinced of the evil of slavery and led the early fight against it, but he had a careful sense of the possible and accordingly made haste very slowly. Among much of the elite it was also a question of good versus evil, on which many would brook no compromise. But it was also a power struggle, in which unrecompensed emancipation was considered a blow to the heart of the finances, and therefore the power, of the slaveholding great landowners. The emancipationists struck while the emperor was out of the country, working through his somewhat naive and fervently abolitionist daughter and heir. Henceforth even the great land-owners were alienated from the monarchy. By 1889 the emperor himself was looking for ways to modify the situation, for example asking his ambassador to the United States to examine the working of the American Supreme Court as a model for a possible future repository of the poder moderador. When that same year a group of about fifty officers and 500 soldiers and cadets managed to enlist the prestige of the senior and most respected general behind a coup, almost no one came forward to support the Empire.

The military had therefore assumed the power to determine the nature of the Brazilian polity. There was precedent for such power, the old poder moderador, and if the military did not yet assume this in theory they certainly did so in practice. But the military was not the emperor; it had no legitimate right, even in republican theory, to assume such a power. Even worse, the military, unlike the emperor, was not a single entity but a separate army and navy and, within those, separate individuals and factions. This actual disunity made such an immediate and total farce of presumed military control that the military president of the republic had to ally with the great landowners and their provincial militia units in order to preserve the republic and Brazilian unity at all. Thus in practice the activist faction of the military was discredited and had to retire behind the scenes, and civilians took control—though with generous attention to military budgets to make sure matters stayed that way. By 1900 the new situation, under the Old Republic (1889-1930), had stabilized.

It was during these thirty years of shaky authority that Brazil established itself as an independently productive cultural unit. In colonial times most intel-lectual production had been in the hands of the Church, particularly the Jesuits—with the spectacular but isolated exception of O Aleijadinho, a crippled leper who produced some of the most remarkable sculptures in the Americas to adorn the churches of the gold fields. Otherwise there were some descriptions of the country and some writing of good poetry—which in Brazil is about the same as saying there was some writing. Only in 1808 did the first printing press arrive, and under the early Empire there were some fair novels. But the cultural independence of Brazil became definite with the humanistic stories of Machado de Assis (1839-1908), somewhat the Dostoevski of Brazil, and even more with the publication in 1902 of Euclides da Cunha's nonfiction **Os Sertoes** (published in English as **Rebellion in the Backlands**), sometimes called the Bible of Brazilian nationality. Brazilian culture has since continued to evolve, produc-ing even in non-literary fields such world-class figures as Oscar Niemeyer and Candido Portinari.

Meanwhile the Old Republic was finding roots in old Brazilian practice. It was the second civilian president, Manoel Ferraz de Campos Salles (1898-1902), who created a workable formula, in effect inverting the old imperial

practice. The local dependency hierarchies were consolidated wherever possible
into statewide machines powerful enough to manage their states, powerful
enough in combination to be a base of authority for the federal government
itself. This was not entirely accepted; a very abortive revolt occurred as early
as 1904 against this "politics of the governors." But the two states of Sao Paulo
and Minas Gerais together with the federal district controlled by themselves
some half the resources of the country, so as long as these two could agree
on policies and candidates and took care not to offend the strongest others,
they could unify and control Brazil. By 1910 this was already showing some
strains, and the Big Two had to settle on a compromise presidential candidate
from Rio Grande do Sul, who happened to be the leading general of the time
and so caused a temporary hysteria among the politicians about a military
re-entry into politics. Also in 1910 the government became strong enough
to begin intervening actively in the smaller states, upsetting their entrenched
machines in favor of, as things turned out, even more entrenched machines.

Meanwhile Brazil continued to change. The urban groups partly responsible
for the 1889 revolution had been left out of the final settlement, since they
were not part of the rural political machines; when they exercised influence,
it was even more **ad hoc** than other settlements made for each election. But
the cities were no longer the "merely immense villages" (Bello 1966:1) they
had been under the Empire; they were the centers of a, still just barely beginning, industrialization. The regime did nothing about this; the last president
of the Old Republic even referred to the labor problem as only a police problem.

The Great Depression introduced a new set of strains. Finally in 1930
the conglomerate of state political machines split, with Sao Paulo and Minas
Gerais supporting different presidential candidates and unable to agree on
a compromise.

At the same time military discontent had been rising again, and with
it **tenentismo.** The classic example came in 1922, when a group of junior officers
(**tenentes,** lieutenants), angered at the election of a supposedly anti-military
president, "revolted," i.e. announced the need for a change of government
in the expectation that the forces of right and justice were only awaiting such
a call to action--an expectation not entirely foolhardy, given the Hispanic
traditional emphasis on abstract justice and especially the events of 1889.
When the call was not answered they made an example of themselves of which
only two survived. The ideological upheavals of the 1930s provided the other
needed ingredient, the atmosphere of sweeping change of existing institutions.
When in 1930 the ruling machine broke up the result was a revolution by parade,
and in spite of dissension afterwards among the winners, this revolution like
that of 1889 was effective.

The revolution of 1930 and its aftermath of dictatorship are important
for two things that did happen and one that did not. First, it marks the public
re-entry of the military into the core of Brazilian politics; henceforth no candidate could become president without military acquiescence. Second, the age
of Getulio Vargas, president from 1930-1945, introduced the lower middle
and labor groups as elements of the political process, if at first only to counterbalance the old rural machines. Henceforth "populism," a vague favoring of
the workingman as against mysterious upper-level and foreign exploiters, was
an intrinsic part of affairs. Third and most important, the revolution did not
succeed in creating workable institutions for Brazil. It did give a certain degree
of dignity and even benefits to the low-status groups, but this was completely
managed from the top down. The Vargas regime operated by a very Brazilian
pragmatism, a set of arrangements called "The System," the usual multilateral
negotiation out of difficulties and pious attention to formal legality, but now
with no noticeable connection between the two. (The great symbol of the Vargas
era might be the constitution of 1937, which in four separate articles 1) empow-

ered the president to rule by decree until a national legislature could be elected and convened; 2) authorized such elections only after a plebiscite approved the constitution; 3) barred such plebiscites during states of emergency; 4) declared a state of emergency.) The postwar democratic resurgence created a democratically elected government with a fully effective vote for the previously disfranchised urban groups, but in a party situation that made presidential responsibility to the voters extremely difficult and legislative responsibility a low comedy. At the same time the military received formal responsibility "to guarantee the constitutional powers and law and order" (Constitution of 1946, article 177); a Brazilian ambassador even noted in so many words that "the Armed Forces of my country have traditionally acted as a moderating power on the constitutional life" (Burns 1966:384). As of 1946 the military's assumption of the poder moderador, however disliked in some quarters, became formally a part of the System.

Since the old electoral machines proved incapable of dealing with the new liberalized vote, this proved to be a very shaky arrangement. In 1950 Vargas was the overwhelming popular choice for president again, and compromised enough with the powers that were to be allowed to run and win. In 1955 the winning candidate won with only 36% of the vote. In 1960, for the first time in Brazilian history, the incumbent government failed to elect its own designated candidate, and the winner had run essentially in defiance of party organization and entrenched dependent relations. His problems were such that in 1961 he resigned, and he was followed by two more unsuccessful, short-lived governments. By 1964 the entire government, including the military commanders and most of the state governors, had decided that this could not go on. Thus there was a third spontaneous revolution by parade, in which a consensus of the ruling elite and many lower-level citizens simply withdrew its confidence from the official administration and so forced it out. Again there were no significant casualties.

By this time Brazil was industrializing rapidly and everyone was speaking of the Land of Tomorrow. Now there was to be a very large-scale organization, under military management of a **poder moderador** just as strong as the emperor's had ever been and lasting until the proper institutions for the Brazil of Tomorrow were found. So far the search has proceeded for almost twenty years.

Thus the history of the Brazilian Peace during the last century has been a steady but very gradual decline of consensus, so gradual that the Brazilian insistence on the politics of compromise and aversion to large-scale violence have successfully maintained the Peace itself. The coup of 1964 did not abolish the System but rather only sheared off an increasingly unworkable electoral system supposedly designed to legitimate it, just as the coups of 1889 and 1930 had resulted primarily in the destruction of other institutions that had not adapted to their changing situations. But now there is very little left to shear off, and the military regime's success at establishing new institutions has been at best very limited. The regime tried to legitimate itself with economic progress, but the worldwide oil crisis struck the Brazilian economy as hard as any other, and there is a general perception that any actual progress has been made at the expense of the low-income groups. Polarization has become such that only 16% of the population, the middle- and upper-income groups, is committed to the regime against challenges from below (**Luso-Brazilian Review**, vol. 15, n.2).

In some ways the situation resembles that of late Republican Rome. The Roman Republican Peace and constitutional system suffered a decline for some 113 years, from the passage of the Land Law of 200 BC allowing the formation of huge landed estates to the end of the Peace in 90 BC and breakup of the system in 87 BC. There followed fifty years of unlimited civil war and blood purges, then a military empire (Melko and Weigel, 1981). In

Brazil too the military has become a core of the political system; the Vargas heritage emphasizes "populism," the people against the exploiters; **tenentismo** provides a tradition of political crusades. Both the massive internal alienation and the traditions needed to exploit it seem to be well in place. Unless a re-institutionalization of the Brazilian polity is found very soon, the Brazilian Gaius Marius may already be waiting in the wings.

Reflections

Brazil is a rimland Peace, with a settled frontier only in the far south, a permanent war zone. It is also one of four peace periods to have continued from monarchical to national times and one of three Hispanic American Peaces, the only one in both categories. While all the others maintained a very careful institutional continuity, Brazil shows a singular disregard for specific formal institutions, ignoring them at first and almost casually removing them during the last century. The change from colony to independent nation is the sole exception; it seems that when the situation is dangerous, Brazilian flexibility and pragmatism will use institutions to **dar um jeito**, improvise the best solution of the moment, as easily as any other instrument.

In comparison with Spanish America, Brazil is much more rural, hierarchic and orderly. Spanish America certainly had its rural development areas, but its core was the old Indian civilizations, where the Spanish population lived from enforced tribute, residing in the cities. In Brazil the Portuguese dispersed to the countryside and the leaders depended not on tribute but on plantation production. Spanish America was built around royal government in the cities; Portuguese America found the royal government almost irrelevant. Only in the late Empire did the economic situation begin to develop problems for this. To date Brazil has managed to maintain its peaceful and pragmatic flexibility, but as urban/national problems assume more and more importance this lack of institutionalization may yet end the Peace.

11

The Costa Rican Peace (1842–1948)

From the time of its emergence from Spanish rule in the early nineteenth century, Central America has been regarded as a tinderbox. The countries occupying this region are very subject to frequent internal rebellion or coup. In their relationships with each other, they are of a strength and population comparable enough so that in times of minor changes in leadership or internal coherence, any one of them could interfere in the affairs of any other. With regard to external powers, none is strong enough to resist invasion and all are subject to pressure from major powers. Since the Monroe Doctrine was promulgated by John Quincy Adams in 1823, these countries have for the most part been protected from such invasions, at least from Europe, but the role of their protector in preserving peace has been ambiguous and controversial.

Origins

Despite the unfavorable circumstances existing in Central America, one of its states, Costa Rica, has managed to remain detached from the embroilments of its neighbors, and at the same time to have remained free from violent internal conflict, for more than a century.

The Costa Ricans have been aware of the contrast. They have developed a belief in their own superiority to their neighbors. They were richer, their wealth was more equally distributed, their literacy rate was higher, their presidents succeeded one another in an orderly, democratic fashion.

Costa Rica was nearly uninvolved in the Spanish Empire. It had few Indians and no ready-made civilization and so no incentive for heavy Spanish settlement; it was at the edge of the edge of the viceroyalty of New Spain, far from any governmental concerns; the trade routes ran elsewhere. When the area was settled in the late 1500's it quickly became a frontier zone of small and isolated farms, unable to support any self-perpetuating rural hierarchy or, for that matter, even the elsewhere troublesome distinction between peninsular and American-born Spaniards.

After Spanish rule had been overthrown in the 1820's, the five provinces of Central America twice attempted to form a federation. In between there was an imbroglio involving the new Mexican Empire that caused some fighting in Costa Rica. Then in 1835 the world suddenly arrived and for seven years Costa Rica was the scene of coups, conspiracies, party conflicts amounting to small civil wars, and invasions from both Central and South America. The last of these invasions occurred in 1842, by an army led by Francisco Morazan, former Federation president who was seeking to regain power. But the Costa Ricans rose up against him and he was captured and executed.

After that there was considerable political controversy, but almost no military action. Costa Rica did not experience an invasion or major uprising until 1948, although bands of sometimes violent robbers were not uncommon in the northern province of Guanacaste. But on the whole we can say that between 1842 and 1948 peace was characteristic of this rather small country—at under 20,000 square miles one of the smallest on the American mainland (but still larger than Switzerland).

Characterization

The pattern of life in Costa Rica struck a North American diplomat, James Stephens, as being unique. He found the Costa Ricans orderly and hospitable, "not like the rest of Central America." A pattern of stability, democratic institutions and peaceful transfer of power has been widely observed by historians of Costa Rica (Bell, 1971:3).

This orderly, democratic pattern was not apparent in the earlier years of the Peace. About 1830 Costa Rica began large-scale coffee production, and this provided the economic base for formation of an oligarchy. The small producers of coffee became dependent on the processing facilities of the larger ones. These oligarchs struggled for power, but while at times civil war threatened, only the 1860 return under arms, and quick arrest and execution, of a former president involved anything approaching warfare. During the next ten years there were frequent changes in government and a growing tendency toward violence, but in 1870 General Tomas Guardia established a dictatorship which broke up the oligarchy. His leading opponents were exiled rather than shot, and a program of rapid economic expansion submerged most other discontent. By 1889 the new entrepreneurs and the remnants of the old oligarchy had formed and enforced a consensus in favor of free and genuine elections, the first such in Central America. For the duration of the Peace this remained hallowed tradition, the one exception involving a defense minister who seized the presidency during a strained period in 1917, and then ruled so arbitrarily as to be forced out by popular opinion two years later. (Specifically by a parade of schoolchildren and teachers: The president's brother tried to disperse them with a fire hose, which the children hacked into a poor state of usefulness with their machetes. As the laughter died down, the president resigned.) The general stability of the system may be seen in the total lack of pomp, mystery and even protection surrounding the president, who, for example, was fully expected to stand in line at the local movie theater to buy his own ticket.

Most of the land was divided among small farmers, hard-working Basques and Galicians. This pattern of land division distinguished Costa Rica sharply from other Central American states, which traditionally were dominated by a few powerful landowners, with much of the remaining population employed as landless tenant farmers.

The different land pattern also led to a different political pattern. The same families were not always in control, and the large number of free farmers made Costa Rica more susceptible to republican patterns, although freely contested elections were not held before the end of the nineteenth century. The elite that selected the candidates included, besides old landed families, professional men and a funded gentry.

Coffee had been the major product in the early nineteenth century. Under Guardia production of sugar and coffee were increased, trade was enlarged, railroads were constructed. The railroads in turn encouraged the production of bananas. So the economy became more varied, and commerce and industry provided alternative means of gaining a living.

The country prospered. Population increased from 80,000 in the first

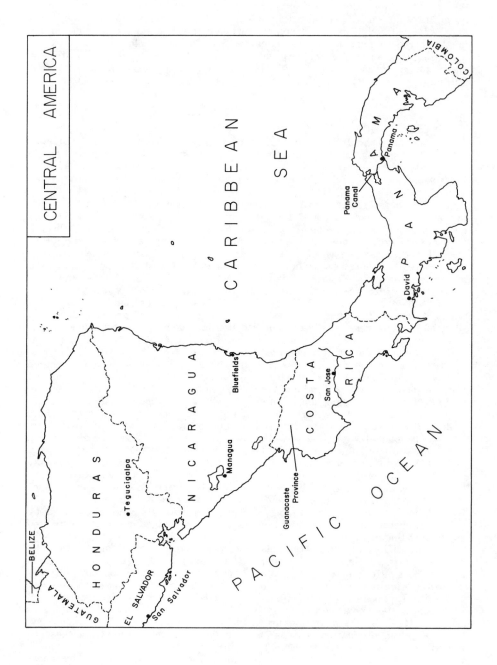

CENTRAL AMERICA

BELIZE
GUATEMALA
HONDURAS
•Tegucigalpa
EL SALVADOR
San Salvador
NICARAGUA
•Managua
Bluefields
COSTA RICA
San Jose
Guanacaste Province
PANAMA
David
Panama
Panama Canal
COLOMBIA

CARIBBEAN SEA

PACIFIC OCEAN

census of 1844, to 800,000 a hundred years later. The population was 80 percent Caucasian, less mixed than in neighboring countries. About one-seventh of the population was of mixed Spanish and Indian blood. Black immigrants from the West Indies came into the country in the twentieth century, particularly to work on banana plantations. There were racial tensions in these areas and in the newspapers of the 1920's and 30's concern was expressed that a change in racial composition of the country would lead to a decline in quality of culture.

Though Catholicism was the state religion, other religions were not prohibited. As in many Latin American countries, Catholicism was more important to women than to men, and therefore taught in homes but not necessarily practiced. It was not necessary for political success to profess Catholicism, and in most descriptions of the country, relatively little attention is given to the Church.

Social conditions within the country were relatively favorable compared with those of most countries. A 1927 census revealed that more than half of the houses in the country were owned by occupants, most without mortgages. There were relatively few very wealthy farmers, though these played a vital role in that they acted as bankers for small farmers and rented expensive machinery required or at least desirable for preparing coffee for market. Few signs of deep poverty were to be seen either in cities or in the country. Social customs tended to be conservative, with the family playing a stronger role than the community.

Costa Ricans were proud of their system of universal public education for men and women, which was reflected by the 1920's in a literacy rate far exceeding that of other Latin American countries and of many European countries as well. In contrast to most Latin American countries, the majority of schools were coeducational, with the result that literacy rates improved for women as well as men. By the twentieth century this development was reflected in the appearance of a number of well-stocked bookstores and well-edited newspapers fully exercising freedom to criticize the government.

This educational breakthrough was slow to be reflected in the creative development within the country. There was relatively little native art compared to other Latin American countries owing to the high percentage of Spanish population. Throughout the nineteenth and twentieth centuries there was a strong tendency to borrow from foreign cultures, particularly the French, both in styles employed and in preference for literature, painting and theater. Only in the 1920's did Costa Rican painters begin to paint their own landscapes. In literature there was some domestic development in the twentieth century in poetry and essays, much of it social protest. By the 1930's and 40's, there were at least two names that would have been recognized beyond the borders of Costa Rica: the poet and essayist Roberto Brenes Mesen and Carlos Luis Fallas, author of **Mamita Yunai,** a novel depicting the life of banana workers. As the Peace terminated, the cultural movement was still in its ascendency.

After 1842 Costa Rica rarely participated in conflicts with neighboring countries. In 1852 she did raise an army of 9,000 when a North American adventurer, William Walker, temporarily took control of neighboring Nicaragua and invaded Guanacaste. But when the Costa Rican Army advanced, Walker retreated, and the action against him was fought in Nicaragua. In the 1880's when the dictator of Guatamala, Justo Rufino Barrios, attempted to unify Central America by force, Costa Rica prepared to fight; but Barrios, who had a powerful, well-equipped army, was killed in El Salvador during the second battle of his campaign, and the threat dissolved instantly.

The Costa Ricans persistently resisted a series of movements to federate or reunify the Central American countries. On at least three occasions three or four other Central American nations agreed to federation or union, but Costa Rican public opinion was opposed, and the Congress refused to ratify proposed agreements, even when Costa Rican delegates to conventions had accepted them, even when it was agreed that their president should be president of the confederation. The Costa Ricans always took the line that federation was desirable some time in the future, but the time was not ripe. The Costa Ricans opposing federation believed the stability of their nation was attributable to their non-involvement in Central American politics. They believed their schools better, their elections more democratic, their economy stronger. There was possibly also a racial factor shaping their aloofness, a fear of being inundated by Negroes and Indians from the north. The economic ties between Costa Rica and Central America were weak. Most of Costa Rican trade was with Colombia, Britain and the United States.

Costa Rica, like other Latin American states, expressed considerable hostility toward the United States, the strongest power in the Western Hemisphere. But the power and inclination of the United States to intervene in Latin American affairs may have contributed to Costa Rican peace. For one thing Costa Rica, like other Central American nations, maintained no standing army in the twentieth century. Their reserves totaled no more than 500. They could maintain such a policy because their two immediate neighbors, Panama and Nicaragua, were equally weak, and because the United States would intervene in the event of invasion from any other great power. Also, in 1932, on a rare occasion in which a defeated Costa Rican presidential candidate did threaten rebellion, the United States offered its good offices, and a peaceful agreement was reached.

Termination

Between 1842 and 1948, there were two possible interruptions to the Peace: the military action against Walker in 1852 and the Guardia coup of 1870. The action against Walker resulted in major casualties for the Costa Rican Army, although the battle took place in Nicaragua. The 1870 coup, by all accounts, was "almost" without bloodshed.

Costa Rica had not long passed its century of peace, however, before its usually reliable election system malfunctioned, and the resulting conflict decisively ended the Peace. Even so, the system quickly recovered itself, and as far as internal affairs are concerned, it could well be that the conflict of 1948 eventually would be seen as a minor interruption in a much longer period of peace. Costa Rica's location in Central America, however, does not make the possibility of continually avoiding external intervention seem very likely.

In 1948, when Otilio Ulate Blanco won a close presidential election, the incumbent president, Teodoro Picado Michalsky, appealed to Congress to void the election because of fraud. It did. A general strike followed, and then a rebellion was mounted by Jose Figueres to insure Ulate's inauguration. When a junta led by Figueres was installed in the capital, San Jose, Nicaraguan troops intervened in behalf of Picado. Figueres asked for intervention of the Organization of American States, a political alliance dominated by the United States. The OAS complied, Figueres retired, and Ulate was inaugurated.

This had the look of a typical Latin American rebellion at the time, and it was so regarded. But it was obviously not typical of Costa Rica, and in fact as it turned out it was not typical of Latin America either. Figueres intervened in behalf of a conservative candidate, although he was himself a liberal. His junta stayed in power only a short time. Figueres subsequently did come to power, but as the elected president, and when his four-year term ended, he retired.

In retrospect the 1948 rebellion appears to have succeeded in maintaining the governmental structure that had served Costa Rica so well for so long.

There were several other factors worth mentioning that related to the 1948 rebellion. There had been a relative economic decline in preceding decades. Both the coffee and the banana business had become less efficient, as coffee was produced in other countries and competition lowered prices, and as banana trees exhausted marginal soil and production declined. In the thirties Communism became an issue and also resulted in a more searching examination of the social system, so that inequities and poverty became more apparent. The issues of Communism and social reform sharpened the differences between parties, and may have contributed to the greater part played by fraud and dubious electoral tactics in both the elections of 1944 and 1948. Finally, Figueres himself was a charismatic and ambitious leader who had preached a doctrine of revolution. That he served only one term as president and did not become another Guardia may be attributed to the Costa Rican pattern and constitution, with more than a little help from the OAS.

Reflections

Costa Rica seems to have succeeded in imposing a pattern that has worked well in providing peace and prosperity in the Western World in the teeth of a more immediate and prevalent pattern that dominated the continent around it. Its story suggests the importance of watching for exceptions to any series of generalizations.

In a sense, once the Costa Rican pattern took shape, the general Latin American pattern actually served as reinforcement. The Costa Ricans took pride in their difference, their prosperity, their free elections, their system of education. The more dictators dominated other Central American and Caribbean countries, the more elections elsewhere were upset by rebellions, the more the Costa Ricans could point to the superiority of their own system.

Costa Rica is much criticised for having prevented the reunification of Central America, but perhaps the Costa Ricans were justified. By following their general policy of non-involvement, they maintained peace and prosperity, whereas other Central American countries more interested in union were less peaceful and prosperous.

The lack of military power or respect for the military has contributed to the Costa Rican Peace. In Latin America, whoever could gain the support of a significant part of the army could challenge the government. But in Costa Rica, for most of the twentieth century, there was no army. Rather Costa Rica was defended by naval power that could not be won over to rival political leaders, for it was in the interest of the United States to discourage conflict among neighboring small powers. Though Costa Rica did not have the advantages of insularity, her two immediate neighbors, Nicaragua and Panama, were weak. Any other power would have to invade by sea.

12

The Canadian Peace
(1885-　　)

"Two bloods, slow to be reconciled in one body"

Origins

The establishment of a Peace within North America involved three major problems: settlement with the indigenous population, conflicts over title among the Europeans and the United States, and conflicts among the Europeans. The eventual resolution of these problems produced two separate countries both largely of British background, the United States and Canada. The United States is not treated herein as a Peace, partly on grounds of continuing violence. The Indian wars, which were formal organized encounters involving regular professional armed forces, concluded only in 1890, less than the required century ago. Even after 1890 there were some four thousand racial lynchings in the United States, some with thousands of spectators.

Canada on the other hand never suffered such intense and prolonged conflict as the Revolutionary and Civil Wars, or even the Indian wars. Most of what it did suffer was attacks from the United States, which for almost a century after the Peace of Paris of 1783 considered the continued British presence in Canada as an anomaly just waiting for correction. The 1860's were particularly tense. In 1861 there was a real possibility that Britain would come into the American Civil War on the Southern side, so real that Britain rushed 14,000 troops into Canada against possible American reprisal. After the war, well-trained and armed Union veterans of Irish descent, acting as part of the Irish revolutionary Fenian Brotherhood, planned several invasions of Canada as part of a general challenge to Britain. One in June, 1866 involved some 600 to 900 Fenians, who met and defeated a British detachment. Canada called out 21,000 militia troops against this, but a few days later President Johnson decided to declare American neutrality in the conflict and the Fenians withdrew. There were other attacks and rumors of other attacks and several wild alarums in Canada in response. Also in 1866 a Massachusetts general introduced a bill in Congress simply to "admit" the new states of Nova Scotia, New Brunswick, Canada East and Canada West to the union. Only with the Treaty of Washington in 1870, with the promise of withdrawal of British regular troops from North America, did the United States formally concede that Canada was in fact a constituted separate national entity in North America.

The Canadian Confederation itself was the major result of this continuing American pressure. Britain had been willing enough to send troops as late as the war scare of 1861, but the very next year, with the war scare over, Canada itself refused to appropriate even half a million dollars for its own defense.

With so little Canadian interest, and with the growing realization after Antietam that the North was going to win and Britain would be faced with a great power in North America, British interest in defending Canada evaporated. There had already been some talk of unification of the British North American colonies, and London seized on this as a useful screen behind which to conduct a reasonably dignified and orderly departure. Within Canada itself there was much disagreement on the subject; in Quebec the Confederation leadership did not dare even have a public vote around the issue. But London insisted, and "imposed" unification "by ingenuity, luck, courage, and sheer force," such that a Canadian delegate in London reported back that Canada had been less granted autonomy than "cast off in summary fashion" (Waite 1962:323, 328). The Confederation was no sooner started than Nova Scotia elected a legislature committed two to one for secession (which London refused); Manitoba and Saskatchewan had to be conquered; British Columbia and Prince Edward Island were in effect bought in with promises of subsidies; Newfoundland spent the next eighty years singing lines about "Come near at your peril, Canadian wolf." The Confederation was Thursday's child and had far to go, and the beginnings were less than promising of the trip.

The last major problem was also major mainly because of the continued possibility of American involvement. The prairies west of Ontario were occupied by a group called the **Metis**, semi-nomadic buffalo hunters of mixed French, Scottish and Indian background, heirs of the old fur-trapping **voyageurs.** They did not want annexation into Canada (or for that matter into any law-enforcing polity), but over in Ottawa Prime Minister Sir John Macdonald, more than any other man the founder of Confederation, felt that the prairies were needed to make Canada viable, and America would take them if Canada did not. A Canadian force simply moved into Meti territory and admitted it as the province of Manitoba. The Metis fled to Saskatchewan and for fifteen years accumulated discontents, partly because of the disappearance of the all-important buffalo herds. They called their leader Louis Riel and in 1885, joined by some of the remaining Indian tribes, went into open rebellion. Macdonald acted instantly, rushing 4500 troops over the westward-reaching railroad and crushing the rebellion before the United States had a chance to intervene. So ended the last formal military action on Canadian soil and began the Canadian Peace.

Characterization

"Two bloods. . .slow to be reconciled in one body" (Hutchison 1942:4): The Canadian Peace is particularly the story of a bitter inter-ethnic war that did not happen. When Britain conquered New France in 1763 the French settlers were allowed to keep their own laws, church and identity, but this alien body in British America proved indigestible. Britain decided to unite it with the British colony of Upper Canada (later Ontario), as a way of yielding to pressures for self-government without creating a self-governing French entity within the British Empire. It was hoped that under the terms of the union of 1841 the French Canadians would be contentedly elevated into Englishmen, thereby solving that problem; instead they quickly reclaimed the capital of the union and re-established French as an official language. By 1864 the future Prime Minister Sir Wilfrid Laurier was able to think that the age of ethnic conflict was over.

Oddly enough, it was re-opened by the Peace settlement itself. Louis Riel had executed an extremist opponent from Ontario, so when Riel was captured in Saskatchewan, Ontario was all for hanging him as a murderer. Quebec was not so noisy on the subject, so Macdonald decided peace in the house would be better kept by a salutary hanging. Quebec erupted over this, declaring that

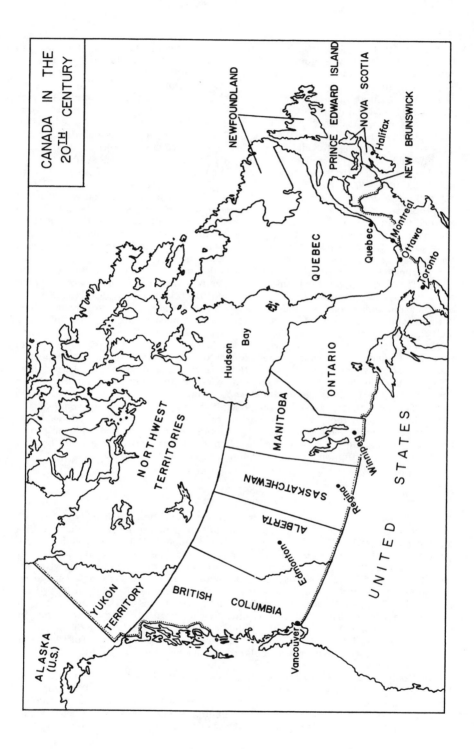

CANADA IN THE 20TH CENTURY

Riel was killed mainly for being French. Henceforth French Canada was on permanent alert for anything remotely resembling an assault on French rights. And this sensitivity could reach very far indeed: In both World Wars there was a conscription crisis in which Quebec fulminated over having French Canadian boys drafted to fight British battles. Nor was this sensitivity entirely unjustified; the fathers of Confederation had said not one official word promoting biculturalism, and outside Quebec such institutions as existed for the preservation of French culture tended to wither on the vine. In large part this was the French Canadians' own fault; while for example Manitoba had been roughly half and half French and British on admission in 1870, by 1890 the end of French migration west had left Manitoba to the British, who had no interest in preserving the remnants of French autonomy. French Canada was withdrawing into the bastion of Quebec (with some outliers particularly in New Brunswick), and even there emphasized the old village-and-countryside values that were becoming increasingly out of date. The industrial revolution moved largely into Ontario, mostly to the Great Lakes area, and such further economic development as occurred in Quebec was accomplished by the British minority, in the English language.

Nevertheless French culture survived in this English world. In part this came of careful attention to events in Ottawa; if French Canadians were bitterly divided over some federal policies, they were united in knowing that **quebecois** individuality could be badly damaged by an uncaring federal government. Prime Minister William Lyon Mackenzie King (1921/1948) made a particular art of cultivating quebecois support, by having as his principal lieutenant the party boss of Quebec—a tactic that worked so well as to become part of Canadian political folklore. But the best that could be expected was that the Confederation would leave French culture alone.

The mechanisms of survival within Quebec are more important. Indeed **survivance** was the code word for an integrated set of values that made the Quebecois somewhat the Jewish Pale of Canada. French Canada found its refuge in the Catholic Church. Nor was this particularly even the Gallican Church. After 1870 France was ruled by the ungodly Third Republic, and while Quebec was somewhat divided between one side pro-French and the other that felt France not to be French enough, on the whole the second group held the floor. **Survivance** was attached to a priesthood which, and for the same reason, matched Ireland's in its uncompromising exaltation of the papacy and strictest possible interpretation of Church doctrines and prerogatives. In Quebec the question was not whether the pope speaking **ex catedra** was infallible but whether in each local jurisdiction every bishop and **cure** shared the same unchallengeable authority. British Canada developed the standard general tolerance of religious dissent found in, say, the United States, and developed uncounted minor sects as a result; French Canada was the Church, distinct, separate, uncontaminated, and absolutely intending to stay that way. But this separateness worked, preserving both French culture and the Canadian Peace.

The focus now returns to Canada at large. With foreign relations no longer a deadly problem, the major issue became definition of the Confederation itself. The initial marriage of Ontario, Quebec, New Brunswick and Nova Scotia had been less than close, and expansion westward produced further division. Because of Canada's extreme northern position this development was linear, along the southern border, producing at least as much regional identity as characterized the colonial United States. By 1900, for purposes of policy decisions, Canada consisted essentially of five regions: the Maritimes, Quebec, Ontario, the Prairies, and British Columbia. On the other hand, this multiple division has contributed to continuation of the Confederation. Only very occasionally will some issue find one province feeling itself persecuted into a permanent minority, and Quebec, the usual victim of such feelings, was as already noted also divided against itself regarding federal programs.

Canadian constitutional development also worked to assuage injured autonomies. The fathers of Confederation had hated the very idea of federalism; it was alien to British practice and next door in the United States had just set off the bloodiest war in recent history. Their great hope was for Canada to be simply another "Kingdom" of the British Crown, but London was not about to flaunt any such word before American sensibilities about North American colonialisms. If the word "dominion" seemed meaningless, at least that very lack of meaning provoked no dangerous hysteria on the floors of the American Congress, and the situation could develop as it would.

It developed thanks to a technicality. If Canada now had a constitution, in Britain this constitution was no more than the British North America Act, a statute law to be interpreted in the standing tradition of all statute laws: that is, as narrowly as possible. The Judicial Committee of the British Privy Council acted as interpreter in such matters, and for decades its decisions were almost all in favor of increasing provincial autonomy, to the point that at times Canada has had very nearly to negotiate treaties with its own provinces.

Even the national political parties have a strong tendency toward provincial bases, and not just in Quebec: Social Credit in Alberta is perhaps the outstanding example. This conflict has created a pendulum effect in dominion–provincial relations, such that for example the 1950's were a period of dominion "usurpation" of central power, the 1960's a period of much greater consultation and recognition of the provinces' claimed rights. The system also seems to produce unusually long periods of leadership under particular individuals. At the dominion level for example, Macdonald served as prime minister from 1867 to 1873 and also 1878 to 1891, Laurier from 1896 to 1911, Mackenzie King from 1921 to 1930 and 1935 to 1948, and Pierre Elliot Trudeau almost continuously from 1968 to 1984. But this is only a reflection of a practice that seems rather strange from the viewpoint of the turbulent electoral history of the United States, such that one analyst speaks of New Brunswick as following the "frightfully un-Canadian practice of alternating parties in office" (McCormick, 1980).

The Liberal Party has ruled Canada almost continuously since 1935, based on an almost guaranteed return of almost every member from Quebec. But the same holds true in the provinces: Nova Scotia was solidly Liberal, Ontario almost as solidly Conservative, for three-quarters of a century; Saskatchewan was Liberal from 1905-1944 with one break, then socialist from 1944-1980 with one break; Social Credit owned Alberta from 1935-1971; and there were shorter reigns. But the votes are honest and the opposition parties continue to exist (two of them in Ontario, three in Alberta) as available replacements should the, so to speak, ruling dynasty falter. This combination of continuity and flexibility seems worth further study.

Canadian foreign policy during the Peace has been considerably less complicated than before, thanks to the resolution of the really dangerous difficulties with the United States. In large part it has consisted of a four-pointed triangle, with Canada, Britain, and the United States being the three official actors and the "two bloods" question pushing a more than shadowy presence into every question that might impact on relations between Ottawa and Quebec. The basic theme has been gradual separation of Canadian foreign policy from control by London, principally because in such settlements as the Treaty of Washington of 1870 and the Alaskan Boundary Question of 1903 Canada perceived Britain as selling out Canadian interests in order to curry favor with the United States. But the relationship between Canada and Britain was complicated by the ethnic question. Quebec had no desire whatever to do anything at all in support of British imperialism, but on the other hand has depended on residual British sovereignty as a final shield against domination by the British Canadians. On the whole anti-imperialism has ruled policy decisions, beginning not later than the occasion when Canadian Prime Minister Sir Wilfrid Laurier, a French Canadian, while on an official visit to Britain was given an intimate confidence on British racial superiority and Canada's proper role in supporting British hegemony.

The actual occasion for separation came in 1922. After World War I Britain signed with Turkey the Treaty of Sevres, by which Turkey yielded the Straits around Istanbul to international control and most of the rest of western Asia Minor to Greece. But the Turkish Republic repudiated the treaty, defeated the Greeks, and began advancing on the international zone. Britain prepared to resume World War I on the question of the Straits, a problem of very little interest to Canada. Moreover, the British Prime Minister, without informing the dominions in advance of the coming crisis, simply announced it in a telegram assuming their support and authorizing them to send troops. Worse yet, the news was released to the press before the Canadian Prime Minister, Mackenzie King, had even received the official telegram. King saw the chance to gain Canada's point by no more than his usual tactic of intensively, in this case even flamboyantly, doing nothing. Henceforth automatic dominion adherence to British foreign policy was a dead letter, and when in 1926 an imperial conference took up British–dominion relations, the only course available was recognition of full autonomy, enshrined in the Statute of Westminster of 1931. (Significantly, Canada did ask for exemption from that clause of the Statute of Westminster which ended Britain's power to disallow Canadian laws. This power was Quebec's final defense against intrusions from British Canada, so that was one piece of autonomy that Quebec did not want Canada to have.)

Moving now to reflections of the Peace in other areas, the patterns of the Canadian economy followed those of the United States. Thus a period of expansion and industrialization in the late nineteenth and early twentieth centuries was punctuated by fluctuating prices and sharp depressions culminating in the Great Depression of the 1930's. Recovery came with World War II and lasted until the 1970's, when Canada began to share in the American pattern of declining growth, rising unemployment and increasing inflation. At least in part because some one-half of Canadian investment came from the United States, the patterns of the Canadian economy seem geared to America's, whether governmental policies are the same or different.

In matters of culture American dominance has been even more obvious, and a particular source of anguish to many Canadians. Much has been said about the lack of any particularly Canadian aesthetic. A Canadian magazine ran a contest a few years ago in which readers were to complete the phrase "As Canadian as. . .": The winning entry was, "As Canadian as possible under the circumstances." A special Royal Commission reported in 1951 that Canada had an international reputation only in painting. If a Canadian writer truly writes from his own experience, he is still likely to be perceived as an American writing in Toronto. However, Canadian scholarship has been productive, putting forth in the twentieth century such world-renowned scholars as Northrup Frye, Hans Selye and Marshall McLuhan, and the recent crisis in internal relations has gone some fair way toward evoking a new sense of nationalism in other areas as well. If the period has not been internationally first-rank, it nevertheless has been creative.

There is finally the great question of Canadian life of the last two decades. The first 75 years of the Canadian Peace depended considerably on the British-French Canadian settlement that produced the, so to speak, Quebecois Pale. But in the early twentieth century the industrial world was already creeping into Quebec. Since for decades this involved mainly the British enclave in Montreal, the Pale remained unconcerned. But after World War II young French Canadians began to notice that there was a world outside the farms and villages, and then to refer to the conservative clerical custodians of old

Quebec as **"les bonzes"** (Buddhist monk-priests). In 1959/1960 with the end of the regime of Maurice Duplessis, the Pale began to collapse. A "Quiet Revolution" saw twentieth-century technocrats take over Quebec, and the world of these technocrats has been not outside of but directly competitive with the equally technocratic world of late-twentieth-century British Canada. Quebecois reactions to this competition vary over a wide range, but the most famous (though hardly the most extreme) has been that of Rene Levesque's **Parti Quebecois,** aiming to resolve the competition by throwing out one of the competitors. This has created some negative reactions—for example in British flight from Quebec—and some positive ones—for example in a resurgence of interest in French language and culture even in the Prairies. The rule of the provincially-oriented Parti Quebecois in Quebec City has not harmed the voting base of the national Liberal Party at all; in the last election this even increased. In the 1980 referendum on Quebecois independence under one or another label, 59.6% of Quebec voted no, including a slim majority of the French Canadian population; in August 1979 a poll found that only 29% of the population of Quebec believed Canada would eventually break up, as against 47% in 1969. (The figure for all Canada was 18%.) The future of Quebecois nationalism therefore remains uncertain, but there is at least no immediate prospect that this problem will end the Canadian Peace.

Reflections

The binational nation is a rarity, simply because of the obvious inherent contradiction in such an arrangement. This study has included several multi-national realms, with Poland the most obvious, but these were not nations; the arrangements behind each Peace did not depend on national identity. The British Peace was truly multinational, but on the basis that lowland Scotland was similar enough to England for similar institutions and the highlands were simply repressed until they could be absorbed, while Ireland below the Anglicized ruling elite found its refuge in the Church. Otherwise, such experiences as in Cyprus, Yugoslavia and Israel/Palestine suggest that the binational nation is an invitation to trouble. But Switzerland on the other hand, by making a nation of a political instead of an ethnic culture, has become a very successfully institutionalized Peace, and French Canada has at times rejoiced in Canadian parliamentary institutions even more than some sections of British Canada. So one can hardly write off the Canadian Peace as predestined to failure.

As compared to other cases Canada again demonstrates the usefulness of a location away from the centers of development, in its case accentuated by the presence of a (during the Peace) friendly if somewhat overpowering neighbor. Prime Minister Trudeau has summed up the problems of such a relationship in his simile that Canada's situation is rather like sharing one's bed with an elephant: Necessarily you are aware of the presence of the beast, even if at the moment it doesn't happen to be pushing. The relationship has also served peace at large, with Canada acting as occasional intermediary between its next-door elephant and its old protector the lion, particularly in Mackenzie King's fabled ability during World War II to lubricate the rough, brittle and very large edges of the egos of Franklin Roosevelt and Winston Churchill. In the world of the 1980's there are very few places still on the edge of developments, and probably only the relatively empty north would still qualify even in Canada. But as of 1985 Canada will have achieved a century of peace—though no Royal Commission has been appointed to celebrate the occasion.

13

The Pacific Peace
(1788–   )

An Edge of Worlds

Just from its name, one might fondly hope the Pacific Ocean to include at least one good Peace. In fact it has so many, so closely interrelated, that the rule of contiguity is hereby invoked to include the whole lot under a single umbrella. All of them show a single central theme. In terms of sheer geographic area the Pacific Ocean should be the heartland of the world; even as an ocean it provides pathways between more different civilizations and ecologies than does any other geographic feature. But the vastness of the place overwhelms even its best-adapted people; if the ocean as a whole is an edge of many civilized worlds, it also divides Polynesia into such widely spread bits as to make it a world of edges. Geoffrey Blainey noted this factor specifically for Australia in his **The Tyranny of Distance,** and that same tyranny applies to every consideration within the Pacific Peace. It also imposes a certain necessity on this essay: There are so many individual developments that only a few can be studied in detail. Thus most attention is given Australia, New Zealand and Hawaii.

Origins

Australia and New Zealand can best be considered as a unit. The only immediately striking difference is Australia's tremendous distances, but in terms of communication time early New Zealand had the same problem; from far south to far north was a two-month journey. The major actual difference was in the native population. In Australia the aborigines were still essentially paleolithic, without agriculture or large cultural units; in New Zealand the Maori were for some decades the suppliers of the British colony. Australia could begin as a Peace; the aborigines were simply pushed aside, and while many of them were killed by Australians who wanted them out of the way, their skirmishes with armed settlers never became serious enough to provoke organized military reaction. In New Zealand the clash between the West and Polynesia brought in 11,000 imperial troops at the height of the war.

The war was essentially over just one problem. The Maori had the land; the British settlers wanted it. Due both to the increasing unwillingness of the Maori to sell and to the incompatibility of Maori and British concepts of property, this transfer process became increasingly strained. The war was set off primarily by a British official whose position in the bureaucracy depended on ever-continuing transfers, and who thus agreed even to transactions designed by Maori chiefs to cause trouble between the British and other chiefs claiming the same land. When in 1872 after 12 years of fighting the British government

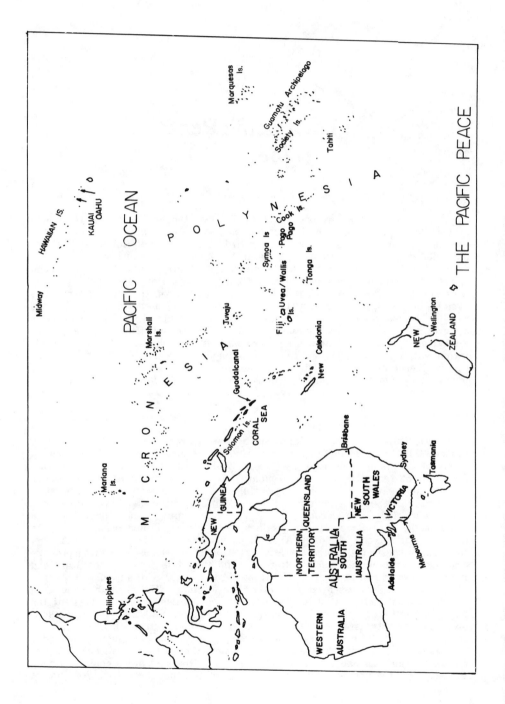

THE PACIFIC PEACE

investigated the matter, it was found so embarrassing that the claims committee adjourned without official findings and settled privately. But the war had definitely subjected the Maori. They were allotted four seats (out of more than seventy) in the New Zealander General Assembly; since this representation presumably gave them a voice in decisions they could then be looted at leisure. And since they were physically defeated and knew it, they turned to a program of peaceful adaptation of British material techniques while at the same time preserving such **Maoritanga**, Maori-ness, as was possible.

The Hawaiian Peace, on the other hand, began long before Western annexation, but under direct Western influence. The incoming sea captains were quite willing to sell arms to any local chief with the price of them, and Kamahameha I was the winner of the first Pacific arms race. His unification was, however, somewhat incomplete: The king of Kauai had submitted as a vassal, not been conquered, and when Kamehameha died in 1819 Kauai still retained its war-making capacity.

Theories aside, the new ruler of Hawaii was Kamehameha's widow Kaahumanu. She had the problem of being a woman, a major bar to power in Hawaiian thinking. But this same thinking revolved particularly around the system of **kapu,** taboos, and for decades Hawaiians had been watching visiting Westerners violate the **kapu** system in every possible way with no observable retribution. Some of them had taken to violating it in private, or would do so when drunk, or would forget it completely when visiting or working outside the kingdom. Kaahumanu arranged to discredit it publicly, and when those chiefs upholding the system revolted and were defeated, **kapu** was dead. Such other opposition as remained within the nobility was bought off by opening the lucrative sandalwood trade to the nobles, who quickly lost their conservative inhibitions in a wild spending spree. Then in 1824 the old king of Kauai died and Kauai revolted, was overwhelmed, and the Hawaiian civil wars were over.

Characterization

Australia and New Zealand began their share of the Peace with a tremendous advantage. Both are offshoots of the British Peace, which after more than three centuries had long since settled the basic peacekeeping institutions beyond even the possibility of question. Australians and New Zealanders thought of themselves as Britons overseas, and most conflicts that developed within the system were similar enough to those in Britain not to need separate discussion.

But Australia in particular did have its own individuality. The Australian Peace began as of colonization in 1788, but its basic institutions were by no means yet in place. British Australia was the result of one, possibly two, needs. British policy was to make convicts useful to the country, by sale into what amounted to term slavery. America had been the principal sales field, but the revolution and independence ended that, though the last shipment of convicts to America was as late as 1788. One experiment with a new site in Africa failed disastrously; a proposal for a second was not even tried. In 1786 London decided on Australia. The result was thus initially not a colony but a jail, possibly with the secondary purpose of naval support base.

Since Australia was to be a jail, its first governor was in effect a warden, not a parliamentary executive. This persisted for over three decades, during two of which the jail was run by the guards for their personal profit from a British subsidy. The fifth governor, Lachlan Macquarie (1810-1821), ended this corruption, reformed the administration, and restored the emphasis on penology, but with changes that inevitably led to the conversion of Australia into a more standard colony. He emphasized rehabilitation, bringing ex-convicts even into the government and treating them as free Britons. The actual colonists and especially the officers of the local garrison, products of a very class-conscious England and now located on a frontier where pretensions of aristocracy were at best very hard to maintain, rejected this absolutely and denounced Macquarie to London whenever possible. There seems even to have been some effort to penalize the descendants of convicts. Macquarie's emphasis on rehabilitation led to more humane treatment, such that supposedly convicts in Britain were asking to be sent to Australia in place of officially more lenient sentences. But in the long run most important, on 7 May 1815 Macquarie founded the first settlement on the far side of the coastal mountains, beginning the movement into the vast plains of interior Australia. During his governorship one of the ex-guards returned from England with an improved variety of sheep to pasture on these plains, and the British textile factories were beginning an expansion that needed geometrically increasing quantities of wool. Wool was the foundation of self-supporting Australia, the real basis on which the jail became a colony with unimpeachable claim as a self-supporting entity to be also self-governing, the resource which could expand to swallow a continent. By 1850 the coast from Brisbane to Adelaide was occupied 200 miles and more deep by the pastoralists. Civilization had arrived on sheepback.

For thirty years these two factors, convicts and sheep, were the keys to internal Australian development (except in South Australia, which was never a convict settlement and had an early emphasis on grain). At times the pastoralists were even ahead of the official explorers. It was a bumptious life, with the low population density characteristic of pastoralism being complimented by a disrespect for authority, especially British authority, predictable from convicts, ex-convicts and their descendants of whom a fourth came from Ireland. Policemen in particular might well have applied for protection by the game laws. But the pastoralists wanted cheap, easily managed labor, which particularly meant convict labor, and once they had it they expanded so quickly that the government gave up on registry of landholdings and simply issued licenses to pasture. The pastoralists would then squat on unused land, provide minimum wages and working conditions to their hired or convict shepherds, and (with a great deal of administrative capacity, hard work and sheer luck) grow rich. These squatters and their attitudes were so clearly in charge that people described the situation as a "squattocracy." By mid-century they could apply enough pressure, backed up in this respect by most of the rest of Australia, that the four oldest colonies were granted self-government. But no sooner had they won this than their neatly ordered world was dealt a tremendous blow. As one of them commented on the disasters of 1851, it was a horrible year: first drought, then floods, then to crown all, gold!

The Australian gold rush changed many things. The old problem of ex-convict versus free settler was simply washed out of existence by a flood of immigrants from everywhere. The convict system itself was smashed; some were sent to Western Australia as late as 1868, but in general the parliamentarians in London decided it would be less than timely to make the second worst punishment in Britain, free transportation to a gold rush. With the vast injection of capital there was much other expansion, and wool, if still king, saw quite a few other contenders rising. In effect the gold rush began just in time to insure that the squattocracy would not monopolize the new representative institutions, and since the constitutions of the colonies could be changed by simple majority vote, universal male suffrage became the rule in Australia while it was still just an agitator's dream in Britain.

It remained to adapt British parliamentarism to the peculiar circumstances of Australia and New Zealand. Part of this was a general process of the industrializing world: The workingmen had concerns alien to traditional society, and traditional society reacted to unionism and strikes with repression, especially in Australia. Labor complained after one strike that the only difference between Government and Opposition was that Government sent in the Gatling guns and Opposition denounced them for not doing it soon enough. Towards 1890 labor became Labor, moving into politics with their own candidates and introducing the revolutionary principle of party discipline. Previously politicians had been elected mostly on personal qualities, primarily charm and an expertise at raiding the public treasury in their constituents' interests. Beginning in 1890 there were dependably cohesive voting blocks in each legislature, able at first to act as a balance of power and later to form governments in their own right. Labor had found a peaceful means of influence, and in New Zealand particularly this caused such early social reform that the country became known as a kind of laboratory of the left, of a "socialism without doctrines."

The only remaining potentially peace-threatening problem was the adaptation of British parliamentarism to a congeries of colonies whose actions were beginning to impact on each other. New Zealand had this problem from the beginning, being a country of small population cut up by mountains into isolated settlements. The answer in its constitutional arrangements of 1852 had been a quasi-federation, a principle so alien to British tradition that the provinces came to be governed by "superintendents." But New Zealand rapidly grew together, and in 1874, with all but one of the provinces lapsing into a permanent insolvency that required federal subsidy even for day-to-day operations, the provinces were simply abolished in favor of a British unitary government.

But in Australia the colonies were the unitary governments, with only occasional and almost unheard whispers of a larger entity. By the 1880's these whispers became much louder, some for an Australian federation, some for an Australasian federation including New Zealand and Fiji, some for an Imperial Federation of all the parliamentary states of the British Empire, a project particularly cherished in New Zealand. In the event, in 1900, it was federation for Australia alone, with New South Wales a last stubborn holdout that eventually acquiesced. Since then there have been loud complaints of growing central power, that the states have been left "without a feather to fly with," but overall the situation seems most comparable to that of the United States before the Civil War. At least in the early years the two largest states, New South Wales and Victoria, could in agreement have dominated Australia, but they have very seldom found anything on which they agree. The other states have also emphatically cultivated their own identities. Western Australia even voted two to one in a 1933 plebiscite to secede from the federation, a secession overruled by London on a technicality, and has made further noises about secession as recently as 1981. In the early 1970s a Labor federal government found itself negotiating with each of the states in turn on terms for a federally-sponsored health plan, and when negotiations were completed the plan looked rather little more than an agreement for the federal government to hand out money and the states to receive it. Otherwise the closest thing to a crisis in recent Australian and New Zealander history occurred in 1975: the Governor-General of Australia, being titular chief executive as representing the Queen, actually used his theoretical authority and turned out an elected government. But the change was validated by the electorate, and after much sound and fury the crisis was forgotten. Peace in Australia and New Zealand seems quite safe.

Thus by 1901 the problems of peace had moved from the domestic to the foreign scene. This had been a long time coming. As long before as 1853 France had annexed New Caledonia, but Britain was allied to France and so ignored Australian concern. In the 1870's Germany began moving in and in 1883 Queensland colony in Australia even tried to pre-empt German expansion into New Guinea, but Britain wanted no trouble with Germany and so invalidated the annexation. In 1902-1905 Japan became a Pacific power, alarming Australia even more, but Britain was negotiating a treaty with Japan and so again ignored Australian concern. When in 1914 Britain went to war, Australia and New Zealand considered themselves automatically at war also. Young Australians and New Zealanders went off to defend the empire, but anything Gallipoli did not teach about modern warfare was hammered in relentlessly by the nightmare endlessness of the insatiable trenches. Australia lost three-quarters more dead in World War I than in World War II; New Zealand had a death rate per capita six times that of Belgium, where the war was partly fought. Still, this was a European war; Australia and New Zealand remained safe at the far edge of the world. When in 1931 the Statute of Westminster gave the dominions full control of their foreign affairs, Australia did not even bother to ratify it until 1942, New Zealand not until 1947. Likewise New Zealand did not bother with a Department (not yet a ministry) of External Affairs until 1943; in 1934 the Australian Department of External Affairs still had a total staff of two.

In 1941 the world arrived; Pearl Harbor was followed by a Japanese assault towards Australia and New Zealand. Their forward mobile defense against Japan centered on two British capital ships off Southeast Asia; on 10 December 1941 Japan sank them both. The outer defense line was impregnable Singapore: On 15 February 1942 Japan took it, with 15,000 Australian prisoners. The inner defense line was Indonesia; during January and February Japan overran that, while Australian troops were still arriving to defend it. Only the southeast coast of New Guinea still stood, and on 19 February 1942 the first Japanese bombers hit Australia.

This, as matters developed, was the high-water mark of the Japanese flood, and the Australian Peace was not significantly broken. One may wonder whether this was sheer luck; certainly Australia and New Zealand did their share of the fighting in World War II, but if any of four hotly fought battles (Coral Sea, Midway, New Guinea, Guadalcanal) had gone the other way, there might have been need to test Churchill's promise to abandon even the Mediterranean if need be to provide troops and ships to repel an invasion of Australia. Nevertheless for the moment Australia and New Zealand remain well out on the periphery of all but the largest catastrophes, so foreign affairs should also provide no great threat in the immediate future.

Regarding next the societies and cultures produced by this Peace, with England's stiff class system replaced by the sense of achievement by actual accomplishment that is characteristic of frontiers, both Australia and New Zealand almost immediately became profoundly egalitarian. The rampant individualism characteristic of early Australia became rather more disciplined after the frontier of usable land was reached in the 1870's, and nowadays it is as much a fond tradition as an actuality—so to speak a "bunyip larrikinism," a just-pretend impulse to troublemaking, exercised in lighter moments to prove it is still there or just as a good excuse for breaking loose. Contrariwise, the convict life and then the frontier produced a widespread sense of cooperation against an overwhelming environment, "matiness" or "mateship," that as mutual loyalty became a mainstay of the union movement and still remains characteristic. New Zealand, built on a smaller scale and without the convict influence, became self-consciously more British than the British, with some sense that the remaining population of England was mainly an underfed underclass without the gumption to migrate to New Zealand.

Culturally Australia and New Zealand were for a long time dependent on Britain. Many talented people, such as Lord Rutherford, Katherine Mansfield and Sylvia Ashton Warner, felt they had to go to Europe for fullest exercise of their talents, and the cultural product of the colonies tended much more towards imitative formality than creativity. But there have been home developments: Rolf Boldrewood (T.A. Browne), a leading novelist of the nineteenth-century middle class; Steele Rudd, a frontier humorist. Patrick White's post-

Hemingway realism won a Nobel Prize; Morris West's novels of the Vatican and Catholic life have reached onto the world scene. In the last few years Australian films have also become well known. Culturally too, although the colonial years on the edge of the Western world remain a reservoir of useful themes, Australia and New Zealand appear to have entered the world at large.

This study now moves to Hawaii, the remaining major region of the Pacific Peace. The Hawaiian civil wars were over as of 1824, but there remained the problem of the onrushing West. To some extent Kaahumanu embraced the West, formally converting Hawaii to a strict missionary Protestantism that became the new official religion of the kingdom. But this did not stop the onrush. In 1839 a French warship forced the government to stop persecution of the Catholics; at other times partial French and British occupations were ended only when the home governments repudiated their naval officers' actions. Moreover the Hawaiian ability to resist was crumbling. By the 1840's the old Hawaiian nobility, the **ali'i,** had become a non-functional appendage of the state and the people at large were becoming an amorphous group still loyal to whatever course the monarchy chose but largely excluded from it. Kamehameha III (1824-1854) reorganized the kingdom root and branch, thereby providing at least an immediate accomodation to Western interests in plantation agriculture, but in effect only the monarchy remained of what had been Hawaii, and it was employing foreigners even in ministerial posts.

The great threat was from the United States. As early as the 1840's the Tyler Doctrine proclaimed Hawaii free of all foreign intervention except America's, and in 1853 Kamehameha III felt constrained to negotiate a treaty of annexation, though he died before it could be completed. The economy came more and more into American hands, and the Americans came more and more to dislike the possibility that the monarchy might end this. When in 1893 the new queen showed every sign of doing exactly that, they constituted themselves "the intelligent part of the community" and took over the government. When later a botched counter-revolution resulted in the capture of some 200 loyalists, they gave the queen a choice between formal abdication and the mass execution of her captured supporters, and police raids, with some allegations of torture, were launched against other potential opposition. The only reported deaths totalled three. One may at least say that the old order died peaceably.

A change of administration and policy in Washington delayed formal annexation until 1898, but this made little real difference. As of 1893 Hawaii was an aristocratic republic; indeed it became so classical an example as to resemble protohistoric India right down to the caste system. At the top were the **haoles,** some 5% of the population, mixed American, north European and Hawaiian in descent and thoroughly and self-consciously American in culture. At the top of the top were what might be styled the **haole ali'i,** mostly descendants of American missionaries and Hawaiian **ali'i;** 70% of the key officers in the new government belonged to this core group, and their careful attention to genealogy and the **kapus** of social convention would have been recognized instantly by the old order. In the second layer were the remaining commoner Hawaiians, fast declining due to disease and intermarriage, plus the, so to speak, commoner immigrants. In an intermediate layer were Latin European immigrants, mostly Portuguese, who acted as day-to-day supervisers of the lower orders. At the bottom were some three-quarters of the population, Orientals imported for plantation labor in huge numbers: By 1890 the population of Hawaii was over half Japanese and almost a quarter Chinese. Then when America annexed the Philippines, the plantation owners added a hundred thousand Filipino laborers as well. This does not seem a brew for peace.

But Hawaii was now American, and American practice dictated that certain sociopolitical forms be followed. Government by hereditary aristocracy had to be somehow disguised. This was possible. There was a voting population, but for three decades the more or less Hawaiians had an outright majority, and they voted as their recognized chiefs told them to vote. Therefore their recognized chiefs were carefully cultivated into the system. Beyond this, Hawaii was essentially an export monoculture (sugar), with most second-rank businesses also being of plantation or associated commercial nature, almost all owned by the **haole ali'i**. The ballot, however secret in theory, was closely watched in practice, and people kept or lost their jobs depending on their votes. The **haole ali'i** then constituted themselves the leadership of the islands' Republican Party, a recognized American institution, and agreed on candidates before the elections. Democratic Party organizers found it prudent in many places to work only at night. Presumably this massively interlocked directorate could have been overthrown by intervention from Washington, but Hawaii was far away and very different, and even territorial governors appointed by Democratic presidents tended to stay within the system. For sixty years it worked.

There were strains. The system assumed that the lower orders would accept their subordinate position and remain resident foreigners. The Japanese particularly did this. But Hawaii was now American, with all the American cultural emphasis on individual self-improvement and social mobility. The children even of the Japanese began absorbing this, as well as picking up values from the other ethnic groups, speaking a Japanese larded with Hawaiianisms that startled the old folks back home. The ethnic compartments proved as watertight as so many sponges. Intermarriage was only the most blatant expression of this, and by the 1950's some one-third of all marriages in Hawaii were more or less mixed. Every ethnic group had its own collection of jokes, insults and stereotypes about every other ethnic group, and the haoles in particular erupted in hysterical racism over occasional specific incidents, but the peaceable tolerance of the old Hawaiians set the standard. Ethnic lynchings were very rare, ethnic riots unknown. In this fluid society only a catalyst was needed to bring about major change, and on 7 December 1941 it arrived. More than battleships was sunk at Pearl Harbor. With lower-order Hawaiians, including Japanese, serving with distinction in American units in World War II, with the GI bill of rights providing college educations on the mainland to Hawaiians who could never otherwise have afforded them, with the whole economy beginning to diversify, the old aristocratic republic tottered and finally, in the 1950's, collapsed. For almost thirty years now, Hawaii has moved freely within the flexible American two-party system, and shows every sign of continuing that way.

Space limitations preclude detailed discussion, but some mention should be made of the many small areas elsewhere in the Pacific Ocean where peace arrived in the nineteenth century and has stayed to date. This means effectively all of Polynesia plus partly Polynesian Fiji and Melanesian New Caledonia and the New Hebrides. Only Samoa technically does not qualify, since its last (and bloody) civil war was as recent as 1899. For easy labelling this will be called the Polynesian Peace, covering at least dozens and arguably a hundred separate situations. But there are common themes.

The natural condition of both Polynesia and Melanesia was war. Yet the colonial period has been an age of peace. The natural assumption is that colonial rule means peace, but this is too simplistic: France took New Caledonia in 1853 and a revolt there in 1878 massacred whole settlements of Europeans. Nor, by and large, did the Europeans simply sail in, hoist a flag or two, shoot a few natives, and call it peace. First they had to convince the natives.

This proved a remarkably quick process in almost all instances, for two reasons. One was simply that war was not fun any more. Where previously it had been a man-to-man affair in which individual prowess gave victory and prestige, the advent of firearms meant that any half-grown adolescent could end the career of a warrior of vast experience and standing, and from such a distance that the adolescent could not even claim personal credit. Moreover, those chiefs who appreciated the new situation could turn themselves into real warlords, introducing massacre on a scale that made everyone from high chief to serf very aware that the old days were gone forever. War had become big business.

Second was the immediate ruin of the old religion. The Polynesian worldview may best be described as magical: Gods, men, weather, crops, everything was bound in an intricate and indissoluble network in which observance of religiously sanctioned ritual connected all the parts, keeping them in balance. The West brought a whole new set of parts, and Polynesia and Melanesia simply had no place for them. The old Polynesian god of disease had no power over European germs, and pandemics slaughtered whole populations. The god of war was helpless against firearms, and as for wealth, if Polynesia was civilization **au naturel,** the West was civilization **de luxe,** bringing desirable commodities in such quantity and variety that whole new religions, the so-called cargo cults, were founded to bring the goodies in magically and continued to be founded as late as World War II. Their own conditioned worldview made the Pacific islanders look to the Western religion as the ritually magical control system behind all this, and Christian missionaries were only too willing to enlighten the heathen and stand as advisers on all the proper applications of Christianity. In many cases they went rather too far; nineteenth-century nationalism combined with Christian certitude to convince many missionaries that the customs of their particular Caucasian tribe did indeed rank with the Bible as the ordained law of the universe. If on first look the Polynesians accepted this uncritically, on second look the flaws in the assumption did appear, and a process of elimination and adaptation created missionary states run by rather more tolerant and secular missionaries. But once the remaining heathen had been dealt with by whatever means were convenient, and excepting an occasional bout between Catholic and Protestant bearers of the faith, one point was universally taught: War was not a fit activity for Christians, it was an offense against God and would disrupt the new order of things. While in the old days war had been a very positive concept, reasonably safe and potentially very rewarding, the new system made it as least as strongly negative. And so it gradually ended.

There was also a major external input. If Europe was an overwhelming factor in Pacific affairs, the Pacific was not nearly as important to Europe. There were germs of conflict, but considerations nearer home always supervened. Thus when in 1842 France proclaimed a protectorate over the (British) missionary kingdom of Tahiti, public opinion in both Britain and France raised a real war scare, but the foreign ministries were too concerned with Anglo-French cooperation against the autocracies of eastern Europe to let Tahiti be a problem. Likewise in the 1880s disputes among Britain, Germany and the United States over each others' positions in Samoa escalated to the point that all three sent flotillas to the islands, but Bismarck was already backing off in favor of settling matters by international conference when a providential hurricane wrecked the American and German ships and with them the chance of immediate confrontation. In World War I German vessels put some 100 shells into Pape'ete, Tahiti, killing two people, before steaming on to depredations nearer home; in World War II a Japanese submarine put four shells into Pago Pago, American Samoa, injuring one man on a bicycle. But those are what count as major incidents. By and large the Pacific was simply so remote from exterior concerns that the more common situation was as in 1938, when the United States, looking for staging bases, sent an occupation force to Canton Atoll and found the British already there. The two occupation forces compromised: They would share out the beer, and leave it to Washington and London to share out the island. And so it went.

Thus the basic situation. But if the Western powers made a point of reasonably amicable division of the spoils, this was not to mean that the Pacific islands were any less treated as just that, spoils. The colonial expansion of the middle 1800s was the death warrant of the missionary kingdoms. France was the first offender in the field, seizing the Marquesas and Tahiti as commercial and naval stations regardless of the legalities of sovereignty involved. But if partition and annexation were to be the fate of the Pacific islands, the prior existence of the missionary kingdoms made it a generally peaceful transition. There were already Europeans, the missionaries, in key positions in the kingdoms; the colonial powers needed only substitute their own agents, with no drastic changes in public appearances. There were exceptions: Samoa was a merry anarchy and remained so until 1899, with each Western contender trying to establish its own favorite Samoan faction in a figurehead monarchy while the factions happily played the Westerners off against each for support, at one point even militarily defeating a German force sent to rationalize the situation. France ended going the farthest in assimilation, largely pushing aside the Melanesians in New Caledonia in favor of government by mining enterprise and turning Tahiti into a market economy that left little place for the old chiefly subsistence system (but leaving the third French Pacific possession, Uvea/Wallis and Futuna, under the old chiefly government). British policy tended toward increasing reorganization of its colonies on British lines until World War I, then reversed course toward increasing native participation in the new institutions. Everywhere the new churches provided new channels for competition and prestige.

By consensus the Great Experiment of the area has been the kingdom of Tonga. Unlike everywhere else in the Pacific, Tonga was not merely a collection of localisms on which a rather creaky superstructure had been erected within living memory. Tonga had an imperial tradition involving at least Fiji and Samoa, possibly Uvea/Wallis and arguably Mangaia in the Cook Islands, and dating back almost a thousand years. Whatever peace and unity had been achieved earlier were disrupted in the early nineteenth century by the introduction of firearms, but the winner of this warlord competition proved a most exceptional man. King George Tupou I (1845-1893) converted the young to missionary Christianity and allied with a most exceptional missionary, the more or less Reverend Shirley Waldemar Baker. The partnership of these two is a source of endless controversy, but it created the one and only Polynesian missionary kingdom to survive the Western onslaught and remain intact today. George Tupou I and Baker did this with a constitutional system which, if it did not magically and instantly transform Tonga into a junior edition of a European great power, did create a government both recognized as such by the Europeans and flexible enough to accommodate the subordinate Tongan chiefs and the people to the realities of change. Power belonged to the king, but less by fiat than by careful adjustment. Besides the predictably central position of the missionary church there were two key elements. For the sake of the people in general, not just theoretical ownership but practical control of the land was centralized in the Crown, and alienation to foreigners was made not just illegal but unconstitutional. Land could not even be leased to foreigners if any Tongan stood in need of it. In effect every potential head of household was guaranteed the means of support of his family. Beyond this, George Tupou I used his acquired warlord power to reorder Tongan society, but conservatively, with traditional forms carefully maintained. Serfdom was abolished and all Tongans became free; on the other hand, hereditary nobility remained firmly in place, and the hereditary nobles were very powerful in both the first two reigns. Finally, every available support, both traditional and imported, was marshalled for the legitimacy of the new Western-style Crown. The situation was not perfect; George Tupou II (1893-1918) proved so incompetent that Britain found itself with grounds to establish a protectorate. But British interference generally remained specific and limited, and as Queen Salote Tupou III (1918-1965) reunited the realm behind the throne the British gradually withdrew.

And so came the major development in the Pacific area in recent years. Half of World War II was the Pacific War, and if the Japanese never reached the Peace area, the Americans certainly did. What had been mostly a low-level coconut economy, further thrown back by the Depression, was suddenly the rear area for an oceanic offensive culminating in the atomic age. What with jet airliners and communications satellites the world has no more edges, and the Polynesian Peace has felt the changes much more than the already wealthy and technically advanced countries. Medical advances have been particularly important; collapsing death rates have meant skyrocketing populations, in some of the smallest, most constricted land areas in the world. For the moment a classical Malthusian challenge is being held off by tourism, government services, temporary work abroad, and outright emigration. There are other local challenges, but with the possible exception of a major ethnic problem in Fiji none appear to be any immediate threat to the Peace. If Polynesia of the atomic age is not quite the idyllic South Seas of fond Western legend, it at least far surpasses most of the other new countries of the postcolonial world.

Reflections

The Pacific Peace makes one point loud and clear: It can be a very good thing to be unwanted. A location on the edge of the world means a certain lack of interest and neglect by outsiders, but when the outsiders are as predatory as the West has frequently been, this is the loneliness of the lamb after the departure of his neighbor the lion.

It also helps to have ready-made Peace systems. Every part of the Pacific Peace benefited from this in some degree; it made Australia and was decisive in New Zealand and Hawaii, and made modernization much easier in the rest of Polynesia. It is probably superfluous that, after some initial excesses, these imported Peace systems proved readily adaptable to local conditions; adaptability is a characteristic of successful Peace systems. Whether this adaptability will extend to the much greater complexities brought in by the late twentieth century, remains to be seen.

14

Settings

The "setting" of a Peace is the political and physical environment in which peace occurs. There are a number of possible classifications, but the following seem pertinent:

Power Relationship. What is the setting of the Peace with relation to its neighbors? Is it surrounded by great powers, or relatively isolated? If surrounded, does it possess enough power to influence its setting?

Centrality. Is the peaceful society protected by land or sea barriers, or by difficult terrain?

Climate. Does the peaceful society have a tropical, temperate or subarctic climate?

Autonomy. Is the government of the peaceful society located within that society, or is it controlled by a government that is located elsewhere?

Prevailing Military Situation. Is the prevailing situation in the setting one of general peace or of general war?

The settings of each of the peace periods, and sometimes sub-peace periods, are summarized in Table 2. There are 12 cases, but these can be expanded to 21 if we count the major subregions that had some autonomy and often different dates.

Beginning with power relationships, then, three basic situations seem to occur.

1. Isolations. Situations in which the peaceful society does not interact much with and is little threatened by external societies, e.g. Australia.

2. Interpower Relationships. Situations in which the government of the peaceful society has sufficient power to exert major influence on interstate relations in the configuration in which it exists, e.g. Poland.

3. Interstice Relationships. Situations in which the government of the peaceful society has little power to influence interstate relations in the configuration in which it exists, e.g. Switzerland.

In a Peace containing more than one state the separate states may have different settings. Sometimes the setting changes over time. Sometimes a government's immediate setting is different from its greater setting. Scandinavia and Costa Rica had the power to influence the setting immediately around them, but not Europe or Latin America respectively. Hawaii was initially isolated like Australia and New Zealand, but technological development placed it in an interstice situation by World War II.

Looking at the major cases, seven were in interpower situations, four were in interstice settings and only one was isolated. If the sub-cases are included, however, the number of interstice relationships goes from nine to twelve, and the isolated to four or five. It does not appear that any of these three situations is essential to peace.

There are on the list, however, no dominant powers, those like the France

TABLE 2. SETTINGS

Peace	Sub-Peace	Power Relationship	Autonomy	Location	Physical Barriers	Climate	General Wars
Venetian		Interpower	Yes	Central	Water	Temperate	None
Hungarian		Interpower	Yes	Central	None	Temperate	None
Polish		Interpower	Yes	Central	None	Temperate	None
Brandenburger		Interstice	Yes	Central	None	Temperate	Thirty Years
Spanish Imperial	(Iberian)	Interpower	Yes	Peripheral	Mountains	Temperate	Thirty Years, Napoleonic*
	American	Isolated	No		Terrain	Tropical	
British	(English)	Interpower	Yes	Peripheral	Water	Temperate	Napoleonic, World*
	Scottish	Interstice	No		None/Water		Napoleonic, World*
	Irish	Interstice			Water		Napoleonic, World
Scandinavian	Swedish	Interpower/Interstice	Yes	Peripheral	Water	Sub-Arctic	Napoleonic, World
	Danish	Interpower/Interstice	Yes	Peripheral/Central	None	Temperate	Napoleonic*
	Finnish	Interstice	No	Peripheral	Water/terrain	Sub-Arctic	World*
	Norwegian	Interstice	No/Yes	Peripheral	Water/terrain	Sub-Arctic	World*
	Icelandic	Isolated	No/Yes	Peripheral	Water/distance	Sub-Arctic	Thirty Years, Napoleonic, World
Swiss		Interstice	Yes	Central	Mountains/terrain	Temperate	World
Brazilian		Interpower	No/Yes	Central	Jungle	Tropical	None
Costa Rican		Interpower/Interstice	Yes	Central	Water	Tropical	World
Canadian		Interstice	No/Yes	Peripheral	None/water	Sub-Arctic	World
Pacific	Australian	Isolated	No/Yes	Peripheral	Water/Distance	Temperate	World
	New Zealander	Isolated	No/Yes	Peripheral	Water/Distance	Temperate	World
	Hawaiian	Isolated/Interstice	Yes/No	Central	Water	Semi-Tropical	World
	Polynesian	Interstice	No	Peripheral	Water	Semi-Tropical	World

*War contributes to termination of peace.

of Louis XIV or Napoleon, that were clearly the greatest power of the times, the one to which other major powers principally reacted.

Another way of looking at location with relation to others is to ask whether the peaceful society was located in the center of political activity or at the periphery. Switzerland, for instance, is considered remarkable because it has maintained peace while being in the very center of European activity. The Scandinavian countries are considered to have an advantage because they are at the periphery, out of the main line of activity.

Among the twelve major cases, six seem to be on the periphery of a system. The British Isles, the Scandinavian countries and the Iberian Peninsula are at the periphery of the European state system. Spanish and Portuguese holdings in Latin America were at the periphery of a Caribbean center and Canada was at the periphery of American interaction in the nineteenth and twentieth centuries. The nations involved in the Pacific Peace were at the periphery of world activity, except for Hawaii, which was peripheral to two systems.

But Hungary, Poland, Brandenburg and Switzerland were in the heart of the European system. Venice was in the center of a bicivilizational system surrounding the Adriatic. Brazil was in the center of the South American system in the past two centuries and Costa Rica, though peripheral to South America, was in the middle of Central America. Thus it appears that if peripheral location does provide an advantage, it is not crucial; nations in central locations also can achieve long periods of peace.

Another factor sometimes mentioned with reference to peace is the presence of physical barriers. Those that occurred within the cases considered here are mountain barriers, difficult terrain, water barriers and sheer distance.

In five cases there seem to have been no significant barriers that would have prevented or discouraged invasion: Hungary, Poland, Brandenburg, Canada (vis-a-vis the United States), and Denmark.

In five there were significant water barriers: the Venetian, British, Scandinavian, Costa Rican, and Pacific.

There were mountain barriers in two: the Swiss Alps and the Iberian Pyrenees.

Difficult terrain protected three: the forests of Sweden and Finland and the jungle of Hispanic America and Brazil.

Distance was a factor for Canada (vis-a-vis Europe) as well as Australia and New Zealand during World War II, and perhaps for Iceland in earlier periods.

All of these physical factors played a role at one time or another, and some may have been decisive in some circumstances in preserving peace. Still, peace was preserved for long periods in Poland, Brandenburg and Hungary despite the absence of either a peripheral location or any kind of physical barrier.

Generally climate does not appear to have been a factor, except that northern countries like Canada and the Scandinavian countries may have been less attractive to invade. The malarial heat of Costa Rica, on the other hand, does not appear to have been a deterrent to other Central American countries invading one another and did not deter the United States from intervening in Central American affairs.

During the medieval period of Western history, war was recurrent, but never general. During the modern period there were three periods of general war of special duration and intensity: the Thirty Years War (1618-1648), the Napoleonic Wars (1793-1815) and the World Wars. The wars of Louis XIV (1672-1715) might have been included but were not.

Ten of the twelve cases existed at least partly in modern times and but one of these, the Polish, existed during one of the general wars. Of these, the Brandenburger was ended by the Thirty Years War, the Spanish Imperial by the Napoleonic Wars and the British by the World Wars. It also could be argued that the British were not involved in the Thirty Years War because their peace was at the time being interrupted by the English Revolution, or that the English Revolution was part of the Thirty Years War.

But a number of the peaceful societies survived one of the general wars without interruption to the peace. The Spanish Imperial was not terminated by the Thirty Years War, the British, Scandinavian and Brazilian survived the Napoleonic Wars, and the Scandinavian, Swiss, Brazilian, Costa Rican, Canadian and Pacific peace periods all were uninterrupted by the World Wars. All of these, however, except the Swiss, were peripheral rather than central in relation to their respective systems. So it would appear that a relatively peaceful general situation is not essential to peace.

One question arises from this consideration of war/peace settings. Which is more common, peace or war? This study of one thousand years has turned up only a dozen peace periods. If we had been more diligent, or had counted all our sub-periods as separate, we might have found two dozen. By contrast, studies done by Sorokin (1937), Singer and Small (1969), and Bouthoul and Carrere (1978) list hundreds of wars over the past three centuries. There has hardly been a year in that period when a war has not been going on somewhere.

Yet (and so far no one has done this), if one were to make a schematized chart showing all the centuries vertically, and all the land territories of the world horizontally, and then to color black all the periods of war delineated by our war scholars and all the violent revolutions that have occurred in the same period (if anyone has researched that), it is almost certain that the chart would be basically white, with black spots and blotches here and there. Most of the time most countries are not enduring wars or violent revolutions in their home territories. As such a study becomes increasingly smaller in scale the problem arises of the proper factoring in of individual and small-group acts of violence. But some impression remains that peace is normal, violence exceptional.

In this chapter we have considered settings with relation to other powers, centrality of location, physical barriers and terrain, climate, autonomy, and presence or absence of general wars. It seems that the presence or absence of any of these political or physical conditions is not essential to the preservation of peace.

15

Origins

By definition peace originates out of conflict. A period of war and/or rebellion ends, and out of the terms of settlement, peace emerges.

Rebellions are more common than wars in history, so it is not surprising that they are more common in conflicts that lead to peace. In the twelve core areas of peace, only three had their beginnings in the termination of war: the Polish victory over the Teutonic Knights at Tannenburg, the defeat of the Dutch in Brazil, and the thwarting of the Morazan invasion in Costa Rica.

In nine cases the peace begins with the termination of an internal struggle. Five of these were rebellions which ended in the suppression of the rebellion by the government that was to establish peace: the suppression of the last town rebellions by the Elector of Brandenburg, the suppression of the counter-revolution in Neuchatel by the Swiss government, of Riel's Rebellion in Saskatchewan by the Canadian government and of the Kauaian Rebellion by the Hawaiian government. The fifth rebellion, the Flabanico uprising in Venice, was successful, and the rebels initiated the peace.

Three of the internal conflicts were civil wars: the Arpad Succession struggle in Hungary, which brought the Angevin monarchs to power, the Wars of the Roses, which ended with the accession of the Tudors in England, and the Castilian civil wars. The Icelandic feuds may or may not have been civil wars.

Bringing in the subcases somewhat modifies the pattern. Four of these began with internal conflicts: the pro-Stuart rebellions at different times in Ireland and Scotland, the Maori War in New Zealand, the anarchy of Regency Brazil. The New Zealander conflict could be classified as a civil war.

Subcase wars include those with the Indians in Spanish America, Norway's Hanseatic War, the Great Northern War, the Swedish invasion of Denmark, and the Russian invasion of Finland. The Indians were repelled or seduced; the Russians were successful; the Swedes and Hanseatic League were successful but withdrew.

Table 3 considers the origins of peace from the standpoint of the conflicts out of which peace began.

The variety of kinds of conflict preceding the peace periods is much more striking than the common elements. Of the 21 origins, 13 came from internal conflict, eight from interpower war. But the internal conflicts included every imaginable kind: rebellions, civil wars, dynastic wars, government suppression and feudal skirmishing. The rebellions included the nobility rebelling against the Crown and nationalists against the state; the civil wars included succession struggles, indigenous against immigrants, and some conditions that seem describable only as anarchy. The external wars were not always state against state, but sometimes involved settlers against indigenous populations and once against a kind of Caesar (Morazan).

Usually the makers of the peace are the victors in the war, but even

TABLE 3
THE ORIGINS OF PEACE

Peace of Sub Peace	Last Conflict	Type of Conflict
Venetian	Flabanico Uprising	Rebellion
Hungarian	Arpad Succession Struggle	Civil War
Polish	Battle of Tannenburg	Interpower War
Brandenburger	Town Rebellions against John Cicero	Rebellion
Spanish Imperial		
Iberian	Castilian Civil Wars	Government Suppression
Spanish America	(Various) Indian Wars	Interpower War
British		
English	War of the Roses	Civil War
Irish	Pro-Stuart Rebellions	Rebellion
Scottish	Pro-Stuart Rebellions	Rebellion
Swiss	Neuchatel Rebellion	Rebellion
Scandinavian		
Icelandic	Family Feuds	Feudal Conflict
Norwegian	Hanseatic War	Interpower War
Danish	Swedish Invasion	Interpower War
Swedish	Great Northern War	Interpower War
Finnish	Russian Invasion	Interpower War
Brazilian	Dutch Colonial Wars	Interpower War
Costa Rican	Morazan Invasion	Interpower War
Canadian	Riel's Rebellion	Rebellion
Pacific		
Hawaiian	Kauaian Rebellion	Rebellion
New Zealander	Maori War	Civil War
Australian	None	None
Polynesian	Various Invasions	Mostly Interpower War

that rule applies badly in Scandinavia, where the Norwegians, Swedes and Danes made peace out of defeat, and the Icelanders and Finns could not be described as victors.

It appears, then, that so long as conflict does not involve continuing basic constitutional issues, it may be resolved into a successful Peace. Anything less—positions of groups within an accepted framework, or extirpation of one side of a basic conflict—can be settled by acceptance of a mechanism for adjusting these disputes peacefully. It is therefore the nature of the peace rather than the nature of the war (beyond irreconcilable conflicts) that determines whether peace will endure.

It may be, also, that different results would have been obtained if we had looked not only at the conflict preceding the peace, but at the entire contexts of the situation preceding peace. These differ immensely, however. Sometimes, as in the case of Canada, the story of origins is half the story of the peace. Other times, as in the case of Poland, a single act of diplomacy suddenly creates a situation in which peace is possible.

16

Leadership

The heroes of peace do not stand out as do the heroes of war. Most of the centuries of peace we have described have not even been so perceived, so those who contributed to them are not perceived as peacemakers, though they may be regarded as important figures in the bringing of order and stability.

In the modern democracies, leadership is decentralized and often exercised for only a short period, so that Britain, Scandinavia, Switzerland, Canada and the Pacific powers are not likely to have a great man around to impose his name on an age. The nearest we can come to that is a woman, Victoria, who was not remarkable but lived a long time, and gave her name to a period that in retrospect looks peaceful, though lasting less than a century.

Where monarchies exist, often there is a single person who did impose his viewpoint on a society, and whose leadership clearly did make a difference when the peace period was being formed. Charles Robert of Hungary, Ferdinand and Isabella of Spain and Henry VII of England clearly played such a role. Others performed similar functions after the basic situation had been set for them by someone else: Ladislas II in Poland following Casimir the Great; Frederick II and Albert Achilles following Frederick I in Brandenburg; Kaahumanu and Kamehameha III following Kamehameha I in Hawaii. You could compare to them the role of Alfred Escher and Jacob Stampfli in making a Swiss constitutional system work after the earlier leadership of Henry Dufour and Jonas Furrer had provided the necessary political contexts and the constitutions (see Table 4).

Others have taken a going situation that is hard to attribute to a particular person, and brought about the crucial changes or refinements that made the peace or its continuation possible: Gustavus III in Sweden, siding with the commoners against the nobility; Tomas Guardia in Costa Rica breaking up the rule of oligarchy and making constitutional government possible; Elizabeth I presiding over the working out of the doctrines of the state religion; Domenico Flabanico, simply following existing law.

Often these crucial functions have been performed by groups in which no single leader is identified, though perhaps a closer reading of the history would reveal previously unnoticed leaders. The merchant oligarchy of Venice carried out such a function, without a specific doge or other leader playing any single crucial role; the evolution of the Scandinavian governments took place in notable constitutional patterns without the overwhelming presence of any one individual.

What is it that Peace leaders do? That is not easy to say in terms of specific acts: there is no recurrent pattern of draining marshes, codifying laws, or taming the nobility. But they do succeed, in some way, in bringing an expectation of order, a sense that the way things are is better than they were, or that they cannot be improved by violence.

Usually there is some kind of settlement with those already sharing power. It may be suppression as in the case of Frederick II and Albert Achilles of Brandenburg; it may be that the dominant class is confirmed in power, as tended to be the case with early modern leaders such as Charles Robert or Ladislas II. It may be that a wider range of classes were admitted to power, as tended to happen in the more recent periods, with Gustavus III of Sweden of Tomas Guardia. Constitutional reform may be involved, as in the case of Escher and Stampfli in Switzerland or Gustavus III in Sweden.

If one word were required for what these leaders do, it might be reconciliation. They provide an appearance of order out of previous chaos, they bring together disparate units, resolve conflicting interests either by compromise or by firm support of one side.

There is a certain recurrent set of personality characteristics to be observed in these reconcilers. They are firm, patient, persistent types, inclined to be sober: Charles Robert, Albert Achilles, Ferdinand and Isabella, Henry VII. They are not usually hale fellows well met. They also seem to have placed a certain emphasis on intrigue and duplicity. But they bided their time and were masters of the possible.

Once the system has become established, it is no longer essential for the leader to be such a dominant personality. There are a few examples of hard workers: the emperors Sigismund and Charles V and King Philip II. But Sigismund and Charles were overworked by their empires, not by the areas of peace. Philip II was devoted to keeping the machine running, but in looking at other situations, or even at subsequent kings in his own country, it seems apparent that he did the hard work because he liked it, and that he could have achieved better results by delegation.

Some of the rulers in these long middle periods have achieved fame, but as much for the magnificence of their courts or for sheer longevity as for their special abilities. Louis the Great, Sigismund I and II of Poland, Joachim II of Brandenburg were monarchs of above average capability who presided over courts that owed their luster to preceding builders. Victoria of England might be very little known if she had not reigned a very long time. Some of these, like Louis and Victoria, were widely popular, but popularity does not seem to be a necessary quality for leaders in peaceful times.

Indeed, the majority of leaders who came to power in these middle periods were mediocre, just like the rest of us. They did not come to power through any merit of their own, but because they inherited their position through a system established by their predecessors or, in democratic periods, because they came to power in a system that rewarded team play, or at least public conformity, as much as ability. There are many of these: a Philip IV in Spain, a John Cicero in Brandenburg, a Lord North in Britain, few of whom come to be mentioned in these pages. Some hereditary monarchs are cited principally for failing even mediocrity: Philip III and Charles II of Spain. Strong leaders may arise in ordinary periods, but generally they stay within the system and do not stay in power as long as hereditary leaders.

When a major crisis arises, there are sometimes reformers emerging, but in most cases they fail. Janos and Matthias Hunyadi were not able to restore peace to Hungary beyond their own time. Frederick William came too late to save Brandenburg. Sigismund Vasa, attempting to introduce foreign ideas, was a major cause of the termination of peace in Poland. William III of Britain and Pedro II of Brazil, however, had many of the characteristics of a reconciler both in personality and action: they made compromises, both political and financial, and worked long and diligently. So Britain and Brazil survived revolution and entered a second phase of peace.

The English reforms of the nineteenth century, however, do not seem to constitute the same kind of phenomenon. The leaders there, Lord Grey and Benjamin Disraeli, were political figures riding the political tides, as Disraeli frankly acknowledged. Nor was this the beginning or a new phase of peace.

TABLE 4. LEADERS

PEACE	FOUNDERS	RECONCILERS	MIDDLE RULER	TERMINATION RULERS	REFORMERS
Venetian				Pietro Gradenigo	
Hungarian	Charles Robert	Charles Robert	Louis the Great	Sigismund	Janos Hunyadi
Polish	Casimir III	Ladislas II	Sigismund I	Sigismund Vasa	Sigismund Vasa
Brandenburger	Frederick I	Frederick II Albert Achilles	Joachim II	George William	Frederick William
Spanish Imperial	Ferdinand & Isabella	Ferdinand & Isabella	Philip II	Ferdinand VII Charles III	
British	Henry VII	Henry VIII Elizabeth I	Victoria	Charles I Neville Chamberlain	William III
Scandinavian		Gustavas III			
Swiss	Henry Dufour Jonas Furrer	Alfred Escher Jacob Stämpfli			
Costa Rican		Tomás Guardia		Teodoro Picado	
Canadian	John Macdonald	John Macdonald	Mackenzie King		
Pacific	Kamehameha I	Kamehameha III			
Brazilian				Pedro I	Pedro II

Grey and Disraeli were, rather, adequate leaders managing normal transformations. Had they never been born, it seems probable that there would have been equally capable leaders managing similar transformations in similar ways.

Finally, we come to the leaders who failed, or who, at any rate, were in power when peace came to an end. And here we come to such a mixed array that it is hard to argue that lack of leadership is much of a factor in the termination of peace. Only Ferdinand VII of Spain, who came to power in 1808, the year of termination of the Spanish Imperial Peace, can be termed really incompetent. George William faced an overwhelming crisis indecisively, but his indecisiveness might not have been noticed had he ruled a few decades earlier. Charles III, who ruled Spain when peace ended in America, was probably an adequate monarch who appointed competent deputies. Prime Minister Neville Chamberlain of England has been much abused for his failure to understand Hitler, but he was an active and vigorous leader.

Three of the leaders in periods of termination were strong and decisive, but their decisiveness may have had more to do with ending peace than the failures of the weak and indecisive leaders. If Doge Pietro Gradenigo had not had the courage to become involved in mainland politics despite local unpopularity, the Venetian Peace may have continued. If Sigismund Vasa had bowed to the will of the Polish nobility, peace would have lasted a few decades longer, though the "Deluge" that was to follow proved he was quite correct in wishing to establish stronger forms of government. And if Teodoro Picado had not challenged the validity of a very dubious election, the Costa Rican Peace might be continuing through the 1980's.

It would appear, then, that leadership plays an important role in the formative periods of peace. While the situation remains fluid, the decisions of the leaders can be of crucial importance. But once the peaceful situation has been defined, the leaders tend to support the defined system, or to do very little. That three terminations have occurred because of the actions of strong leaders, each in a different way breaking established patterns, indicates that this is a possibility. Otherwise terminations of peace do not seem to be due to deficiencies of leadership.

17

Polities

Peace is associated with a particular territory, and most often that territory is a particular country. In two cases more than one country was involved, where the same factors seemed to apply to several, as in Scandinavia. Only once in the West was the cited area an empire: the Spanish. This association with territory is probably an artifact of the available data. We have no Russian Peace, but it is probable that there were regions of Russia that had more than a century of peace, and likewise there were probably others besides Brandenburg to be found among the thousand-odd principalities of the Holy Roman Empire.

Given these limitations in the process of selection, nevertheless there is no obvious relationship between peace and size. The twelve major peace periods come in many different sizes. If we divide them into what were roughly regarded as small, medium and large territories by standards that at least preceded the age of air travel, we get a fairly even division.

Small (Under 50,000 sq. mi.)	Medium (50,000-200,000 sq. mi.)	Large (Over 200,000 sq. mi.)
Venice	Hungary	Spanish Imperial
Brandenburg	Poland	Scandinavian
Switzerland	Britain	Brazilian
Costa Rica		Canadian
		Pacific

Address by sub-areas would yield a greater bias toward the small countries, but there would remain plenty of medium-sized ones too: Spain, England, Sweden, Norway, Finland and New Zealand would be classified as medium while Australia would be among the large territories. Size **per se** does not seem to be a necessary requirement for peace.

In the settings chapter we have already dealt with the question of power, and again shown that in the Western world this has not been a decisive factor. Nations that were powerful in relation to others and nations that were not have both succeeded in achieving long periods of peace (Ch. 14, Table 2).

When we look at the kind of government predominating in these societies, however, a salient factor is immediately noticeable. Most governments were hereditary monarchies before the nineteenth century. Since 1800 there has been a trend toward dominion by ministries, with a nominal monarch or no monarch at all, and this may be noted earlier in Britain and Sweden. In the centuries since Montesquieu there also has been a trend toward formal separation of three branches of government, but in most cases this theory has been obviated by a practical subsumption of the executive by the legislative. Moreover, legitimation by popular consent rather than hereditary divine right has become universal.

140

Of the seven governments of peaceful societies that existed before the nineteenth century, six were hereditary monarchies. The only exception is the Venetian oligarchy, which was becoming less representative by the end of the Peace.

In the past two centuries, most of the governments of peaceful societies have moved toward the representative side of the continuum. This includes the governments of the major peace areas: the British, Swiss, Costa Rican and Swedish. Brazil moved from semi-responsible monarchy to republic and recently back toward dictatorship. Ireland, Norway, Iceland, Canada, Australia and New Zealand were in a process of separation from the central government, during which they had partial representation in the legislature of the governing nation and were developing, either gradually or in sudden jumps, greater autonomy and eventually independence. The Irish perceived the process as moving too slowly, and ultimately this perception resulted in the termination of their Peace. Scotland and Hawaii moved in the opposite direction, securing full representation in the legislature of a larger nation. Denmark lost her Peace before a process of constitutional modification had gotten very far. Only Finland secured peace under a despotic government. In practice, popularly responsible government has become the only kind recognized as valid in the modern peace periods.

In most of the analytical sections of this work, it has appeared that peace can exist under a number of different kinds of circumstances. It is refreshing, therefore, to discover a particular circumstance that does seem to favor peace. In a previous, more general study of a wider range of peace periods, one of the authors found no difference between representative and despotic forms of government (Melko, 1972; 1973, 178-188). But in the past two centuries in Western history the distinction emerges very clearly. Considering that we were focusing on areas of peace and not governments, and that the distinction has not been evident until this analysis, it seems as though it must be significant, in both senses of the term.

This would appear to be a subject for further research. But one possible reason for this phenomenon emerges from a consideration of the individual cases. We have seen a number of variations of governments moving from despotic to representative situations in painful steps, often with a great deal of nonviolent conflict, sometimes helped over rough spots by outstanding leadership, often as in the case of Ireland, Finland and Costa Rica, losing the peace in the process. Even despotisms have acknowledged the power of the representative image by adopting legislatures and periodic elections. So where a despotism thwarts the process of the emergence of representative government, it apparently can do so only by repressive policies that occasionally lead to violence, either by the government or by elites responding to the government.

Another area of research that would seem to be suggested by this finding is the relation between republican forms and foreign policy. Of particular interest are the findings of Dean Babst, who has argued that "freely elected governments" do not fight each other (1964, 1972). Assuming that "freely elected" means approximately what representative means here, Babst finds that representative governments fight despotic governments, and despotic governments fight each other, but representative governments do not fight each other. A recent study by Tatu Vanhanen (1979) indicates by several political, economic, educational and demographic measures that there has been a long-term trend toward democracy over the past two centuries.

It would appear, therefore, that in the past two centuries representative governments have had a better chance for long periods of internal peace, and have been far less likely to fight one another. If this finding were confirmed by a more careful consideration of the criteria for representative governments, we may have isolated an important factor in reducing violent conflict among and within nations.

Such being the case, the question arises: why? Here comparison of the successful representative peace periods to the despotic successes is enlightening. Both kinds had some institutionalized mechanisms whereby the interests of individuals, and particularly powerful individuals who might otherwise have disrupted the Peace, could be reconciled to the interests of the state. In the Hispanic Peace, for example, this was a combination of the **poder moderador** with a certain tendency to ignore unwelcome laws even when validated; in the Scandinavian Peace all-powerful interests tended to be coopted into the state in an interlocking network in which everyone found some place. In the Eastern European peace periods, the great nobility was given power in the form of responsibility for managing huge estates, controlling the lesser nobility, and fighting distant wars, as well as rewards in the form of great wealth, conscript labor, and preferential taxation.

But elections, when perceived as honest, are an enormously flexible instrument for registry of such interests and even when corrupt can be so if the corruption is a weighting factor in favor of real interests. The sheer power of election in this process can be appreciated particularly well by the number of farcical imitations grandstanded by evanescent despotisms in those countries where political change seems almost to be measured in revolutions per minute. The magic wand does not work without the magic; nevertheless they keep trying, as if in hope that the magic will somehow be there. Legitimation by election has not been the one and only successful method of insuring internal peace, but in the past two centuries it has certainly proven effective.

There was a variety of succession systems, some of them evolving while the peace was in progress. A number of the monarchies used a system involving succession to the first-born son. These generally worked if a son were born, but not having seraglios the monarchs were sometimes unlucky, and the absence of a son could produce a crisis, as it did on the death of Louis the Great of Hungary. In most of the modern systems the parliamentary system eased the problem of succession, since the leader was the head of the party or combination of parties in power, this leader being elected by the party or negotiated if there were a coalition of parties. This system seemed to work very well, and there are no instances of violence because of a failure of succession.

There were other systems of succession. In Venice the doge was elected by an advisory council that gradually became a ruling council. In Poland the monarch was elected by the nobility, though usually the monarch elected was the eldest son. Both of these systems evolved while peace was in progress. The Polish system was much maligned, and the election of Sigismund Vasa probably did hurry the termination of the peace, but all the same that election was managed without violence, as were all the others during the two-century peace period. The Costa Ricans used a variation of the American political system, directly electing the president without allowing a candidate to succeed himself, and this system did lead to a termination of the Costa Rican Peace when the results of an election were challenged.

A polity may have a reasonably clear and coherent system of succession, but still not have stability. The succession system may be challenged frequently, because such a system has been corrupted or has never been fully accepted, or because patterns of challenge exist within the political culture. Dynastic wars have been among the most common peace-destroying challenges. It should be noted, however, that there have been occasions in Scandinavia, England and Brazil where a coup d'etat may have saved the Peace. But political stability seems to be the norm in peaceful societies. The representative systems often have intense political battles, many of them fought behind the scenes, but once an official has been chosen by recognized methods, his incumbency is usually assured.

There is no special organization of law or system of justice observable in these societies. Some states, like Poland and Australia, were busy with legislation as they entered a new situation. All were involved in changes in laws by legislation or edict as social conditions changed, or as taxes were perceived to be needed. But the effectiveness of such systems seemed to have less to do with their content than with their capacity to satisfy or contain powerful classes, interest groups or autonomous regions. What seemed to be more important was not the nature or content of the justice system so much as the division and delegation of power.

This division of power may be looked at in several ways. We may consider the division by strata, among classes or elites. We may consider it by polity, the distribution between central and regional authorities that are in some way geographically or politically distinguished. And we may look at the distribution of both over time: Is the central government acquiring or delegating more power?

In terms of elites, a practical decentralization seems to be the prevailing pattern. Spain and Portugal had strongly centralized monarchies, but both had recognized provisions for, in effect, ignoring unwelcome central decrees. Likewise the Scandinavian monarchies were traditionally centralized, but equally traditionally used local leaders and local consent to govern the localities. The British kings were also strong, but for much of the time the nobles contested royal dominance through Parliament. Poland and Hungary each had a nobility very successful in preserving its rights, and the Brandenburg electors needed the support of the nobility against the towns. Venice was governed by an oligarchy with a doge who was at most first among equals.

Among the modern governments, all without exception have had a considerable elite, with leadership hedged by party and electoral rules. Whereas hereditary monarchs like Louis the Great or the Sigismunds of Hungary and Poland might rule for three to five decades, modern presidents and prime ministers often exceed a decade, but hardly ever reach two decades of consecutive rule. Neither of the most famous British leaders of this period, Gladstone and Disraeli, was ever in power for more than half a dozen years at a time. Pedro II, it is true, ruled for several decades, an enlightened anachronism.

In terms of territory, most of the states had a central authority that was dominant over regional authority. But where there was a distinctly separate region, there was always a tension concerning the amount of regional authority allowed. In Norway and Finland a great deal of autonomy was permitted. In Scotland and Hawaii, the tension was resolved by full incorporation within the greater state, in Scotland by the initiative of the major power, in Hawaii by autonomous advocacy. In Spanish and Portuguese America, Australia, New Zealand and Iceland, autonomy was a geographical reality, whatever the wishes of the central state. In Ireland the degree of autonomy was always a political issue and peace came to an end there, as it did in Finland, when the indigenous leaders felt they had insufficient autonomy or that the autonomy they had was threatened. Problems of autonomy for Ireland, Norway, Finland, Iceland, Brazil, Canada, Australia and New Zealand were ultimately resolved by the granting of full independence.

Very often a process of decentralization is evident. Power moved from the monarch to the nobility in Hungary, Poland and Brandenburg; from doge to oligarchy in Venice; and from central government to a wider range of elites in all the modern governments. Brazil moved from centralized empire to federation. Its recent return to centralized dictatorship could signify impending termination of the Peace. The British experienced a major interruption to their long Peace when the Stuarts attempted to reassert monarchical authority, but then successfully centralized using the representative authority of Parliament. Thus even in the face of formal centralization, a high degree of either practical local autonomy or of local representation in the central government appears to be very much the rule.

There seem to be two salient findings concerning the polities of these peaceful societies. In modern times, all of them had representative governments. And throughout the millennium all of them were more likely to be decentralized than centralized, in terms of elites, territory and process.

18

Economies

It often has been noted that war can have a stimulating effect on economies. The great depression ended in World War II, which led to full employment as all available populations were needed to produce goods for a total war. The totalitarian nations, which rearmed first, recovered from the depression more quickly than the Western democracies. And after World War II, the long period of withholding of purchases of durable goods led to a tremendous demand. This demand stimulated production and expansion which in turn resulted in general prosperity through the fifties and into the sixties.

One would wonder, then, if peace might not have the opposite effect. Are periods of peace also periods of stagnation, unemployment and poverty? Considering the cases of long peace in the Western World, the answer seems to be that they are not. The majority of them were prosperous. Among the earlier cases, Venice was a vigorous trading society; times were prosperous in the Golden Age of Hungary; Poland experienced a great period of agricultural production and an increase in trade; Tudor and Stuart England were alive with agricultural and early industrial activity, greatly stimulated by world expansion, colonization and trade.

On the other hand, the Spanish Imperial Peace was hardly a period of unmitigated prosperity. Great wealth flowed into the country, but apparently flowed out again, leaving inflation and declining production behind, although there are revisionists who believe that the early modern period was not such an economic disaster for the Iberian Peninsula however frequently the government may have gone bankrupt. Brandenburg was hardly prosperous; the land was difficult to cultivate and Germany in general seems to have been economically backward in the sixteenth century. The economies of the Scandinavian countries that were peaceful before the nineteenth century—Iceland, Norway, Denmark—were slow to develop and the Brazilian economy was backward until the twentieth century.

So there is a mixed picture in this earlier period. Peaceful societies were sometimes prosperous, sometimes not.

When we reach the last two centuries, however, the image of dynamic, prosperous societies predominates. England led the industrial revolution and Scotland joined in the prosperity; Switzerland became a symbol for prosperity as well as peace; Norway and particularly Sweden were often presented as models of economic development and high living standard in the twentieth century; the Pacific economies, despite periodic depressions, were lands of opportunity and wealth; likewise the Canadian economy had its ups and downs, but still is one of the most prosperous in the world.

Still, such prosperity is not universal. Costa Rica, though better off than other Central American nations, was a relatively poor country; Brazil developed unevenly; Iceland was poor well into the twentieth century; Finland did not equal its western Scandinavian neighbors in economic development;

and Ireland experienced a famous and disastrous famine in the middle of the nineteenth century, nor did the Irish ever share fully in British industrial development.

So it would appear that peaceful nations were more often than not prosperous, but that peace was no guarantee of prosperity, nor was absence or loss of prosperity concurrent with absence or loss of peace.

Nations may be prosperous, but the prosperity may be narrowly shared, and the vast majority of a population may live in poverty. Among the prosperous peaceful nations of the medieval and early modern period, however, this appears to be true only of Spain. The Venetian world had a high percentage of middle-class small businessmen, and low taxes and trade and manufacture provided plenty of employment in shipyards and on ships. Hungary was known for its low taxes, and small landholders fared well, though not the town dwellers. Prosperity for the Polish nobility may not have been so widely distributed, and again the towns were not thriving. England is famous for its sturdy yeoman, a symbol of wide distribution of wealth and capacity for productivity, both on farm and in town, but enclosures and industrialization did impose poverty, unemployment and displacement on some parts of the population.

The prosperous nations of the modern period also seem to have been involved in activities that distributed wealth. England, the Scandinavian Countries and Switzerland made great efforts in the twentieth century to develop social systems that supported the poor, and England expanded these policies to the dominions which, besides, were lands of opportunity for those who could raise funds for the oceanic voyage. Only in Brazil is this at best recent and still questionable.

Another factor that should be considered is the economic environment, both inside and outside. Were the processes of production and distribution encouraged, left alone, or inhibited? Among the prosperous nations just discussed, they were generally encouraged or left alone. Taxes were raised to support the welfare systems, and it would require an economic analysis beyond anything attempted here to determine whether the taxation policies of twentieth-century Sweden or Great Britain were likely to take a greater portion of funds for capitalization than those of the governments of Louis the Great or Sigismund I. But the only case in which the government seems clearly to have inhibited the process of development was in Spain, where the government in its preoccupation with financing itself lost sight of this need. And even making allowances for laissez-faire philosophy, private organization proved to be woefully inadequate in providing relief during the Irish potato famine of the 1840's. It was, however, another seven decades before the Irish Peace came to an end, so the famine did not prevent peace from continuing.

Environments, of course, go beyond countries. Sometimes what happens in any one country is largely linked to the greater environment. That was notably true of Brandenburg with regard to Germany, and Canada as it was affected by the United States. Spain and Great Britain, on the other hand, were to a great extent creators of their economic environment, and in the long run each had serious problems from the economic reactions outside, Spain because internal inflation drained silver and gold, Britain at a later date because industrial imitators built more modern facilities.

Costa Rica and Brandenburg, relatively poor countries, may have been shielded from discontent by greater poverty surrounding them. Venice, Hungary, Poland, Britain, Switzerland, Sweden and Norway were often considerably more prosperous than surrounding nations. Iceland, though poor, was relatively isolated from comparison. Only Ireland, balancing a most unstable Peace, was markedly poorer than her neighbors. Australia, New Zealand, Hawaii and Canada, though distant from other places, provided economic improvement for many immigrants.

On the whole, it would seem, the peaceful societies were economically better off than neighboring lands or other lands that would invite comparison.

There were several different kinds of economies, varying according to the times. Hungary, Poland and Brandenburg and later Costa Rica, Hawaii and Brazil were largely agricultural; Venice and Britain were maritime and mercantile, but Spain, Costa Rica and most of the Island nations also depended on sea trade; Hungary and particularly Poland depended greatly on land trade; Britain, Australia and New Zealand had periods in which husbandry predominated. All the peaceful societies in the nineteenth and twentieth centuries, with the exception of Costa Rica, became industrial manufacturing centers.

Natural resources do not appear to have played a great part in the histories of the majority of the peaceful societies. Gold was important to Hungary, Spain and colonial Brazil, and coal and steel to industrializing Britain. The availability of land affected the histories of Spanish America, Canada and the Pacific societies. But Venice, Brandenburg, Britain, Switzerland, the Scandinavian powers and Costa Rica were not especially endowed with resources. In the case of Spain it is questionable whether the resources helped or interfered with the development of the economy.

Before the twentieth century, except for the canals of Venice, none of the peaceful societies was blessed with an exceptional system of transportation or communications. The unifications of Canada and Australia, it is true, were supported by the completion of railroads.

Prosperity and Peace seem to have no specifically necessary connection. A long economic rise can be associated with war (as in Continental Europe) or Peace (as in Britain, some Commonwealth countries, and Scandinavia); a long decline may occur with no notable effect on a Peace, as in the Spanish Empire. If any lesson can be safely drawn, it is that in a peaceful society the economy is likely to be, not necessarily prosperous, but well integrated with other elements of the system. Even so public a catastrophe as the later Spanish Habsburg economy did not interfere with Peace when this condition was fulfilled.

19

Societies

In the introduction to this volume the problem was noted of the society at war abroad, at peace at home. To label such a society as a Peace seems at least partly self-contradictory; surely the presence of the foreign war has major effects on the domestic Peace.

The situation arises often enough to provide plenty of cases for analysis. Only three of the twelve peace periods studied herein lacked external conflict: the Brandenburger, the Swiss, and (only partly) the Scandinavian. All the others suffered outside war of some kind. The exact kinds were quite various: dynastic wars involving nobility and mercenaries, secondary wars involving professional standing armies; and total wars involving total civilian mobilization and reenforcement of the armed forces by volunteers and conscription.

The most recent of the total wars, World Wars I and II, involved Britain, Canada and the Pacific nations. World War I took an immense total of lives in Britain and New Zealand in particular, so that a substantial number of families sustained the loss of a near relative and their members, surely, would have reacted very strongly to the idea that their societies were at peace. Moreover, as critics say, war and discussion of war were everywhere. Not only were many people involved in war-related work, but they were also fearful that their side might lose the war and they would be invaded, a fear that had substantial basis of fact for Australia in World War II. On the other hand, this same World War II brought with it an immense economic recovery for these countries, reenforcing the idea presented by Marxist economists and others that war is essential to continued prosperity in capitalist economies, and the idea, explored and rejected in the previous chapter, that war is necessary for continued prosperity in any economic system.

In situations in which war was not total it is possible to ascertain social effects, but it would be hard to say these pervaded the society. Mark Fabryci suggests that one reason Poland remained an agricultural society was that the nobility concentrated its efforts in preparing for and fighting wars on the Lithuanian borders. Military careers also provided occupations for many younger sons of the nobility who were not needed to maintain the lands nor were recruited into the clergy. After all, in medieval times it was the business of knights to fight. When they went off on crusades, merchants and travelers were relieved (Bloch, 1962). When there was a long period of peace, what could be the business of a professional warrior? The Lithuanian and Balkan wars may indeed have contributed to peace in Poland and Hungary.

In modern times, wars both total and local provided opportunities for the youth of Australia and New Zealand, who left to fight and often die in distant places neither to defend their countries nor because of lack of local opportunity, but for the reasons of youth, adventure and the opportunity to see the world. Still a different class, the merchants of Venice, fought or traded according to whichever would bring the greater profit. In most of these situations individuals seem to have felt no sense of duress or protest but rather of duty in this use of physical violence. Away from home, warfare was sought, or at least not avoided.

The social structures of most of these peaceful societies were not unusual for their times. In Hungary, in Poland, Brandenburg and Brazil, perhaps in Spain in the seventeenth and eighteenth centuries, the great nobility was dominant, and the townsmen and monarchs were less powerful. In Venice the great merchants prevailed. In England the breaking of the peace in the seventeenth century involved a temporary recovery of power for the nobility. In the nineteenth and twentieth centuries there was a decentralization of power among landholders and industrialists and a general extension of the franchise.

In the earlier systems there was not a great deal of vertical mobility. Even in commercial Venice the great families more and more dominated, and it could not have been easy to move up socially, even with luck and new wealth. The British and Spanish systems did provide opportunity overseas, at least a route for vigorous activity by the discontented and the social systems of the last two centuries have provided for vertical mobility partly because of the possibility of horizontal mobility. For the Scandinavian countries, such horizontal mobility was largely restricted to emigration. \

Horizontal mobility suggests moderate population, but it is not easy to find a relation between peace and population density. Most of the societies had increasing populations during their period of peace, and a few were densely populated: Venice, Britain, Costa Rica. Others, like Brandenburg, Norway and Iceland may have been crowded in relation to the poverty of the soil. But only in Costa Rica does overcrowding appear to have been one factor among others in the breaking of a period of peace. Native populations in the Pacific societies suffered catastrophic declines, mostly from disease introduced by the immigrants.

These precipitous population declines in the Pacific societies serve as a reminder that peaceful societies are not always pleasant to live in. Plagues were the bane of medieval societies and both Norway and Venice experienced them during their peace periods, though the great Black Death of the 1340's may have missed Hungary. When the plague struck, it would last in a given city or village about a year. During such a time, new victims would be claimed every few days--daily in the cities--and would die a terrible lingering death over several days. Venice was also subject to devastating storms, floods and fires.

In considering the effects of total war, we have already touched on the subject of government pervasiveness and control. On the whole, governments of the peaceful societies were not pervasive, did not control the lives of their subjects. The state may have been limited by agreement with the aristocracy, as in the case of Poland and Hungary, or by institutional ineffectiveness, as in Spain and Brazil, or by contract, as in Switzerland, Britain, the Scandinavian countries and those overseas. An attempt by the British monarchy to override these limits contributed to an interruption of the Peace in the seventeenth century.

While many of the peaceful societies were ethnically homogenous, there were also a good many instances of successful integration or at least peaceful co-existence of ethnic and racial minorities. A number of national groups occupied Hungary, so that in some periods the Magyars were a minority; Lithuanians moved into Poland in considerable numbers; the Spaniards coexisted with native populations of the New World as did the New Zealanders and Canadians, though the Australians tended to drive them out; Canada absorbed a succession of ethnic immigrants; Switzerland is a land of four languages; Costa Rica accepted a substantial minority of black West Indians and Hawaii acquired a world reputation for its successful integration of different races and ethnic groups. Conflict between Caucasians and Maori delayed peace in New Zealand, and the decline of the banana industry with resultant black dispersal could have been a factor in the Costa Rican conflicts of 1948. But on the whole, the peaceful societies were successful at racial and ethnic assimilation. Only Australia had a policy that created and maintained a homogeneous, Caucasian population.

Peace also continued through periods of immense social change. In the past two centuries most societies in the West have experienced a transition from a rural, smallholder agrarian economy to a more mechanized, more urbanized type of economy, with all the political and social changes such a transformation entails. In the earlier societies change seems to have been more gradual.

One kind of change does not seem to have been easily accommodated: the change from manorial farming to modern agriculture. Only the British and Scandinavian peace periods survived this kind of transition. In Brazil this same change may yet end the Peace.

A review of the societies themselves, then, suggests a few negative findings that contradict some widely held images. Generally the fighting of external wars does not transform the society itself; frequently the peaceful societies are socially decentralized; often they are ethnically or racially heterogeneous; and frequently they survive major periods of social change.

20

Culture

Every human society has a culture, and it is the culture that individualizes, gives color and texture to the society.

This chapter will be devoted to four aspects of culture: religion, civilization, aesthetic creativity and outlook. These are not easy to sort out and have a way of interacting with one another. Religion refers to the perceived religious structure and its place in the society as distinguished from the characteristic of religiosity. Civilization refers to Western civilization, which has been a determinant in the selection of the societies. Aesthetics includes not only art, but also literature, language, science, philosophy and other indicators of creativity and vitality. Outlook, a term preferred by Carroll Quigley (1962) refers to the collective worldview, values, patterns and general atmosphere of the society; it is the most difficult aspect to get hold of, and the one that most tends to become entangled with the others.

One function of religion in many countries is to contribute to the unity of state and peoples. If there is a single religion shared by all, this provides a strong magnet for the loyalty of the subjects. Obeying the state and obeying God are one. This also means, however, that dissent is difficult because denial of the state religion is denial of the legitimacy of the state itself. Spain became the epitome of this kind of state, and religious persecution was part of the fabric of its Peace, to the extent that the Inquisition may be said to have existed partly by popular demand.

Spain, however, has been the extreme. Most Western peaceful societies regarded religion as central to the fabric of the Peace, even given minority religions and a lack of any continued importance of the religion's particular beliefs, but in general when religion became state-controlled and -enforced it also lost much or all of its power of inspiration. In medieval Venice and Hungary as in all medieval realms religion was a central and integral feature, but such disputes as existed were over appointments, powerful positions, rather than religious matters. Venice was near certain disputes on the mainland but did not get involved in mainland controversies; when later it did, it ended the Peace. Hungary existed at a time when Catholicism was still the only conceivable choice, and when Protestantism arrived on the scene and created the possibility of a second choice, the Peace ended.

Likewise in modern Costa Rica there was a single state religion, long past being an issue, long become a prop of the state and otherwise a sterile backdrop. In five cases, the British, the Scandinavian (Danish and Swedish sectors), the Brazilian, the Canadian and the Pacific, the atmosphere was increasingly secular for more drastic reasons. In Britain, Denmark and Sweden the Church had been annexed to the point of being swallowed by the State— indeed the swallowing of Church property had been a major motive for the exercise—and became more and more an official formality, of debatable relevance even to such speculations as Swedenborg's. In Norway and Iceland the transition to Protestantism occurred during the Peace and caused some of the greater tumult of the times, but died down quickly.

In the Canadian and Pacific cases, religion was generally an irrelevancy, excepting that it formed a highly emotional core for Quebecois resistance to Anglo-Canadian assimilation. Thus in these cases religion had so lost its power to inspire that religious controversies became little more than arguments over bureaucratic privilege. Finally, in Hawaii, such a mixmaster of civilizations had developed by the later nineteenth century that tolerance was the only possible course, and the secular emphasis of the intruding American culture made this choice easy.

In four countries, Catholic-Protestant controversies were serious issues requiring some delicate maneuvering on the part of governments. Poland remained Catholic, but was tolerant of increasing Protestant minorities. Britain and Brandenburg both converted from Catholicism to Protestantism, with much caution and consideration on the part of secular leaders, and generally with protection or at least provision for Catholic minorities. These maneuvers often threatened peace, especially in Britain after the execution of Mary, Queen of Scots, led to the threat of the Spanish Armada, and ultimately brought about the termination of peace in Catholic Ireland. Switzerland entered its Peace in a secularized period, but its constitution was carefully constructed to insure the religious freedom of Catholic minorities.

Thus the rule seems to be that religion and peace are compatible in either of two situations: if the religion continues to be a strong source of motivation but is uncontested, or if it is contested but no longer a strong source of motivation. Even Spain illustrates this, since Judaism, the official reason behind the Inquisition, was forced out or into hiding as of the first year of the Peace, and thenceforth the Inquisition existed mainly to probe beliefs that no one would express except in private, and to verify genealogies. The Inquisition was thus in effect for most of its life a deep investigation into something that was no longer there, which made it quite tolerable to the Peace.

The question of civilization is relatively simple in a consideration of the Western world, since it is generally accepted that all these cases belong to a single Western civilization, however defined. The one possible exception would be Hawaii, which was under Polynesian rule as of the beginning of the Peace and has had a massive East Asian influx since. But Western influence was even heavier, and even the unification of the islands may be attributed to it. Certainly for the last century Hawaii has been essentially Western, though with contributions from other civilizations possibly stronger than anywhere else in the world.

Venice had conflicts and trade with Byzantine civilization, and Byzantine culture certainly had an impact on the Venetians. In this period, however, the young expansive civilization the Venetians represented was certainly a threat to the peace of the mature Byzantine civilization, but the converse was not true, at least not on the home islands. There the Hungarians, Normans, and German emperors were more dangerous threats. The Hungarians faced a major attack from the Ottoman Turks, representatives of Islamic civilization, but this was neither as serious nor as devastating as the attacks by fellow Christians that overwhelmed Brandenburg during the Thirty Years War. There is little evidence, then, to indicate that conflicts between civilizations are more dangerous to peace than conflicts within a single civilization.

When the term "culture" is used in a narrower sense, it is often understood to refer to the aesthetic creativity of a society. And there has been a perception that conflict is stimulating, peace boring. These twelve peace periods present a mixed picture. Some have been aesthetically creative, some have not. Four have produced creative artists, writers or composers of world renown: Spain, Great Britain, Scandinavia and Switzerland. The British creativity was expressed in several spurts in the fifteenth and sixteenth century, and again in the nineteenth and twentieth, with great achievement in literature, less in art and music, and in the seventeenth and eighteenth in science and invention. The Spaniards had one great century, the seventeenth, which featured painting and literature. The Swiss had a burst of creativity in several fields that was remarkable for so small a country. The Scandinavians produced at least two world famous playwrights, two outstanding composers, and a great film director in the late nineteenth and twentieth centuries.

Two of the societies, Poland and Brazil, each produced a burst of indigenous creativity that did not receive world attention, but was truly distinct from alien influences.

Venice, Hungary, Brandenburg, Costa Rica and Canada did not have great aesthetic periods. The Hungarians imported a great deal, first from the Renaissance, then from the Enlightenment. The Venetians borrowed from Byzantine civilization, the Costa Ricans from France, though some local talent in poetry and art was emerging toward the end of the peace. Canada borrowed but also tried to create her own art, which has somehow remained submerged in that of the U.S. | Brandenburg neither created nor borrowed greatly.

So only six of the twelve societies had major creative periods, only four really transcending their own nation. Some rather extensive random sampling would be needed to ascertain whether this was an average achievement or not, but it appears that long periods of peace do not seem to prevent the possibility of creative development.

Nor does there seem to be any pattern of creativity relating to peace. Britain and Switzerland were creative throughout their peace periods, Spain and Poland mostly in the middle period. Scandinavia, the Pacific societies and Costa Rica experienced late creativity. So creativity may occur during any phase of a peace period, and bursts of creativity may be repeated more than once.

The last category, outlook, does not lend itself very well to tabulation or counting. How strong, for example, was the perception of peace in these countries? The Swiss have been very conscious of it, and built their institutions to support it. The Scandinavians seem to have become aware of its value in the nineteenth century. Britons occasionally expressed an appreciation of peace, and the Costa Ricans saw themselves as being more peaceful than their neighbors. On the other hand the Venetians were as willing to fight as trade, and the Poles saw war as their vocation. The Canadian and especially the Pacific frontiersmen were willing to fight when necessary, if not a bit more. The Hungarians, Brandenburgers and Spaniards did not list peace among their greatest values. So only in a minority of the states was peace perceived as having special value.

One well-known prototype of peace comes from the Roman Empire, as interpreted by Gibbon, Spengler, and Toynbee: a world-weary kind of peace in which people are tired of incessant fighting and willing to accept any rule that will stop it. This view has been reinforced more recently by Robert Wesson (1967) and S.N. Eisenstadt (1963), who have pictured empires as being oppressive and uncreative. But most of the societies in the Western world have not been empires, and the two that were—the Spanish and British—were vital colonial empires, not conquest states within their own civilization. The impression from the majority of the peaceful societies is one of vitality, not weariness, from the Venetians ever hatching new plans for increasing trade and making money, through the golden ages of Hungary and Poland, the active participation in world affairs of Spain and Britain, the opportunism and alertness of the Swiss, the pioneer expansiveness of the Canadians and Australians. The inhabitants of these countries may be perceived as having been rude or gauche to our cosmopolitan tastes, but they were hardly weary.

There is one other factor in some of the cultures that is difficult to isolate, but it has to do with a pattern of relationship that either does not include violence as a viable alternative or in any event puts it rather low in the sequence of options one might choose. The model for this outlook is the constitutional development in Scandinavia, which today has become a center for peace research. We know from Ibsen and Strindberg that the pattern of conflict was high in these countries, but there were restrictions on ways of expressing it. In the last resort, suicide was more acceptable than homicide.

In Switzerland the pattern of peaceful resolution has been consciously inculcated, a matter of external and internal survival. In Britain it gradually emerged as a widespread norm. There are proper ways to act, and violent solutions are not acceptable. Police patrolled without weapons, prime ministers walked the streets without guards. Riots with relatively low casualties in the latter half of the twentieth century were perceived as shocking. Canada, another center of peace research, never had the violent patterns of its neighbor to the south. Australia, a more rough and ready country, always made a great ideal of matiness on an egalitarian basis. The Costa Ricans consciously saw themselves as more civilized, less given to violent solutions, than their neighbors. The Spaniards, whatever may be said about Latin temperament, were bound, as we have seen, by codes of gentlemanly conduct that applied to lower levels of society as well as higher. Even the Venetians, though ever willing to fight, preferred to trade and make a profit. The Hungarian and Polish nobility were warriors by profession, but gentlemen among themselves. But the patterns are less convincing in the last three cases.

In the cases of Venice, Hungary, Poland, Spain and Britain, there were places to fight, places where young men could take out their aggressions in legitimate form. Australians and New Zealanders showed themselves ready and willing to kill people and risk being killed whenever the opportunity arose. In societies that provided opportunity for exercise of violence as well as those that didn't, there are some evidences in literature of edginess and strong social conflict. This is particularly true of Norway, Sweden, Australia and New Zealand. But literature is designed to explore conflict rather than harmony. And certainly the novels of Patrick White, at least, have long patches of unaggressive normality. On the whole these societies, along with Switzerland, Brandenburg, Costa Rica and Canada, do not seem to exhibit an extraordinarily high level of social neurosis.

Peaceful societies in the West, then, are at least moderately creative, reasonably vital, and not especially neurotic in their social interaction. Usually they are not specifically focused on peace as an objective, but their norms suggest other modes of interaction than violence. Peace and religion are compatible if religion is a strong source of motivation but uncontested, or if contested, no longer a strong force.

21

Foreign Relations

Chapter 14 on Settings considered the peaceful societies in relation to their political environment. The most common situation was for the peaceful society to be governed by a power that was strong enough to influence the state system surrounding it. But some of the states were interstice states too weak to influence the situation, and some were more or less isolated from other powers. We have seen that the majority of the governments of these powers were autonomous, that they were more likely to be central than peripheral, that they were partly protected by some kind of physical barrier, that they most frequently experienced a temperate climate, and that their setting had involved at least one general war during the peace period (Table 2:p.130).

Within this general framework, how have nations managed to maintain peace when they were inferior to their neighbors? The most extreme situation seems to have been the acceptance of alien rule. This seems to have occurred a number of times, often after conflict. Frequently this relinquishment of autonomy was palliated or even ameliorated by the acceptance of a common monarch, as happened in Stuart Scotland, Iceland with Norway and Norway with Denmark and Sweden.

Sometimes a country was protected because it was in the sphere of influence of a great power. This was true of Canada and Costa Rica with relation to the United States. Iceland, Canada, Australia and New Zealand hoped to bring themselves some protection in the twentieth century by joining in formal alliance with the United States and a number of Western European countries, the Commonwealth countries previously having been protected by Britain, as, perhaps, was Iceland.

But when power is equally divided among a number of neighbors, small powers have found it expedient to remain neutral, as Switzerland and Sweden have done throughout the century. When a weak nation has its back to the wall, and the multipower situation changes to reveal one dominant power, it can revert to a policy of tribute or appeasement, buying off the surviving great power by making trade concessions or supplying raw materials. This is what Sweden did when first France and later Germany became dominant powers in Europe.

There is only one example of freely accepted federation of two roughly equal powers to create a peace: that between Poland and Lithuania. There is an analogy between this and the unification of Scotland and England under the Stuarts, except that Lithuania was much more of an equal than Scotland. Moreover, and this is the only case, peace was preserved in the territory of the dominant Polish power, but not in Lithuania.

Some countries avoided entangling alliances. Venice and Britain each rested its Peace not on alliances but on its navy. Venice had a standing alliance with Byzantium, more a trade agreement and recognition of mutual interest than an alliance, then an agreement with the Crusaders mainly for division of the loot. Britain's alliances were **ad hoc** for wartime. Costa Rica simply stayed out.

Hungary seems to have been the only power to use buffer states against a potential adversary, but these do not seem to have performed any useful function in preserving the peace. Switzerland, itself a buffer between Germany and Italy, had peace when the greater powers did not.

Sometimes power relations changed during the period of peace. In the cases of Hungary, Poland, Spain and Switzerland, neighbors were growing stronger. In the cases of Hungary and Poland this change in relative power vis-a-vis the Ottomans and Sweden contributed to the termination of Peace. Switzerland, on the other hand, found in the unifications of Italy and Germany a strong catalyst toward its own unification, neutrality and the creation of a long period of peace. Switzerland differed from the other three powers in that it was an interstice state.

When small powers grow stronger in relation to great powers, they are inclined to break their dependent ties and seek autonomy. This happened with four colonial nations: Brazil, Canada, Australia and New Zealand. There seem to be four basic stages in the process: defeat of or settlement with indigenous peoples; achievement of independence from alien nations by warfare or division of spheres of influence; agreement of the local provinces on federation or unification, eventually combined with negotiations with the mother country for autonomy.

For Australia and New Zealand peace was achieved after a resolution of sorts with the indigenous population. The last conflict in Canada involved a resistance from indigenous peoples and immigrant colonial settlers. The phase of unification of different provinces provided much disagreement but little threat of violence, as was also true of the fourth stage, separation from the mother country. This stage, of course, had caused violent conflict in the United States, and was to do so frequently during similar Asian and African separations in the twentieth century.

Hawaii and Iceland could also be viewed as colonial settlements, but they did not grow in relative power, only in capacity for autonomy. Americanized Hawaii chose the opposite solution, full incorporation with a major power with all the rights of other provinces. Iceland chose independence, with the incumbent risks and advantages of an interstice state.

Occasionally in peaceful situations, there are borders between autonomous states that are considered so safe that they are not necessary to guard. These borders provide an automatic buffer for each of the neighbors vis-a-vis the powers beyond. Examples which come to mind are those between Hungary and Poland during the Hungarian and the Polish Peace periods and the Norwegian-Swedish and the Canadian-American borders. The Polish-Hungarian border was originally stabilized by the common dynasty governing the two countries in the time of Jagiello and Jadwiga. But it continued to be maintained by cultural community and common interest, Hungary protecting against the Ottomans, Poland against the Lithuanians and Russians.

The idea of peace as a cultural value has been considered in the preceding chapter. Did this value reflect in policy? Occasionally it did, but more often not. For Switzerland, of course, maintenance of peace is a conscious element of policy, almost a constitutional axiom for the nation. For the Scandinavians it became a central element, so that it has come to be understood that Scandinavian nations will not attack one another. Even when Sweden hoped to recover Finland, invasion was never seriously planned. Peace as a value related to policy also has been mentioned from time to time by British statesmen, notably Disraeli's "peace in our time" after the 1878 Berlin Conference, echoed 60 years later in Neville Chamberlain just before the termination of the long British Peace.

But much more frequently, governments valued peace less than territorial integrity. Most of the governments were unaware they had peace. Peace became part of the rhetoric of the past two centuries, but it is difficult to find this reflected in policies.

The introduction (Chapter 1) to this book refers to previous controversies over the definition of peace as an absence of violence in a society, even though the government of that society may be fighting elsewhere. That definition was defended, in part, on the ground that areas of peace should first be delineated before considering whether these areas remained peaceful because governments managed to preserve them by fighting elsewhere. The problem was considered from the standpoint of exporting domestic troublemakers in Chapter 19. Here it needs to be considered in relation to foreign policy.

Now that some cases have been delineated, what can be said about the relation between peace at home and war abroad? Certainly there have been countries that did not fight externally during their peace periods. This was true of Switzerland and Brandenburg. It was true of Iceland, Norway and Hawaii during the periods in which they controlled their own policy. It was true of Sweden in the nineteenth and twentieth centuries. So it was not necessary for these countries to fight elsewhere in order to preserve internal peace.

Among countries that did engage in external fighting, however, it is difficult to sort out which warfare was expansionist, which defensive, and which had other purposes. Certainly Spain and Britain were expanding world powers during their periods of peace, and much of their fighting involved conquest of territory, however many fits of absence of mind may be perceived by subsequent historians. Poland was engaged in expansive wars in Eastern Europe and so was Hungary in the Balkans, though the latter could be interpreted as buffer preparations for future defense.

The same governments, however, can be perceived to have been fighting defensively. The British coalitions against Napoleon were defensive as was their fighting in World War I. Another naval power, Venice, engaged in at least one defensive battle, their victory over Barbarossa having the same impact as the British victory at Trafalgar. Among the defensive land actions were the largely unsuccessful attempts of the Hungarians to deflect the Ottomans and the battle the Costa Rican army fought against William Walker in Nicaragua.

There seem to have been more foreign conflicts and expeditions that were neither offensive nor defensive. The British and Spaniards fought many battles overseas and in Europe that defended some territory they acquired, but not their homeland. The Venetians engaged in many battles and frays, but they never acquired territory for political advantage, though they did battle for trade rights and agricultural and timber land and sometimes engaged in pure piracy. Some of the Hungarian conflicts in the Balkans, Italy and along the Adriatic seem to have had more to do with glory than either expansion or defense. Australia and New Zealand were still supporting Britain in World War II in a war that had little to do with the defense of their homelands, and may even have weakened them when it became apparent that such a defense might be necessary. If some of the Australians and New Zealanders were enlisting to experience the glory of war, they had much the same motivation as the Polish nobility in fighting in Lithuania.

It seems probable that only a small portion of the external wars of governments of peaceful societies had to do with defending domestic peace. It also seems clear, from the societies that did not fight at all, that warfare elsewhere is not necessary to prevent violence and rebellion at home.

One aspect of these external conflicts seems worth noting, however. The governments that did engage in such conflicts never became overcommitted. Usually they did not get drawn into situations from which they could not withdraw. The one obvious exception is the war in the Spanish Netherlands, which the Spaniards could neither win nor terminate. By contrast the Venetians readily gave up territory when attacked on the mainland; the Hungarians sustained a number of defeats in the Balkans that went unavenged; the Spaniards, after the Thirty Years War, lost more battles than they won. The Costa Ricans, victorious over Walker, withdrew from Nicaragua.

There are some negative findings. International Courts, arms control and collective security seem to have played little part in preserving peace. Nor does there seem to be any clear case of a peaceful society refusing to enter a temporary power vacuum, being aware that conflict would result when power was recovered.

Something may be said about military structures. In most of these cases, there was little technological change during the period of peace. Rib and plank construction did begin during the Venetian Peace, and may have helped Venice maintain a naval advantage. There were changes during the long British, Scandinavian and Brazilian peace periods, though among these only Britain was finally responsible for its own defense. Until World War II it did keep up with the latest technology in the all-important Royal Navy, but the development of air power finally ended the Peace. The Pacific nations barely survived the replacement of traditional naval conflict by carrier warfare. Much earlier the Peace of Poland came to an end in part because the change in the nature of armies from feudal to mercenary left the Poles obsolescent.

Naval power was involved in the defense of a large proportion of the peaceful societies. It was directly employed by Venice, Britain and Spain, but great power naval protection also contributed to peace in Scandinavia, Costa Rica, Canada and the Pacific states. Peaceful societies have had several kinds of military forces, depending on the times. Feudal levies, mercenaries, and conscript armies and militias have all been used. Costa Rica, in the twentieth century, had no army. None of the peaceful societies was known for the size of its land forces; none kept a large standing army.

One military factor that probably contributes to peace is not easy to measure and would be hard to study. That is the normal superiority of the defense. Other things being equal, it is difficult for one nation to attack another, to maintain its forces in the other's territory, to cope with hostile populations, to risk other powers' coming in on the side of the defender. This cannot be demonstrated by evaluating the percentage of times invasion results in gain for the invader unless you can include the probably greater number of times a nation has decided against invasion, in part because of the normal superiority of the defense.

Finally, luck plays a part. The Pacific societies were lucky to be out of range of the Japanese, in terms both of distance and importance with relation to Japanese war plans. Spain was lucky that the settlement of the War of Spanish Succession resulted in a Bourbon dynasty. Costa Rica was lucky that the chance death of Justo Barrios prevented a possible invasion. Perhaps Iceland, beneficiary of the longest peace of all, was fortunate in its poverty and dubious climate.

To sum up, it would appear that the concept of spheres of influence, sometimes castigated as a historical evil outgrown by contemporary nations, has helped preserve the peace of smaller nations. So have unifications of the weak with the strong, though such unifications may be condemned by nationalists. But when nations are relatively equal in power with their neighbors and can benefit from some degree of isolation, they have done well to avoid alliances.

For the most part it appears that wars that governments of peaceful societies have carried on outside the peaceful territory have not been necessary to preserve the peace. It certainly could be argued that a Peace like that of Switzerland is of a higher or at any rate different quality from that of Britain. But the question of the relationship between domestic peace and foreign warfare is one that should be studied more explicitly.

22

Terminations

The enumeration of the terminations is a little different from the delineation of the peace periods themselves. In the first place, eight of the peace and subpeace periods are still continuing: the Swiss, the Scandinavian (Iceland and Sweden), the Brazilian, the Canadian and all four areas of the Pacific. That leaves 13 terminations. But three of the subperiods may be further divided, since they had two phases: the Spanish, English and Norwegian. We may subdivide these into the Habsburg and Bourbon Spanish, the Stuart and Hanoverian English, and the Medieval and Modern Norwegian. The Brazilian also had two phases, the second of which continues. Thus four first phase terminations may be added, making 17 in all (Table 5). (The Polynesian Subpeace is not considered.)

As the table also shows, sometimes the event that precipitated the ending of peace was internal, a rebellion of some sort, and sometimes it was external, an invasion or bombing. Sometimes both occurred.

Internal collapse was somewhat more common. There were eight cases of rebellion and one civil war. The rebellions were of all sorts. There were elite opposition rebellions such as Tiepolo's in Venice, Zebrzydowski's in Poland, the English Civil War and the Figueres Rebellion in Costa Rica. There were ideological nationalist rebellions such as the Sinn Fein Rebellion in Ireland and the 1918 Rebellion in Finland, and to a minor extent the Tupac Amaru Rebellion in Peru. The Brazilian provincial rebellions occurred against an over-centralized regime of suddenly doubtful legitimacy.

In eight cases, peace came to an end because of external factors that usually did not have much to do with the internal condition of the peaceful society. The Thirty Years War ended peace in Brandenburg, the Napoleonic Wars ended peace in Denmark and the Iberian Peninsula, and World War II ended peace in Norway, England and Scotland. War between Sweden and Denmark spilled over into Norway in the seventeenth century. The Bohemian Hussite invasion of Hungary anticipated internal rebellions that were partially related.

In three cases external invasions followed internal crises which in two cases had already broken the peace. The Genoese War followed by several decades Tiepolo's Rebellion, but related to a change signified by the earlier episode; the War of the Spanish Succession was precipitated by the absence of a Spanish heir; and the German intervention in Finland was precipitated by the rebellion as well as the fact that Germany and Russia were already at war.

There were 12 attacks from external sources in the 17 terminations, but only two of these—the Hussite invasion of Hungary and the Napoleonic invasion of Spain—were followed by internal conflict. This could suggest that there was no serious internal problem prior to the invasion or bombing, or that the invasion resolved the internal problem that had terminated the peace, or that an internal counter-response to the external episode ended violence.

Looking at the quality of leadership during these periods of termination,

159

TABLE 5. TERMINATIONS

PEACE	PRECIPITATING OR FOLLOWING (F) INTERNAL EVENT	PRECIPITATING OR FOLLOWING (F) EXTERNAL EVENT
Venetian	Tiepolo's Rebellion	F Genoese Raids
Hungarian	F Peasant/Hussite Rebellion	Bohemian-Hussite Invasions
Polish	Zebrzydowski's Rebellion	F Swedish Invasion
Brandenburger		Thirty Years War
Habsburg Spanish		War of Spanish Succession
Bourbon Spanish	F Two Decades of Anarchy	French Invasion, Napoleonic Wars
Spanish American	Tupac Amaru Rebellion (1780)	
Stuart English	Civil War	
Hanoverian English		World War II Bombing
Scottish		World War II Bombing
Irish	Sinn Fein Rebellion	
Medieval Norwegian		Swedish/Danish Spillover
Modern Norwegian		German Invasion
Danish		British Raids, Napoleonic Wars
Finnish	1918 Rebellion	F German Intervention, World War I
Costa Rican	Figueres Rebellion	
Early Brazilian	Provincial Rebellions (1831-1850)	

there are only two cases in which it seems to be notoriously bad: Ferdinand VII in Bourbon Spain and George William in Brandenburg. And even George William, as has been noted earlier, might not have been regarded as imcompetent if he had not come along at a time where it was particularly difficult to make decisions. Outstanding leaders emerged in Hungary, Brandenburg, Stuart England and Brazil after the peace periods had been broken: Frederick William the Great Elector in Brandenburg, the Hunyadis in Hungary, William of Orange in England and Pedro II in Brazil. But only William, as William III, and Pedro II were successful in restoring the Peace, William because he was willing to cooperate with an able group of Parliamentary leaders, Pedro because fear of further rebellion gave him widespread support.

In two cases, peace broke around the issue of an attempt to change power relationships within the elite. Both Charles I of England and Sigismund Vasa of Poland attempted to strengthen the monarchy, and were challenged by established elites. But in Spain, it was the breakdown of a highly centralized authority that ended the peace, and made it exceptionally difficult to restore.

In Spain, Brazil and perhaps Poland there was a problem of institutionalization of a government form continuing into a time when external forces became powerful enough to challenge it. In Brazil, the continued presence of a legitimate monarch allowed for restoration.

One factor that seems to have been common in peaceful societies is that their governments provided a reasonable expectation of justice. Generally this seems to be so of the societies at the time of termination, but in four of them this capacity had markedly weakened. In the Iberian Peninsula the loss of vigor in the monarch weakened the expectation of justice, since justice and the monarchy were so intertwined; the Spaniards in America exploited native populations harshly, but so had their Indian predecessors and the exploitation was at least predictable. In Hungary, there had been increasing demands for labor and military service, and restrictions on freedom of movement; and in Venice, a long period of rule by terror followed Tiepolo's rebellion.

Workable systems of succession have appeared to be necessary in a peaceful society, and disputed successions have caused interruptions to peace. It is not surprising, therefore, that succession problems were involved in four of the terminations. In Hungary the death of Sigismund without a son caused a long succession struggle, in Poland Sigismund Vasa was elected to the Polish throne after the Jagiellonian dynasty died out; the Iberian Peace was first breached by the war of Spanish succession; and in a modern case, the Costa Rican Peace ended in a struggle over the presidential succession. In Brazil, peace was interrupted by the suddenly questionable position of the Braganza dynasty and the absence of an adult successor.

There does not seem to be any close relationship between termination and economies. Hungary was experiencing some economic difficulty that could have contributed to the conflicts of the 1430's. Peasants were paying increasing taxes after having been lightly taxed, and the nobility was being asked to pay taxes in cash rather than kind. Spain had probably been experiencing a long economic decline, though authorities do not totally agree about that. In any case no one suggests an economic cause of either break in peace. Otherwise the terminations seem to have occurred in periods that were not experiencing appreciable economic transformation.

A number of the conflicts of termination had to do with power distribution among social classes, though this is not easy to separate from problems of centralization and decentralization. But certainly Venice was experiencing a rise of the patrician class at the time of Tiepolo's rebellion, and the great nobility was consolidating its hold in Hungary. In Brandenburg, too, the nobility had gained power in relation to the Elector. Zebrzydowski's rebellion and the English Civil War were also conflicts in which the nobility was seeking to retain power, on these occasions against the monarchy. The collapse of Bourbon Spain, on the other hand, may be attributed in some part to the inability of a weakened nobility to provide even a temporary nexus of authority in place of a failing Crown.

Religion seems to have been a factor on two occasions: in the Hussite invasion of Hungary and in the Catholic–Protestant conflict implicit in the Sinn Fein Rebellion in Ireland.

Changing beliefs played a part in several different terminations. The growth of nationalism was central to the Sinn Fein rebellion and the Finnish rebellion against Russia in 1918. In Poland Sigismund Vasa brought in a very different worldview from that of the Polish nobility. In Spain the discrediting of the monarchy resulted in a widespread loss of faith and belief in authority.

The only foreign policy change that definitely affected peace was the Venetian involvement on the mainland after centuries of remaining aloof. Brandenburg changed its situation by acquiring East Prussia, doubling the territory to be defended and creating a common boundary with Poland, but without this acquisition there still would have been a Thirty Years War.

It is difficult to see any case where the dogged maintenance of a previously successful policy was a factor in the termination of peace, with the exception of the breakup of the Spanish American Empire.

A consideration of changes in military capacity simply reviews ground already covered. The Polish and Brandenburger feudal armies were no match for the standing armies developing on the European Continent in the seventeenth century.

This review of terminations uncovers no golden key. Terminations occur both from internal revolutions and external invasions. Political factors—changes in distributions of power and foreign policy decisions—seem to play a more important part than economic factors. Changes in belief played a part too. Yet, whether one considers changes in power, foreign policy or outlook, there are more cases of maintenance of the status quo than of change.

We have noted that luck played a part in some of the long peace periods. Perhaps, over a period of time, luck tends to run out. Brandenburg was lucky to have no strong neighbors, but then wound up in the center of the Thirty Years War. England was lucky to have a location that enabled naval power to protect her, but technology eventually brought the violence of war to the islands.

But these changes must be expected; not since the invention of fire have we been able to escape the occasional burn. Here luck may be described as the environment in which leadership operates. There will occasionally be such world-devouring catastrophes as the Thirty Years War, in which even magnificent leadership is likely to fail, but for the moment these must be assumed and regretted but not addressed. The question for current investigation is not the great catastrophic bang but the more frequent resigned and fatalistic whimper. How was the environment managed so well for so long? And only then, how did failure come in the end?

23

Recapitulation

Settings

1. Peace was obtained for societies governed by powers of different magnitude, both minor and major. But there never was a century of peace for the dominant power of the day.

2. Most Peace periods were achieved by societies involved with, not isolated from, others. Many more societies so exist in involvement with others, however, than in isolation, and an isolated society (by definition) does not face the threat of external war.

3. Among mutually involved societies, a location on the periphery of a state system provides some advantage for peace as compared to a central location, but is not decisive.

4. Peaceful societies more often than not were protected by at least one physical barrier.

5. Climate does not appear to have been an important factor in the preservation of peace.

6. Autonomy does not appear to be a prerequisite of peace.

7. All but three of the peace periods existed during one of the three general wars that occurred in the West during the past five centuries.

8. There were exceptionally long or recurrent periods of peace in Iceland, Norway, Great Britain and Brazil.

9. The majority of the peace periods that existed during a general war were not ended by that war.

10. When history is examined in terms of each local and short-term development rather than only heavily spotlighted events, peace may be far more common than war.

Origins

1. Long periods of peace originate more commonly from rebellions than from war.

2. Peace emerges from both successful and unsuccessful rebellions.

3. The kinds of conflict from which peace originates are strikingly varied. It is difficult to think of a kind that has not led to a long period of peace.

4. Where peace begins with the settlement of a war, the makers of the peace have usually been the victors in the war.

Leadership

1. In democratic societies, it is more difficult to identify heroes of peace than war heroes.

163

2. Often it is possible to identify a crucial "reconciler" early in the history of a peace.

3. Reconcilers provide order out of chaos, bring together conflicting units, resolve conflicting interests.

4. Reconcilers are inclined to be firm, patient, persistent and sober, rarely jolly or festive.

5. Later rulers in peaceful periods are likely to receive fame for magnificence or longevity rather than for governing abilities.

6. Most leaders who come to power in middle periods of peace are likely to be mediocre.

7. Reformers generally fail to restore peace.

8. Leadership at the end of a peace period does not appear to be inferior to that which prevailed during middle periods.

9. It would appear, then, that leadership plays an important part in the formative phase of a peace period, but not thereafter.

Polities

1. Peace has been achieved more than once in states of all geographic sizes.

2. Hereditary monarchy dominated most of the peaceful societies through the eighteenth century.

3. In the past two centuries, all governments of peaceful societies except that of Brazil have tended toward representative government.

4. Peace has been maintained frequently during processes of change in representation and autonomy.

5. Effective systems of succession are important to the maintenance of peace.

6. Political stability is the norm in peaceful societies.

7. No particular system of law or justice seems necessary to peaceful societies.

8. Decentralization of power among elites is the more common pattern in peaceful societies of the West.

9. Governments of peaceful societies tend to be relatively mild in their treatment of subjects.

10. Tension between central and regional authority has been very common in peaceful societies.

Economies

1. Peace periods are not generally periods of either prosperity or stagnation, unemployment and poverty. Some were prosperous, some were not.

2. The peaceful societies of the past two centuries have generally been prosperous.

3. Peace was no guarantee of prosperity, nor was its loss necessarily concurrent with a decline in prosperity.

4. Peaceful nations that have been prosperous have been fairly effective in distributing that prosperity.

5. Peaceful societies have had many different kinds of economies.

6. Peaceful societies have tended to be active in trade.

7. Natural resources do not seem to have played a great part in the establishment or maintenance of peaceful societies.

8. Few of the peaceful societies, before the twentieth century, were blessed with exceptional systems of transportation or communication.

9. Economic factors seem to have had little to do with the termination of peace.

Societies

1. In three cases in which peaceful societies were involved in general wars, their total societies were very much involved in terms of fear of loss or invasion, and members of families being involved in combat.

2. In most limited wars, societies were not greatly affected by the war.

3. In many peaceful societies, the members of the society were not explicitly aware that they were at peace and had no conception of peace as being valuable.

4. Vertical mobility was common in the peaceful societies of the past two centuries, and earlier in Britain and Spanish America.

5. In Western societies it is difficult to perceive a relationship between peace and population density or change.

6. The governments of peaceful societies were usually not pervasive in their influence on the lives of people living in those societies.

7. While many of the peaceful societies were ethnically homogenous, there is a good sprinkling of cases involving coexistence or integration of ethnic and racial minorities.

8. Peace continued through periods of immense social change in the past two centuries.

9. At least since medieval times, maintenance of a Peace has depended not on conducting organized external warfare, but on the availability of a socially fluid frontier area that may include low-level violence, which could be an important contributing factor to maintaining a Peace.

Culture

1. In most peaceful societies religion was regarded as subordinate to government.

2. All but one of the governments were tolerant of minorities or at least permitted them to live within the realm.

3. There is little evidence from the study of the peaceful societies of the West to indicate that conflicts between civilizations were more dangerous to peace than conflicts within a single civilization.

4. Seven of the twelve societies had major creative periods during the time of peace.

5. Patterns of creativity can be found early, in the middle, and toward the end of the peace periods.

6. If peaceful societies are creative, they have also been pragmatic in outlook, tolerant of variety, and productive of much that was second-rate.

7. Some of the members of the peaceful societies regarded peace as a value, but this was not the case in most of the societies.

8. The inhabitants of the peaceful societies were much more likely to be vital than weary.

9. In quite a number of the societies, there were patterned limitations on violence, or at least non-violent behavior was perceived to be more acceptable.

10. Several of the governments of the societies provided institutionalized opportunities for conflict and violence outside the societies themselves.

11. Societies in which such opportunities were absent do not seem to be especially neurotic.

Foreign Relations

1. Weak nations with strong neighbors have often maintained peace by accepting the rule of these neighbors.

2. Weak nations have also maintained peace by being within the sphere of influence of a major power.

3. When neighboring powers are equal or inferior, the governments of peaceful societies have tended to avoid peace time alliances.

4. Buffer states have not played a major role in the protection of peaceful societies in the West.

5. Peaceful societies in the colonial world achieved peace before they achieved autonomy.

6. Stable borders have contributed to peace on at least three occasions.

7. Most governments of peaceful societies did not pursue peace as a policy.

8. It seems probable that only a small portion of the fighting done by governments of peaceful societies outside their own territory was necessary to the defense of the peaceful territories.

9. Governments of peaceful societies avoided becoming overcommitted in foreign conflicts.

10. International courts, arms control and collective security played no role in any case of peace.

11. Naval power played a role in the peace of several of the societies.

12. Peaceful societies usually did not have large armies, standing or otherwise.

13. It is probable, but not provable, that in most cases defense was perceived to be superior to offense.

14. In several cases in interstate affairs luck played a major role in preserving peace.

Terminations

1. The termination of peace was sometimes precipitated by an internal event, sometimes by an external intrusion.

2. Where external intervention took place, it usually followed a change in the external balance or situation.

3. Generally during the termination of a peace period the quality of leadership is not markedly inferior.

4. In several cases, expectations of justice had markedly weakened at the time of termination.

5. Succession problems were involved in several cases of termination, as they were in a number of interruptions.

6. No close relation is obvious between termination and the economic condition of the Peace.

7. A number of terminating conflicts have arisen from power disputes among social classes.

8. Religion was a factor in only two terminations.

9. Changes in outlook played a part in several terminations.

10. Changes in foreign policy caused termination only once; refusal to change foreign policy is not observed to cause termination.

11. Bad luck was a factor in at least two terminations.

12. On the whole, it proved to be more instructive to study the mechanisms for maintaining peace than it was to study the terminations.

Salient Findings

Of more than ninety discoveries, the following seem most important:

1. In the past two centuries all governments of peaceful societies, with the exception of Brazil, have tended toward representative government.

2. No state in Western history has succeeded in combining regional or general dominance with a century of peace.

3. No peaceful society has based that peace on a large professional armed force.

4. Peace may emerge from any of a wide variety of settings.

And not as a finding but as a point for further exploration:

5. On the local and short-term scale, peace may be far more common than war. This would imply that the propensity for war is a product of increasing complexity and that a Peace is the long-term successful address of these problems. Nothing in these pages contradicts such a proposition, but the number of potential variables and quantity of necessary detailed research involved in supporting it are beyond the capacity of this work.

24

The Western and Ancient Worlds

How does Peace in the Western World compare to that achieved by societies in the Ancient World? In an earlier study of the Ancient World (Melko and Weigel, 1981), similar analytical categories were used, though orientations were sometimes different, so that questions asked in the two studies were not always the same. Still, there are many overlappings in which similarities and differences become apparent.

These assessments, based on comparisons of recapitulations of analyses of common elements in briefly recounted cases, are necessarily approximate. But they may give some insight toward the factors that have been consistent in peaceful societies through a long period of history, and also some areas in which change may have taken place.

Similarities

In general settings, there was a wide range of sizes of peaceful societies, in both area and power. Size in both ranged from city-states to vast empires, though the empires were of different kinds. In both worlds, physical barriers of some sort played a role in most of the peace periods, but climate does not seem to have been important.

Both had areas of very long or recurring peace. There were several in the West, such as in Norway, Britain and Iceland, the longest peace period of all. In the Ancient World there were very long periods in Spain and Phoenicia, but nothing else matches the record of Egypt, where long periods of peace recurred at least three times, and arguably five, over a period of three millennia.

Reconcilers appeared in both ages, but perhaps were more important in ancient times. But in both worlds reconcilers had a capacity for manipulating the particular situation they confronted. After this initial period of building and consolidation, creative leadership seemed to be relatively unimportant, though monarchs often appeared who are remembered for such accomplishments as splendor, conquest or longevity. Capable reformers sometimes arose after the termination of peace, but usually failed to restore peace for any long period.

In the major peace periods the government of the peaceful society was usually located within that society. There was often a tension, however, between central and regional authorities, with a tendency toward decentralization being much more common than toward centralization. Instability of succession was common in both worlds, and where it occurred there was frequently a breach and sometimes a termination of the peace. The expectation of justice seems to have been more important than the development of specific law codes.

Active trade was common in peaceful societies of both ages. Governments were not active in economic intervention, except regarding their own financing, and there were few exceptional natural resources, nor forms of transportation nor communication.

Within the societies of both periods there were few social consequences from ordinary wars, as distinguished from general wars, and usually there was a lack of awareness of the prevalence of peace. Governments were not pervasive in these societies, and no pattern of relationship could be found between peace and population density or change. Ethnic and racial intermixtures were reasonably common in the peaceful societies of either age.

There was a good deal of evidence of creativity within these societies, though not in all, and a good deal of second-rate work was also produced. Unquestionably there was a great deal of vitality in these societies, a willingness to accept a variety of styles, perhaps a tendency toward pragmatic outlooks.

Foreign policies in both epochs were characterized by prudence, caution in relation to neighbors, an avoidance of overcommitment. Frequently the leaders of peaceful societies perceived a common family or ideological bond with neighbors. In both ages buffer states, international courts, collective security and arms control were of little or no importance. In neither age was external fighting absolutely necessary to prevent violence at home. There were few military transformations during peace periods, and peaceful societies tended to have military forces better equipped for defense than attack.

In both worlds, peace could come to an end through either internal rebellion or external intervention. An external intervention was often preceded by a change in the external setting, internal violence by a change in power of elites. Leadership was usually not especially weak at the period of termination, and political factors usually played more of a role than economic factors. It was rare for change in religious or foreign policies to play a role in the termination of peace. It often seemed that peace was lost in a situation that was not more difficult to manage than a series of preceding situations in which peace was maintained. After avoiding a series of stumbling blocks, a government finally stumbled.

Differences

The topic of origins was not included in the analysis of the Ancient World, so comparisons in this rather important area cannot be made.

In the West there was no Peace ruled by a single dominant power such as the Roman or Achemenid of the Ancient World. Western empires were colonial in nature, they never included all their European neighbors, though such was the aim of such occasional Western leaders as Napoleon and Hitler. In the Ancient World, peace existed in generally stable situations, whereas in the West, local peace periods frequently continued through periods of general war. In the West, involved situations and central locations were more common; in the Ancient World isolated or peripheral situations were more common.

Somewhat surprisingly, the variety of governmental forms among peaceful societies seems to have been wider in the Ancient World than in the West. Autonomy seems to have been more the rule in the Ancient World than in the West. Individual leaders of a reconciliation period are often difficult to identify in representative oligarchic societies in the West, but their identity usually was clear in the Ancient World, with the exception of Phoenicia.

The peaceful societies of the Ancient World were usually prosperous; less frequently so in the West. In the Ancient World, prosperity frequently followed peace, and waned before its termination; in the West no such relationship was discerned. Vertical mobility was more striking in the Ancient World than it was in Western societies before the industrial revolution.

The Ancient World included at least three civilizations; the Western World is here treated as a single civilization, though the Hispanic evolution is arguably a separate one. The appreciation of peace as a value is more evident in the Ancient World, though there was a decline of this appreciation evident at the time of termination. The same is true of the decline of creativity.

In foreign relations, peaceful societies of the Ancient World were more likely to be in situations of general stability and predictability. Small and weak peaceful societies in the Western World were more likely to accept the rule of stronger neighbors, or to be protected by spheres of influence. External fighting was rarely defensive in the West, more frequently so among the governments of peaceful societies in the Ancient World. There were colonies in the Ancient World, but a long period of colonial peace was observed only in Roman Spain.

During periods of termination, internal rebellion followed external attack frequently in the Ancient World, only once in the West. The initial incident precipitating termination was generally external in the Ancient World, but might be either internal or external in the West. Changes in external situations before termination were more noticeable in the Ancient World than in the West, and so were cases of termination arising from persistence in existing policies or techniques despite these changes. On the other hand succession problems, declines in expectation of justice, and changes in outlook were more frequently factors in Western terminations.

The Reality of Peace

Certainly it should be clear, by now, that peace need not be regarded merely as an ideal condition to be achieved in some future millennium. Repeatedly for periods of a century or more, during the last three millennia societies have managed to survive without physical violence and more often than not with considerable vitality.

Peace has been achieved in many ways, by many kinds of people; it has been achieved in small areas and large and in different polities, economies and cultures.

When achieved, often through a process of wise and prudent government, Peace often has gone unstudied and unnoticed.

Yet a successful Peace requires such complex balancing of interests, so careful a generalized matching of institutions, concepts and realities which, as individual elements, may be wildly contradictory. Above all, Peace requires such a long-term flexibility and sense of the possible that the more easily appreciated generalship of a single war, however brilliant, is nevertheless on a very small scale by comparison. Alexander of Macedon built an empire and a destiny, but even he failed to build a Peace. In the exploding complexity of the late twentieth century a study of these previous successes and the reasons for their eventual failure may give welcome lessons for present use. Indeed, given what a serious collapse could mean in the atomic age, such study would seem long overdue.

The achievement of peace should be noticed, studied, appreciated and even acclaimed.

Selected Bibliography

General References

Babst, Dean. "Elective Governments—A Force for Peace." **Wisconsin Sociologist,** 1964, 9-14.
_____. "A Force for Peace." **Industrial Research,** April, 1972.
Bloch, Marc. **Feudal Society,** tr. by L.A. Manyon. Chicago: University of Chicago Press, 1962.
Bouthoul, Gaston, and Rene Carrere. "A List of the 366 Major Armed Conflicts of the Period 1740-1974." **Peace Research,** X:3, 1978.
Carr, E.H. **What Is History?** New York: Random House, 1967.
Coudenhove-Kalergi, Richard. **From War to Peace.** London: Cape, 1959.
Eisenstadt, S.N. **The Political System of Empires.** New York: Free Press, 1963.
Gibbon, Edward. **The Decline and Fall of the Roman Empire.** New York: Modern Library, 1954.
Leitenberg, Milton. "Obscene Definition." **The Bulletin of the Atomic Scientists,** p. 2, Sept. 1975.
Melko, Matthew. **52 Peaceful Societies.** Oakville, Ontario: Canadian Peace Research Institute, 1973.
_____. "The Government of Peaceful Societies." **Peace Research,** February, 1972.
_____, and Richard D. Weigel. **Peace in the Ancient World.** Jefferson, N.C.: McFarland, 1981.
Quigley, Carroll. **The Evolution of Civilizations.** New York: McMillan, 1962.
Singer, J. David; Melvin Small, and Susan Jones. **The Wages of War: A Statistical Handbook, 1816-1965.** New York: Wiley, 1972.
Sorokin, Pitirim A. **Social and Cultural Dynamics, III.** New York: American Book Company, 1937.
Spengler, Oswald. **The Decline of the West,** Charles Atkinson translation. London: Allen & Unwin, 1932; reprint, New York: Alfred Knopf, 1980.
Vanhanen, Tatu. **Power and the Means of Power: A Study of 119 Asian, European, American, and African States, 1850-1975.** Ann Arbor, MI: University Microfilms International, 1979.
Wesson, Robert G. **The Imperial Order.** Berkeley: University of California Press, 1967.
Young, G.M. **Victorian England,** 2nd ed. New York: Oxford University Press, 1964.
Ziegler, Philip. **The Black Death.** New York: John Day, 1960.

The Venetian Peace

Baynes, N.H., and H. St. L.B. Moss. **Byzantium.** Oxford: Clarendon Press, 1961.
Browning, Robert. **The Byzantine Empire.** New York: Scribner's, 1980.
Bryce, James. **The Holy Roman Empire,** 4th ed. London: Macmillan, 1963.
Bury, J.B.; J.R. Tanner, C.W. Previte-Orton, and Z.N. Brooke, editors. **The**

Cambridge Medieval History, vol. V, **Contest of Empire and Papacy.** New York: Cambridge University Press, 1964.

Cheetham, Nicolas. **Mediaeval Greece.** New Haven: Yale University Press, 1981.

Crawford, Francis Marion. **The Rulers of the South: Sicily, Calabria, Malta,** vol. II. New York: Macmillan, 1900.

Diehl, Charles. **Byzantium: Greatness and Decline,** tr. by Naomi Walford. New Brunswick, NJ: Rutgers University Press, 1957.

Geanakoplos, Deno John. **Interaction of the "Sibling" Byzantine and Western Cultures in the Middle Ages and Italian Renaissance (330–1600).** New Haven: Yale University Press, 1976.

Hazlitt, W. Carew. **The Venetian Republic.** London: Black, 1915.

Heer, Friedrich. **The Holy Roman Empire,** tr. Janet Sondheimer. New York: Praeger, 1967.

Hussey, J.M. **The Byzantine World,** 2nd ed. London: Hutchinson, 1961.

Lane, Frederic C. **Venice, a Maritime Republic.** Baltimore: Johns Hopkins University Press, 1973.

McNeill, William H. **Venice, The Hinge of Europe, 1081–1797.** Chicago: University of Chicago Press, 1974.

Norwich, John Julius. **The Kingdom in the Sun, 1130–1194,** 2nd ed. Harlow, Eng: Longman, 1970.

_____. **A History of Venice.** New York: Knopf, 1982.

Okey, Thomas. **The Story of Venice.** London: J.M. Dent, 1907.

Sinor, Denis. **History of Hungary.** London: Allen and Unwin, 1959.

Sismondi, J.D.L. de. **A History of the Italian Republics.** Garden City, NY: Doubleday, 1966.

Wiel, Alethea. **Venice.** New York: Putnam's, 1894.

The Hungarian Peace

Dvornik, Francis. **The Slavs in European History and Civilization.** New Brunswick, NJ: Rutgers University Press, 1962.

Eckhart, Ferenc. **A Short History of the Hungarian People.** London: Grant Richards, 1931.

Graus, Frantisek; Karl Bosl; Ferdinand Seibt; M.M. Postan, and Alexander Gieysztor. **Eastern and Western Europe in the Middle Ages.** London: Thames and Hudson, 1970.

Halecki, Oscar. **Borderlands of Western Civilization,** Rev. ed. London: Dent, 1955.

_____. **A History of Poland,** Ninth Edition. New York: McKay, 1976.

Homan, Balint. "Hungary, 1301–1490." **The Cambridge Medieval History,** vol. VIII. C.W. Previte-Orton and Z.N. Brooke, editors. Cambridge, England: Cambridge University Press, 1936.

Kaminsky, Howard. **A History of the Hussite Revolution.** Berkeley: University of California Press, 1945.

Kinross, J.P.D. **The Ottoman Centuries.** New York: Morrow, 1977.

Knatchbull-Hugessen, C.M. **The Political Evolution of the Hungarian Nation.** New York: Arno Press, 1971.

Knoll, Paul W. **The Rise of the Polish Monarchy: Piast Poland in East Central Europe, 1320–1370.** Chicago: University of Chicago Press, 1972.

Kosary, Domokos G. **A History of Hungary.** Cleveland: The Benjamin Franklin Bibliophile Society, 1941.

Macartney, C.A. **Hungary, A Short History.** Hawthorne, NY: Aldine, 1962.

Norwich, John Julius. **A History of Venice.** New York: Knopf, 1982.

Previte-Orton, C.W. **History of Europe, 1197–1378.** London: Methuen, 3d. ed., 1951 (Original 1937).

Sinor, Denis. **History of Hungary.** New York: Praeger, 1959.
Temperley, Harold W.V. **History of Serbia.** London: Bell, 1919.
Tihany, Leslie C. **A History of Middle Europe.** New Brunswick, NJ: Rutgers University Press, 1976.
Waugh, W.T. **A History of Europe From 1378–1494,** 3d. ed. London: Methuen, 1949.

The Polish Peace

Bain, R. Nisbet. **Slavonic Europe: A Political History of Poland and Russia from 1447 to 1796.** New York: Arno Press, 1971 (1980 reprint).
Betts, R.R. "Constitutional Development and Political Thought in Eastern Europe," Ch. XV, pp. 464–480, **The New Cambridge Modern History,** v. II, **The Reformation, 1520–1559.** New York: Cambridge University Press, 1961.
Cambridge History of Poland. New York: Cambridge University Press, 1950.
Dvornik, Francis. **The Slavs in European History and Civilization.** New Brunswick, NJ: Rutgers University Press, 1962.
Davies, Norman. **God's Playground: A History of Poland.** New York: Columbia University Press, 1982.
Ehrenpreis, Wiktor J. "Poland (Up to 1918)" in Joseph S. Roucek, ed. **Central Eastern Europe: Crucible of World Wars.** New York: Prentice-Hall, 1946.
Fox, Paul. **The Reformation in Poland, Some Social and Economic Aspects.** Baltimore: John Hopkins, 1924.
Grant, A.J. **A History of Europe from 1494 to 1610.** London: Methuen, 1952.
Halecki, Oskar. **Borderlands of Western Civilization; a History of East Central Europe.** New York: Ronald Press, 1952.
Heymann, Frederick G. **Poland and Czechoslovakia.** Englewood Cliffs, NJ: Prentice-Hall, 1966.
Knoll, Paul W. "Feudal Poland: Division and Reunion," **The Polish Review** (XXIII:2), 40–52.
Kula, Witold. **An Economic Theory of the Feudal System; Towards a Model of the Polish Economy, 1500–1800,** New Edition. London: NLB, 1976.
Lonnroth, E. "The Baltic Countries" in M.M. Postan, E.E. Rich and Edward Miller, eds. **The Cambridge Economic History of Europe,** v. III **Economic Organization and Policies in the Middle Ages.** New York: Cambridge University Press, 1971.
Macartney, C.A. "Eastern Europe" Ch. XIII, pp. 368–94, **The New Cambridge Modern History,** v. I **The Renaissance, 1493–1520.** Cambridge University Press, 1961.
McNeill, William H. **Europe's Steppe Frontier, 1500–1800.** Chicago: University of Chicago Press, 1964.
Roberts, Michael. **The Early Vasas.** New York: Cambridge University Press, 1968.
Skwarczynskii, P. "Poland and Lithuania," Ch. XII, pp. 377–403. **New Cambridge Modern History,** III, **The Counter Reformation and Price Revolution, 1559–1610,** Cambridge University Press, 1961.
Tihany, Leslie C. **A History of Middle Europe.** New Brunswick, NJ: Rutgers University Press, 1976.
Waugh, W.T. **A History of Europe from 1378–1494.** London: Methuen, 3d. ed.

The Brandenburger Peace

Brandi, Karl, **The Emperor Charles V,** tr. by C.V. Wedgwood. London: Cape, 1939.

Bryce, James. **The Holy Roman Empire,** 4th ed. London: Macmillan, 1963.

Carsten, F.L. **The Origins of Prussia.** Oxford: The Clarendon Press, 1954.

Fay, Sidney. **The Rise of Brandenburg—Prussia to 1786.** New York: Holt, Rinehart and Winston, 1937.

Henderson, Ernest F. **A Short History of Germany.** New York: Macmillan, 1902.

Holborn, Hajo. **A History of Modern Germany.** New York: Knopf, 1964.

Klassen, Peter J. **Europe in the Reformation.** Englewood Cliffs, NJ: Prentice-Hall, 1979.

Koch, H.W. **A History of Prussia.** London: Longman, 1978.

Maehl, William H. **Germany in Western Civilization.** University, AL: University of Alabama Press, 1979.

Marriott, J.A.R., and Charles Grant Robertson. **The Evolution of Prussia.** Oxford: The Clarendon Press, 1946.

Mitchell, Otis C. **A Concise History of Brandenburg—Prussia to 1786.** Washington: University Press of America, 1980.

Nelson, Walter Henry. **The Soldier Kings: The House of Hohenzollern.** New York: Putnam, 1970.

Ranke, Leopold. **Memoirs of the House of Brandenburg, and History of Prussia During the Seventeenth and Eighteenth Centuries,** vol. I, tr. by Sir Alex and Lady Duff Gordon, Original 1849. New York: Greenwood Press, 1968.

Rodes, John E. **Germany: A History.** New York: Holt, Rinehart and Winston, 1964.

Taylor, A.J.P. **The Course of German History.** London: Methuen, 1961.

Wedgwood, C.V. **The Thirty Years War.** London: Cape, 1938.

The Spanish Imperial Peace

JOURNALS AND SERIALS

The Americas
Anuario de Estudios Americanos
Cambridge Economic History of Europe
Comparative Studies in Society and History
Hispanic American Historical Review
Journal of Latin American Studies
Journal of Modern History
Latin American Research Review
New Cambridge Modern History
Past and Present

SPAIN

Braudel, Fernand. **The Mediterranean and the Mediterranean World in the Age of Philip II.** S. Reynolds, tr. New York: Harper and Row, 1972.

Carr, Raymond. **Spain, 1808–1939.** Oxford: Clarendon Press, 1966.

Christiansen, E. **The Origins of Military Power in Spain.** London: Oxford University Press, 1967.

Davies, R. Trevor. **The Golden Century of Spain, 1501–1621.** New York: Harper and Row, Harper Torchbooks, 1937.

_____. **Spain in Decline, 1621–1700.** London: Macmillan and Co. Ltd., 1957.

Deforneaux, Marcelin. **Daily Life in Spain in the Golden Age,** tr. by N. Branch. New York: Praeger, 1970.

Dominguez Ortiz, Antonio. **The Golden Age of Spain, 1516–1659,** tr. by J. Casey. New York: Basic Books, 1971.

_____. **Sociedad y Estado en el Siglo XVIII Espanol.** Barcelona: Editorial Ariel, 1976.

Elliott, J.H. **Imperial Spain, 1469-1716.** New York: New American Library, Mentor Books, 1963.

Fernandez Alvarez, Manuel. **La Sociedad Espanola del Renacimiento.** Madrid: Ediciones Catedra, 1974.

Hargreaves-Mawdsley, W.N. **Spain under the Bourbons, 1700-1833.** New York: Macmillan, 1973.

Herr, Richard. **The Eighteenth-Century Revolution in Spain.** Princeton: Princeton University Press, 1958.

Hillgarth, J.N. **The Spanish Kingdoms, 1250-1516.** Oxford: Clarendon Press, 1978.

Kamen, Henry. **The Spanish Inquisition.** New York: New American Library, 1965.

_____. **The War of Succession in Spain, 1700-1715.** Bloomington, IN: Indiana University Press, 1969.

Livermore, Harold. **History of Spain.** New York: Minerva Press, 1968.

Lynch, John. **Spain under the Habsburgs.** New York: Oxford University Press, 1964 & 1969.

Mariejol, Jean Hippolyte. **The Spain of Ferdinand and Isabella,** tr. by B. Keen and edited. New Brunswick: Rutgers University Press, 1961.

Menendez Pidal, Ramon. **The Spaniards in Their History.** tr. by W. Starkie. New York: W.W. Norton and Co., 1950.

_____, ed. **Historia de Espana,** tomo 17. Madrid: Espasa-Calpe, S.A., 1969.

O'Callaghan, Joseph F. **A History of Medieval Spain.** Ithaca: Cornell University Press, 1975.

Payne, Stanley G. **A History of Spain and Portugal.** Madison: University of Wisconsin Press, 1973.

Ramsey, John Fraser. **Spain: The Rise of the First World Power.** University, AL: University of Alabama Press, 1973.

Seaver, Henry Latimer. **The Great Revolt in Castile, a Study of the Comunero Movement of 1520-1521.** New York: Octagon Books, 1966 (Orig. 1928).

Vicens Vives, Jaime. **An Economic History of Spain.** F.M. Lopez-Morillas, tr. Princeton: Princeton University Press, 1969.

_____. **Approaches to the History of Spain,** tr. and ed. by J.C. Ullman. Berkeley: University of California Press, 1970.

SPANISH AMERICA

Anna, Timothy E. **The Fall of the Royal Government in Mexico City.** Lincoln: University of Nebraska Press, 1978.

_____. **The Fall of the Royal Government in Peru.** Lincoln: University of Nebraska Press, 1979.

Arciniegas, German. **Latin America: A Cultural History.** New York: Alfred A. Knopf, 1967.

Burkholder, Mark A., and D.S. Chandler. **From Impotence to Authority: The Spanish Crown and the American Audiencias, 1687-1808.** Columbia: University of Missouri Press, 1977.

Campbell, Leon G. **The Military and Society in Colonial Peru, 1750-1810.** Philadelphia: Memoirs of the American Philosophical Society, vol. 123, 1978.

Cheetham, Nicholas. **New Spain.** London: Victor Gollanz, Ltd., 1974.

Chevalier, Francois. **Land and Society in Colonial Mexico: The Great Hacienda.** tr. by A. Eustis. Berkeley: University of California Press, 1963.

Diffie, Bailey W. **Latin American Civilization, Colonial Period.** New York: Octagon Books, 1967 (reprint), 1945.

Dominguez, Jorge I. **Insurrection or Loyalty: The Breakdown of the Spanish American Empire.** Cambridge, MA: Harvard University Press, 1980.

Fehrenbach, T.R. **Fire and Blood, a History of Mexico.** New York: Macmillan, 1973.

Fisher, J.R. **Government and Society in Colonial Peru, the Intendant System, 1784-1814.** London: University of London, the Athlone Press, 1970.

Fisher, Lillian Estelle. **The Intendant System in Spanish America.** New York: Gordian Press, 1969 (Orig. 1929).

Gibson, Charles. **The Aztecs under Spanish Rule.** Palo Alto: Stanford University Press, 1964.

_____. **Spain in America.** New York: Harper and Row, Harper Torchbooks, 1966.

Gongora, Mario. **Studies in the Colonial History of Spanish America.** tr. by R. Southern. New York: Cambridge University Press, 1975.

Hanke, Lewis. **The Spanish Struggle for Justice in the Conquest of America.** Boston: Little, Brown and Co., 1949.

Hennessey, Alastair. **The Frontier in Latin American History.** Albuquerque: University of New Mexico Press, 1978.

Lockhart, James. **Spanish Peru, 1532-1560.** Madison: University of Wisconsin Press, 1968.

Lynch, John. **Spanish Colonial Administration, 1782-1810: The Intendant System in the Viceroyalty of the Rio de la Plata.** London: University of London, The Athlone Press, 1958.

Madariaga, Salvador de. **The Rise of the Spanish American Empire.** New York: The Free Press, 1947a.

_____. **The Fall of the Spanish American Empire.** London: Hollis and Carter, 1947b.

Merriman, Roger Bigelow. **The Rise of the Spanish Empire in the Old World and in the New.** New York: Cooper Square, 1962 (Orig. 1918).

Morrisey, R.J. "The Northward Expansion of Cattle Ranching in New Spain, 1550-1600," **Agricultural History** 25:115-121.

Nunn, Charles F. **Foreign Immigrants in Early Bourbon Mexico, 1700-1760.** New York: Cambridge University Press, 1979.

Phelan, John Leddy. **The Hispanization of the Philippines, Spanish Aims and Filipino Responses 1565-1700.** Madison: University of Wisconsin Press, 1959.

Powell, Philip Wayne. **Soldiers, Indians and Silver. The Northward Advance of New Spain, 1550-1600.** Berkeley: University of California Press, 1969.

Sanchez, Luis Alberto. **Historia General de America.** Madrid: Ediciones Rodas, 1972.

Shafer, Robert Jones. **The Economic Societies in the Spanish World (1763-1821).** Syracuse: Syracuse University Press, 1958.

Sierra, Justo. **The Political Evolution of the Mexican People.** tr. by C. Ramsdell. Austin: University of Texas Press, 1969.

Thomas, Alfred Barnaby. **Latin America: A History.** New York: Macmillan, 1956.

Vargas Ugarte, Ruben. **Historia General del Peru,** vols. I-V. Lima: Editor Carlos Milla Batres, 1966.

The British Peace

ENGLAND, BRITAIN AND THE EMPIRE

Ashley, Maurice. **Great Britain to 1688.** Ann Arbor: University of Michigan Press, 1961.

Barbary, James. **Puritan and Cavalier: The English Civil War.** New York: Nelson, 1977.

Bence-Jones, Mark, and Hugh Montgomery-Massingberd. **The British Aristocracy.** London: Constable, 1979.

Black, J.B. **The Reign of Elizabeth: 1558-1603,** 2d ed. London: Oxford University Press, 1959.

Bowle, John. **The English Experience.** New York: Putnam's, 1971.

_____. **The Imperial Achievement: The Rise and Transformation of the British Empire.** Boston: Little, Brown, 1974.

Chesney, Kellow. **The Anti-Society: An Account of the Victorian Underground.** Boston: Gambit, 1970.

Clark, George. **The Later Stuarts: 1660-1714,** 2d ed. London: Oxford University Press, 1956.

Graves, Robert, and Alan Hodge. **The Lost Weekend: A Social History of Great Britain, 1918-1939.** New York: Norton, 1963. (orig. 1940).

Hall, W.P., and Albion, R.G. **A History of England and the British Empire.** New York: Ginn, 1946.

Halliday, F.E. **An Illustrated Cultural History of England.** London: Thames & Hudson, 1967.

Lockyer, Roger. **Tudor and Stuart Britain: 1471-1714.** New York: St. Martin's, 1964.

Lofts, Nora. **Domestic Life in England.** New York: Doubleday, 1976.

Mackie, J.D. **The Early Tudors.** London: Oxford University Press, 1952.

Mason, Francis K. **Battle Over Britain.** New York: Doubleday, 1969.

Morris, James. **Pax Britannica: The Climax of an Empire.** New York: Harcourt Brace, 1968.

Plumb, J.H. **The First Four Georges.** Boston: Little Brown, 1975 (Orig. 1956).

Rowse, A.L. **The England of Elizabeth.** New York: Macmillan, 1951.

White, R.J. **The Age of George III.** New York: Walker, 1968.

Young, G.M. **Victorian England,** 2d ed. New York: Oxford University Press, 1964.

SCOTLAND AND IRELAND

Costigan, Giovanni. **A History of Modern Ireland.** New York: Western, 1969.

Dangerfield, George. **The Damnable Question: A Study of Anglo-Irish Relations.** Boston: Little, Brown, 1976.

Dunlop, Robert. **Ireland From the Earliest Times to the Present Day.** London: Oxford University Press, 1922.

Edwards, R. Dudley. **A New History of Ireland.** Toronto: University of Toronto Press, 1971.

Fitzgibbon, Constantine. **Out of the Lion's Paw: Ireland Wins Her Freedom.** New York: American Heritage, 1969.

Hahn, Emily. **Fractured Emerald: Ireland.** New York: Doubleday, 1971.

Jackson, T.A. **Ireland Her Own.** New York: International Publishers, 1947.

Kellas, James G. **Modern Scotland: The Nation Since 1870.** New York: Praeger, 1968.

Mackie, J.D. **A History of Scotland.** Harmondsworth, Eng: Penguin, 1964.

Magnusson, Magnus and Helen Troy. **Landlord or Tenant? A View of Irish History.** London: The Bodley Head, 1978.

Rait, Robert, and George S. Pryde. **Scotland,** 2d ed. New York: Praeger, 1954.

The Scandinavian Peace

SCANDINAVIA

Andren, Nils. **Government and Politics in the Nordic Countries.** Stockholm: Almqvist & Wiksell, 1964.

Arneson, Ben A. **The Democratic Monarchies of Scandinavia.** New York: D. Van Nostrand Co., Inc.
Bukdahl, Jorgen, et al., eds. **Scandinavia, Past and Present.** Odense: Henriksen, 1959.
Derry, T.K. **A History of Scandinavia.** Minneapolis: University of Minnesota Press, 1979.
Hovde, B.J. **The Scandinavian Countries, 1720-1865.** Boston: Chapman & Grimes Publishers, 1943.
Jones, Gwyn. **A History of the Vikings.** New York: Oxford University Press, 1968.
Lindgren, Raymond E. **Norway-Sweden, Union, Disunion and Scandinavian Integration.** Princeton, NJ: Princeton University Press, 1959.
Millward, Roy. **Scandinavian Lands.** London: Macmillan, 1965.
Scott, Franklin D. **The United States and Scandinavia.** Cambridge, MA: Harvard University Press, 1950.
Toyne, S.M. **The Scandinavians in History.** Port Washington, NY: Kennikat Press, 1970 (Orig. 1948).
Wuorinen, John H. **Scandinavia.** Englewood Cliffs, NJ: Prentice-Hall, 1965.

SWEDEN

Abrahamsen, Samuel. **Sweden's Foreign Policy.** Washington, DC: Public Affairs Press, 1957.
Ander, O. Fritjof. **The Building of Modern Sweden, The Reign of Gustav V, 1907-1950.** Rock Island, IL: Augustana Book Concern, 1958.
Andersson, Ingvar. **A History of Sweden.** New York: Praeger Publishers, 1956.
Elder, Neil C.M. **Government in Sweden.** Oxford: Pergamon Press, Ltd., 1970.
Heckscher, Eli F. **An Economic History of Sweden.** Cambridge, MA: Harvard University Press, 1963.
Koblik, Steven, ed. **Sweden's Development from Poverty to Affluence.** Minneapolis, MN: University of Minnesota Press, 1975.
Lewin, Leif. **The Swedish Electorate, 1887-1968.** Stockholm: Almqvist & Wiksell, 1972.
Masson, Georgina. **Queen Christina.** New York: Farrar, Straus & Giroux, 1968.
Moberg, Vilhelm. **A History of the Swedish People.** New York: Random House, Pantheon Books, 1972.
Oakley, Stewart. **A Short History of Sweden.** New York: Praeger, 1966.
Roberts, Michael. **Essays in Swedish History.** Minneapolis, MN: University of Minnesota Press, 1967.
_____. **The Early Vasas.** New York: Cambridge University Press, 1968a.
_____, ed. **Sweden as a Great Power, 1611-1697.** New York: St. Martin's Press, 1968b.
Samuelsson, Kurt. **From Great Power to Welfare State, 300 Years of Swedish Social Development.** London: George Allen and Unwin, 1968.
Scobbie, Irene. **Sweden.** New York: Praeger, 1972.
Scott, Franklin D. **Sweden: The Nation's History.** Minneapolis: University of Minnesota Press, 1977.
Stomberg, Andrew A. **A History of Sweden.** New York: Macmillan, 1931.
Strode, Hudson. **Sweden: Model for a World.** New York: Harcourt, Brace & World, Inc., 1949.
Verney, Douglas V. **Parliamentary Reform in Sweden, 1866-1921.** London: Clarendon Press, 1957.

DENMARK

Anderson, Robert T. **Denmark, Success of a Developing Nation.** Cambridge, MA: Schenkman Publishing Co., Inc., 1975.

_____, and B.G. Anderson. **The Vanishing Village, A Danish Maritime Community.** Seattle, WA: University of Washington Press, 1964.

Jones, Gwyn. **Denmark.** New York: Praeger, 1970.

Lauring, Palle. **A History of the Kingdom of Denmark.** Copenhagen: Host & Son, 1960.

Miller, Kenneth E. **Government and Politics in Denmark.** Boston: Houghton Mifflin Co., 1968.

NORWAY

Derry, T.K. **A Short History of Norway.** London: George Allen and Unwin, 1957.

Drake, Michael. **Population and Society in Norway 1735–1865.** New York: Cambridge University Press, 1969.

Dyrvik, Stale, et al. **The Satellite State.** Oslo: Universitetsforlaget, 1979.

Jorgenson, Theodore. **Norway's Relation to Scandinavian Unionism, 1815–1871.** Northfield, MN: St. Olaf's College Press, 1935.

Larsen, Karen. **A History of Norway.** Princeton, NJ: Princeton University Press, 1948.

Larson, Laurence M. **The Earliest Norwegian Laws.** New York: Columbia University Press, 1935.

Lieberman, Sima. **The Industrialization of Norway 1800–1920.** Oslo: Universitetsforlaget, 1970.

Midgaard, John. **A Brief History of Norway.** Oslo: Johan Grundt Tanum Forlag, 1963.

Nordskog, John Eric. **Social Reform in Norway.** Los Angeles, CA: University of Southern California, 1935.

Popperwell, Ronald G. **Norway.** New York: Praeger, 1972.

Storing, James A. **Norwegian Democracy.** Boston: Houghton Mifflin Co., 1963.

Valen, Henry, and Danile Katz. **Political Parties in Norway.** Oslo: Universitetsforlaget, 1967.

FINLAND

Jutikkala, Eino with Kauko Pirinen. **A History of Finland.** New York: Praeger, 1962.

Kirby, D.G. **Finland in the Twentieth Century.** Minneapolis, MN: University of Minnesota Press, 1979.

Mazour, Anatole G. **Finland Between East and West.** Princeton: Princeton University Press, 1956.

Mead, W.R. **Finland.** New York: Praeger, 1968.

Nousiainen, Jaako. **The Finnish Political System.** Cambridge, MA: Harvard University Press, 1971.

Smith, C. Jay, Jr. **Finland and the Russian Revolution.** Athens, GA: University of Georgia Press, 1958.

Wuorinen, John H. **A History of Finland.** New York: Columbia University Press, 1965b.

ICELAND

Gjerset, Knut. **History of Iceland.** New York: Macmillan, 1925.

Griffiths, John C. **Modern Iceland.** New York: Praeger, 1969.

Johannesson, Jon. **A History of the Old Icelandic Commonwealth (Islendinga Saga, vol. I).** Winnipeg: University of Manitoba Press, 1974.

Magnusson, Sigurdur A. **Northern Sphinx, Iceland and the Icelanders from the Settlement to the Present.** Toronto: McGill-Queen's University Press, 1977.

Nordal, Johannes and Valdimar Kristinsson. **Iceland 874–1974.** Reykjavik: Central Bank of Iceland, 1975.

Tomasson, Richard F. **Iceland, The First New Society.** Minneapolis: University of Minnesota Press, 1980.

The Swiss Peace

Bonjour, Edgar; H.S. Offler, and G.R. Potter. **A Short History of Switzerland.** Oxford: Clarendon Press, 1963.

De Salis, J.R. **Switzerland and Europe.** University of Alabama Press, 1971.

Gilliard, Charles. **A History of Switzerland.** London: Allen & Unwin, 1955.

Gretler, Armin. **Values, Trends and Alternatives in Swiss Society: A Prospective Analysis.** Praeger, 1973.

Gross, Francois, ed. **Focus on Switzerland.** Laausanne: Swiss Office for the Development of Trade, 1975.

Hasler, Alfred. **The Lifeboat is Full,** tr. by Charles Markmann. New York: Funk & Wagnalls, 1969.

Herold, J. Christopher. **The Swiss Without Halos.** New York: Columbia University Press, 1948.

Hug, Lina, and Richard Stead. **Switzerland.** New York: Putnam's, 1960.

Luck, Murray J. **Modern Switzerland.** Palo Alto: Society for the Promotion of Science and Scholarship, 1978.

Lunn, Arnold. **The Cradle of Switzerland.** London: Hollis and Carter, 1952.

McCracken, W.D. **The Rise of the Swiss Republic.** New York: Holt, 1892.

Martin, William. **Switzerland From Roman Times to the Present.** New York: Praeger, 1971.

Rappard, William E. **Collective Security in Swiss Experience.** London: Allen & Unwin, 1948.

Schurch, Ernest, ed. **Switzerland.** Werner Reist, 1960.

Sorell, Walter. **The Swiss: A Cultural Panorama of Switzerland.** Indianapolis: Bobbs-Merrill, 1972.

Steinberg, Jonathan. **Why Switzerland?** New York: Cambridge University Press, 1976.

Stucki, Lorenz. **The Secret Empire: The Success Story of Switzerland.** New York: Herder & Herder, 1971.

Ziegler, Jean. **Switzerland: The Awful Truth,** tr. by Rosemary Sheed Middleton. New York: Harper & Row, 1976.

The Brazilian Peace

JOURNALS AND SERIALS

Comparative Studies in Society and History
Current History
Hispanic American Historical Review
Journal of Latin American Studies
Latin American Research Review
Luso–Brazilian Review
The Americas

BOOKS

Arciniegas, German. **Latin America: A Cultural History,** tr. by Joan MacLean. New York: Knopf, 1967.

Bello, Jose Maria. **A History of Modern Brazil 1889–1964**, tr. by James L. Taylor. Palo Alto: Stanford University Press, 1966.

Boxer, C.R. **The Golden Age of Brazil, 1695–1750**. Berkeley: University of California Press, 1962.

Burns, E. Bradford. **Perspectives on Brazilian History**. New York: Columbia University Press, 1967.

_____. **A History of Brazil**. New York: Columbia University Press, 1970.

Calogeras, Joao Pandia. **A History of Brazil**, tr. by P.A. Martin. Chapel Hill: University of North Carolina Press, 1963.

Dulles, J.W.F. **Vargas of Brazil**. Austin: University of Texas Press, 1967.

Flynn, Peter. **Brazil: A Political Analysis**. Boulder: Westview Press, 1978.

Freyre, Gilberto. **New World in the Tropics**. New York: Vintage Books, 1963.

_____. **The Masters and the Slaves**, tr. by Samuel Putnam. New York: Knopf, 1964.

_____. **Order and Progress**, tr. by R.W. Horton. New York: Knopf, 1970.

Johnson, John J. **The Military and Society in Latin America**. Palo Alto: Stanford University Press, 1964.

Lacombe, Americo Jacobina. **Brasil: Periodo Nacional**. Mexico D.F.: Instituto Panamericano de Geografia e Historia 1956.

Love, Joseph L. **Rio Grande do Sul and Brazilian Regionalism 1882–1930**. Palo Alto: Stanford University Press, 1971.

Nabuco, Joaquim. **Um Estadista do Imperio**. Rio de Janeiro: Editora Nova Aguilar, 1975.

Oliveira Lima, Manuel de. **The Evolution of Brazil**. New York: Russell & Russell, 1966.

Poppino, Rollie E. **Brazil, The Land and the People**. New York: 1968.

Prado, Paulo. **Retrato do Brasil**, 4th ed. Rio de Janeiro: Livraria Jose Olympio Editora, 1962.

Ribeiro, Joao. **Historia do Brasil**, 17th ed. Rio de Janeiro: Livraria Francisco Alves, 1960.

Rodrigues, Jose Honorio. **Brasil, Periodo Colonial**. Mexico D.F.: Instituto Panamericano de Geografia e Historia, 1953.

_____. **The Brazilians, Their Character and Aspirations**, tr. by R.E. Dimmick. Austin: University of Texas Press, 1967.

Roett, R. **Brazil in the Sixties**. Nashville: Vanderbilt University Press, 1972.

Schneider, R.M. **The Political System of Brazil**. Columbia University Press, 1971.

Stepan, A. **Authoritarian Brazil**. New Haven: Yale University Press, 1973.

Thomas, Alfred Barnaby. **Latin America, A History**. New York: Macmillan, 1956.

Tomasek, Richard D. **Latin American Politics**. New York: Anchor, 1970.

Vianna, Helio. **Historia do Brasil**, 5th ed. Sao Paulo: Edicoes Melhoramentos, 1967.

Wagley, Charles. **An Introduction to Brazil**. New York: Columbia University Press, 1963.

Worcester, Donald E. **Brazil, From Colony to World Power**. New York: Scribner's, 1973.

The Costa Rican Peace

Bell, John Patrick. **Crisis in Costa Rica: The 1948 Revolution**. Austin: University of Texas Press, 1971.

Biesanz, Richard, Karen and Mavis. **The Costa Ricans**. Englewood Cliffs, NJ: Prentice-Hall, 1982.

Gunther, John. **Inside Latin America**. New York: Harper, 1941.

Herring, Hubert. **A History of Latin America.** New York: Knopf, 1953.
Jones, Chester L. **Costa Rica and Civilization in the Caribbean.** New York: Russell and Russell, 1935.
Kirkpatrick, F.A. **Latin America.** New York: Macmillan, 1939.
Martz, John D. **Central America.** Chapel Hill: University of North Carolina Press, 1950.
Munro, Dana G. **The Five Republics of Central America.** New York: Russell and Russell, 1967 (Original 1918).
Parker, F.D. **The Central American Republics.** New York: Oxford University Press, 1964.
Rippy, J. Fred. **Latin America.** Ann Arbor: University of Michigan Press, 1958.
Rodriquez, Mario. **Central America.** Englewood Cliffs, NJ: Prentice-Hall, 1965.
Thomas, Alfred Barnaby. **Latin America, A History.** New York: Macmillan, 1956.
Thompson, Wallace. **Rainbow Countries of Central America.** Chatauqua, N.Y.: Chatauqua Press, 1927.
Wendt, Herbert. **The Red, White and Black Continent: Latin America—Land of Reformers and Rebels.** Garden City, NY: Doubleday, 1968.
West, Robert C., and John P. Augelli. **Middle America: Its Lands and Peoples.** Englewood Cliffs, NJ: Prentice-Hall, 1966.
Wilgus, Curtis A. **The Development of Hispanic America.** New York: Farrar and Rinehart, 1941.

The Canadian Peace

JOURNALS AND SERIALS

Canadian Historical Review
Current History
Encyclopaedia Britannica Books of the Year
Journal of Canadian Studies

BOOKS

Bothwell, Robert; Ian Drummond, and John English. **Canada Since 1945: Power, Politics and Provincialism.** Toronto: University of Toronto Press, 1981.
Bowle, John. **The Imperial Achievement: The Rise and Transformation of the British Empire.** Boston: Little, Brown, 1974.
Brebner, J. Bartlett. **Canada.** Ann Arbor: University of Michigan Press, 1960.
Brown, Robert Craig and Ramsay Cook. **Canada 1896–1921.** Toronto: McClelland and Stewart, 1976.
Bryce, George. **A Short History of the Canadian People.** London: Sampson Low, Marston & Co. Ltd., 1914.
Butler, Rick, and Jean-Guy Carrier, eds. **The Trudeau Decade.** Toronto: Doubleday, 1979.
Creighton, Donald. **The Road to Confederation.** Toronto: Macmillan of Canada, 1964.
_____. **Canada's First Century 1867–1967.** Toronto: Macmillan of Canada.
Dawson, R. MacGregor. **William Lyon Mackenzie King, A Political Biography, 1874–1923.** Toronto: University of Toronto Press, 1958.
_____. **The Development of Dominion Status 1900–1936.** Hamden, CT: Archon Books, 1965. (orig. 1937).
Donaldson, Gordon. **Fifteen Men: Canada's Prime Ministers from Macdonald to Trudeau.** Toronto: Doubleday, 1969.

Falardeau, Jean-Charles, ed. **Essais sur le Quebec Contemporain.** Quebec: Les Presses Universitaires Laval, 1953.

Farr, David M.L. **The Colonial Office and Canada 1867-1887.** Toronto: University of Toronto Press, 1955.

Fraser, Blair. **The Search for Identity: Canada, 1945-1967.** Toronto: Doubleday, 1967.

Hutchison, Bruce. **The Unknown Country, Canada and Her People.** New York: Coward-McCann, Inc., 1942.

_____. **The Incredible Canadian.** London: Longmans, Green and Co., 1953.

_____. **Mr. Prime Minister 1867-1964.** New York: Harcourt, Brace and World, 1964.

Kilbourn, William. **Canada: A Guide to the Peaceable Kingdom.** New York: St. Martin's, 1970.

McInnis, Edgar. **Canada,** rev. ed. New York: Holt, Rinehart and Winston, 1963.

MacKirdy, K.A.; J.S. Moir, and Y.F. Zoltany. **Changing Perspectives in Canadian History.** Dow Mills, Ont.: J.M. Dent & Sons (Canada), 1967.

McNaught, Kenneth. **The Pelican History of Canada,** rev. ed. Harmondsworth, Eng.: Penguin, 1976.

Morton, Desmond. **Canada and War.** Toronto: Butterworths, 1981.

Morton, W.L. **The Critical Years, the Union of British North America 1857-1873.** Toronto: McClelland and Stewart, 1964.

Neatby, H. Blair. **William Lyon Mackenzie King, The Lonely Heights, 1924-1932.** Toronto: University of Toronto Press, 1963.

Oswalt, Wendell H. **This Land Was Theirs: A Study of North American Indians,** 3rd ed. New York: Willey, 1978.

Park, Julian. **The Culture of Contemporary Canada.** Ithaca: Cornell University Press, 1957.

Price, John A. **Native Studies: American and Canadian Indians.** Toronto: McGraw-Hill Ryerson, 1978.

Shortt, Adam, and Arthur G. Doughty, gen. eds. **Canada and Its Provinces, vol. VI, The Dominion, Political Evolution.** Toronto: Publishers Association of Canada, 1914.

Simeon, Richard, ed. **Must Canada Fail?** Montreal: McGill-Queens University Press, 1977.

Waite, P.B. **The Life and Times of Confederation 1864-1867.** Toronto: University of Toronto Press, 1962.

Weinfeld, Morton; William Shaffir, and Irwin Cotter, eds. **The Canadian Jewish Mosaic.** Roxdale, Ont.: Wiley, 1981.

Winks, Robin. "An Orphaned Dominion," **Wilson Quarterly,** Summer 1982.

The Pacific Peace

JOURNALS AND SERIALS

The Australian Journal of Politics and History
Australian Quarterly
Encyclopaedia Britannica Books of the Year
Historical Studies (Australia and New Zealand)
The New Zealand Journal of History

BOOKS

Australia and New Zealand

Aitkin, Don. **Stability and Change in Australian Politics.** New York: St. Martin's, 1977.

Barnard, Marjorie. **A History of Australia.** New York: Praeger, 1963.

Bartlett, Norman. **Australia and America through 200 Years 1776–1976.** Sydney: Fine Arts Press, 1976.

Bedggod, David. **Rich and Poor in New Zealand.** Boston: Allen & Unwin, 1980.

Belshaw, Horace, ed. **New Zealand.** Berkeley: University of California Press, 1947.

Birch, Alan, and David S. Macmillan. **The Sydney Scene 1788–1960.** New York: Cambridge University Press, 1962.

Blainey, Geoffrey. **The Tyranny of Distance: How Distance Shaped Australia's History.** New York: St. Martin's, 1968.

Bowle, John. **The Imperial Achievement: The Rise and Transformation of the British Empire.** Boston: Little, Brown, 1974.

Cameron, Roderick. **Australia: History and Horizons.** New York: Columbia University Press, 1971.

Cameron, William J. **New Zealand.** Englewood Cliffs, NJ: Prentice-Hall, 1965.

Clark, C.M.H. **A History of Australia, vol. IV, The Earth Abideth For Ever, 1851–1888.** Forest Grove, OR: International Scholarly Book Services, 1978.

Crowley, F.K., ed. **A New History of Australia.** Melbourne: William Heinemann Australia, 1974.

Gilchrist, J.T., and W.J. Murray. **Eye–Witness. Selected Documents from Australia's Past.** Adelaide: Rigby, 1968.

Gordon, Bernard K. **New Zealand Becomes a Pacific Power.** University of Chicago Press, 1960.

Grattan, C. Hartley, ed. **Australia.** Berkeley: University of California Press, 1947.

_____. **The Southwest Pacific to 1900.** Ann Arbor: University of Michigan Press, 1963a.

_____. **The Southwest Pacific since 1900.** Ann Arbor: University of Michigan Press, 1963b.

Hancock, W.K. **Australia.** New York: Scribner's, 1930.

Holmes, Jean, and Campbell Sharman. **The Australian Federal System.** Hornsby, N.S.W.: George Allen & Unwin, 1977.

Leach, Richard H. **Interstate Relations in Australia.** University of Kentucky Press, 1965.

Livingston, William S., and William Roger Louis. **Australia, New Zealand and the Pacific Islands since the First World War.** Austin: University of Texas Press, 1979.

McMinn, W.G. **A Constitutional History of Australia.** New York: Oxford University Press, 1979.

Milne, R.S. **Political Parties in New Zealand.** London: Oxford University Press, 1966.

Munday, B.J., and J.R. Grigsby. **Mainstreams in Australian History.** Melbourne: Cassell Australia, 1968.

Older, Jules. "A Genteel Struggle for Equality in New Zealand." **Chronicle of Higher Education,** 14 July 1982, p. 48.

Oliver, W.H. **The Story of New Zealand.** London: Faber and Faber, 1960.

_____, and B.R. Williams, eds. **The Oxford History of New Zealand.** Wellington: Oxford University Press, 1981.

Preston, Richard H., ed. **Contemporary Australia: Studies in History, Politics and Economics.** Durham, NC: Duke University Press, 1969.

Reed, A.H. **The Story of New Zealand,** 11th ed. Wellington: A.H. and A.W. Reed, 1965.

Reese, Trevor R. **Australia in the Twentieth Century.** New York: Praeger, 1964.

Ritchie, John. **Australia as Once We Were.** New York: Holmes and Meier, 1975.

Shaw, A.G.L. **A Short History of Australia,** 2nd ed. London: Faber and Faber, 1961.

Sinclair, Keith. **A History of New Zealand.** Baltimore: Penguin, 1959.

Sojak, Philip L. **New Zealand.** New York: Macmillan, 1946.

Spate, O.H.K. **Australia.** New York: Praeger, 1968.

Turner, G.W. **The English Language in Australia and New Zealand.** London: Longmans, Green and Co., 1966.

Ward, Russel. **Australia.** Englewood Cliffs, NJ: Prentice-Hall, 1965a.

_____. **The Australian Legend.** Melbourne: Oxford University Press, 1965b.

_____. **The History of Australia: The Twentieth Century.** New York: Harper and Row, 1977.

Williams, John A. **Politics of the New Zealand Maori.** Seattle: University of Washington Press, 1969.

Younger, R.M. **Australia and the Australians.** New York: Humanities Press, 1970.

Hawaii (see also Pacific Islands)

Bailey, Paul. **Those Kings and Queens of Old Hawaii.** Los Angeles: Westernlore Press, 1975.

Clark, Blake. **Hawaii.** New York: Doubleday, 1948.

Daws, Gavan. **Shoal of Time, A History of the Hawaiian Islands.** New York: Macmillan, 1968.

Fuchs, Lawrence H. **Hawaii Pono: A Social History.** New York: Harcourt, Brace and World, 1961.

Joesting, Edward. **Hawaii: An Uncommon History.** New York: Norton, 1972.

Kuykendall, Ralph S., and A. Grove Day. **Hawaii: A History,** rev. ed. Englewood Cliffs, NJ: Prentice-Hall, 1961.

Lee, William Storrs. **The Islands.** New York: Holt, Rinehart & Winston, 1966.

Osborne, Thomas J. **"Empire Can Wait": American Opposition to Hawaiian Annexation, 1893–1898.** Kent, OH: Kent State University Press, 1981.

Russ, William Adam, Jr. **The Hawaiian Republic (1894–1898) and Its Struggle to Win Annexation.** Selgrove, PA: Susquehanna University Press, 1981.

Tabrah, Ruth M. **Hawaii: A Bicentennial History.** New York: Norton, 1980.

Teodoro, Luis V., Jr., ed. **Out of This Struggle: The Filipinos in Hawaii.** Honolulu: University Press of Hawaii, 1981.

Wright, Theon. **The Disenchanted Isles.** New York: Dial Press, 1972.

Wyndette, Olive. **Islands of Destiny.** Rutland, VT and Tokyo: Charles E. Tuttle, 1968.

Young, Lucien. **The Real Hawaii.** New York: Arno Press, 1970 (original 1902).

Pacific Islands

Adams, Henry Brooks. **Tahiti: Memoirs of Arii Taimai.** Ridgewood, NJ: Gregg Press, Inc., 1968 (original 1901).

Barclay, Glen. **A History of the Pacific from the Stone Age to the Present Day.** New York: Taplinger Publishing Co., 1978.

Beaglehole, Ernest. **Social Change in the South Pacific.** London: George Allen & Unwin, 1957.

Bourgeau, J. **La France du Pacifique.** Paris: Editions Maritimes et Coloniales, 1955.

Brookes, Jean Ingram. **International Rivalry in the Pacific Islands 1800–1875.** Berkeley: University of California Press, 1941.

Buck, Peter H. (Te Rangi Hiroa). **Vikings of the Sunrise.** New York: Frederick A. Stokes Co., 1938.

Burchett, W.G. **Pacific Treasure Island: New Caledonia.** Melbourne: F.W. Cheshire, 1941.

Derrick, R.A. **A History of Fiji.** Suva, Fiji: Government Press, 1957.

Deschamps, Hubert, and Jean Guiart. **Tahiti, Nouvelle–Caledonie, Nouvelles–Hebrides.** Paris: Editions Berger–Levrault, 1957.

Ellis, William. **Polynesian Researches.** Multiple volumes and publishers.

Gifford, Edward Winslow. **Tongan Society.** Bernice P. Bishop Museum Bulletin nbr. 61. Honolulu: The Museum, 1929.

Gilson, R.P. **Samoa 1830 to 1900.** Melbourne: Oxford University Press, 1970.

Goldman, Irving. **Ancient Polynesian Society.** Chicago: University of Chicago Press, 1970.

Grattan, C. Hartley. **The Southwest Pacific to 1900.** Ann Arbor: University of Michigan Press, 1963.

_____. **The Southwest Pacific Since 1900.** Ann Arbor: University of Michigan Press, 1963.

Gray, J.A.C. **Amerika Samoa.** Annapolis: United States Naval Institute, 1960.

Handy, Willowdean C. **Forever the Land of Men.** New York: Dodd, Mead & Co., 1965.

Harding, Thomas G., and Ben J. Wallace, eds. **Cultures of the Pacific.** New York: The Free Press, 1970.

Hempenstall, Peter J. **Pacific Islanders under German Rule.** Canberra: Australian National University Press, 1978.

Henderson, John W., et al. **Area Handbook for Oceania.** Washington, DC: U.S. Government Printing Office, 1971.

Julien, Charles-Andre. **Histoire de l'Oceanie.** Paris: Presses Universitaires de France, 1946.

Keesing, Felix M. **Modern Samoa.** Stanford University Press, 1934.

_____. **The South Seas in the Modern World.** New York: Octagon Books, 1975 (original 1941).

_____, and Marie M. Keesing. **Elite Communication in Samoa.** Stanford University Press, 1956.

Koskinen, Aarne A. **Missionary Influence as a Political Factor in the Pacific Islands.** Helsinki, 1953.

Livingston, William S., and William Roger Louis, eds. **Australia, New Zealand and the Pacific Islands since the First World War.** Austin: University of Texas Press, 1979.

Luke, Sir Harry. **Queen Salote and Her Kingdom.** London: Putnam, 1954.

Mander, Linden A. **Some Dependent Peoples of the South Pacific.** New York: Macmillan, 1954.

Marcus, George E. **The Nobility and the Chiefly Tradition in the Modern Kingdom of Tonga.** Wellington: The Polynesian Society (Incorporated), 1980.

Morrell, William P. **Britain in the Pacific Islands.** Oxford: Oxford University Press, 1960.

Newbury, Colin. **Tahiti Nui.** Honolulu: University Press of Hawaii, 1980.

Oliver, Douglas L. **The Pacific Islands.** Garden City, NY: Doubleday, 1961.

Pritchard, W.T. **Polynesian Reminiscences.** London: Dawsons of Pall Mall, 1968 (original 1866).

Quain, Buell. **Fijian Village.** Chicago: University of Chicago Press, 1948.

Roberts, Stephen H. **History of French Colonial Policy (1870–1925).** London: P.S. King and Son Ltd., 1929.

Roth, G.K. **Fijian Way of Life.** Melbourne: Oxford University Press, 1953.

Rutherford, Noel, ed. **Friendly Islands: A History of Tonga.** Melbourne: Oxford University Press, 1977.

Scholefield, Guy H. **The Pacific, Its Past and Future.** London: John Murray, 1919.

Stanner, W.E.H. **The South Seas in Transition.** Sydney: Australasian Publishing Co., 1953.

Suggs, Robert C. **The Hidden Worlds of Polynesia.** New York: Harcourt, Brace & World, 1962.

Thomson, Basil. **The Fijians, A Study in the Decay of Custom.** London: Dawsons of Pall Mall, 1968.

West, F.J. **Political Advancement in the South Pacific.** Melbourne: Oxford University Press, 1961.

Williamson, Robert W. **The Social and Political Systems of Central Polynesia.** Cambridge University Press, 1924.

Index